VOLUME 2

CIVIC LITERACY

VOLUME 2

CIVIC LITERACY

BUILDING CIVIC FUTURES IN OUT-OF-SCHOOL LITERACY LEARNING ENVIRONMENTS

EDITORS
LAMAR TIMMONS-LONG, NEW YORK UNIVERSITY
NICOLE MIRRA, RUTGERS UNIVERSITY
ANTERO GARCIA, STANFORD UNIVERSITY

National Council of Teachers of English®

Copy editor: Michael Ryan
Staff editor: Cynthia Gomez
Cover design: Pat Mayer
Interior design: Ash Goodwin

ISBN 978-0-8141-0236-7
eISBN 978-0-8141-0237-4
PDF ISBN 978-0-8141-0238-1

It is the policy of NCTE in its journals and other publications to provide a forum for the open discussion of ideas concerning the content and the teaching of English and the language arts. Publicity accorded to any particular point of view does not imply endorsement by the Executive Committee, the Board of Directors, or the membership at large, except in announcements of policy, where such endorsement is clearly specified.

NCTE provides equal employment opportunity to all staff members and applicants for employment without regard to race, color, religion, sex, national origin, age, physical, mental or perceived handicap/disability, sexual orientation including gender identity or expression, ancestry, genetic information, marital status, military status, unfavorable discharge from military service, pregnancy, citizenship status, personal appearance, matriculation or political affiliation, or any other protected status under applicable federal, state, and local laws.

Every effort has been made to provide current URLs and email addresses, but, because of the rapidly changing nature of the web, some sites and addresses may no longer be accessible.

Library of Congress Control Number: 2025930034

VOLUME 2 | BUILDING CIVIC FUTURES IN OUT-OF-SCHOOL LITERACY LEARNING ENVIRONMENTS

CONTENTS

Introduction

LAMAR TIMMONS-LONG, NICOLE MIRRA & ANTERO GARCIA

"To infinity and beyond . . ."

—Buzz Lightyear

From the Beginning: To Infinity and Beyond

Buzz Lightyear was my (LaMar's) favorite character from the Disney/Pixar film *Toy Story* (Lasseter, 1995); Buzz (as we'll call him for short) was an astronaut who knew the potential of outer space—a place with no boundaries, limitless, and full of possibilities. He is known for his famous line "to infinity and beyond," and, in a book committed to encouraging educators to think expansively about literacy learning beyond the traditional confines of classroom spaces, we find it fitting to begin this introduction with the lessons from this beloved animated character. Buzz inspires us to think outside of, over, and underneath our physical classrooms and go far afield of what is standard in our profession to create spaces where students can thrive. He also reminds us to think and go beyond ourselves and our content to remove the potential limits within education—those that are placed upon us and those that we preemptively place upon ourselves. Within this volume, scholar-educators share their stories in the spirit of challenging all who work with youth to think "to infinity and beyond . . ." by going against traditional forms of educating students and pushing ourselves to provide youth with experiences that shape their character, strengthen their personal and academic skills, and equip them with the necessary tools to build a more humanizing and liberatory tomorrow. To, quite literally, build new worlds.

Spaces beyond the traditional classroom are not easily categorized; they operate from any site outside (and sometimes, in a figurative sense, inside) the confined walls of traditional school spaces in order to cater to the development and support of young people in the fullest sense of those concepts. Beyond the classroom can be clubs, parks, community centers, or transitory snatches of time when educators create/facilitate spaces, moments, and experiences for students between the cracks of their academic classes. The essays in this book consistently play with the idea of speculative education: the practice of imagining desired ways of being with each other grounded in the ethics of equity and justice and then working toward actualizing those dreams moment to moment in our daily work with each other and our students (Mirra & Garcia, 2023). The authors represented in these pages dream and imagine environments outside traditional academic spaces. Together, they invite us all to dream and imagine the impossible becoming possible. We consider how learning, discourse, skills, and criticality can be defined when working with youth outside of "school" time. We ask educators to break down the barriers of the classroom walls and curate spaces that afford students the opportunity to be creative and imaginative.

Dreaming and imagining are not always easy, particularly for teachers and community-learning practitioners beset by narrow utilitarian ideas about the purpose and practice of education in an increasingly polarized society. Yet we must dream because each of us can recall memories or bring to mind stories of nontraditional educational spaces that were crucial to our lives.

So, if it is difficult to immediately jump into dreaming in education, let's first talk about television. The '90s was a time for unique and thoughtful television series that reflected youth of all ages, identities, and racial backgrounds. Networks created shows that reflected elementary, middle, and high school students. Characters attended class, hung out with friends, played sports, participated in clubs, and demonstrated the necessity of creating well-rounded young people. Television shows like *Family Matters* (Bickley et al., 1989–1998) and *Moesha* (Farquhar et al., 1996–2001) convey the possibilities of what could happen outside of classrooms to develop our young people.

Turn on the TV

Moesha (1996–2001) was a television show about a Black teenage girl who attended a high school in South Central Los Angeles. Like many teenagers, she was a curious young woman who excelled in her academic classes. Moesha was a writer and a leader in her own right. Throughout the series, we see her as a prominent writer honing her writing and journalistic skills; she was keen on finding something to write about, gathering information, and then constructing a well-rounded story. While she potentially learned writing skills in academic classes, they were explored, further developed, and applied in depth in her after-school newspaper club. Aside from participating in the school newspaper, she spent many days after school with her friends at the local hangout spot called the Den. It was a place that offered young people a location to come, relax, and be seen, heard, and valued. Andel, the owner, created this place for young folk to be creative, have fun, practice academic and social skills, and learn life lessons from each other. Both the newspaper club and the Den are examples of how nontraditional spaces curated for young people will push them toward utilizing various skills and their imaginations in order to practice becoming better individuals.

Family Matters (1989–1998), another '90s classic sitcom, was about a family called the Winslows who were living in Chicago. Laura Winslow and Steve Urkel were two key young characters in the show: Laura was a successful student who served as a cheerleader for the school basketball team. Of course, being a cheerleader takes hard work and dedication—one must be flexible, have some rhythm, be precise, take risks, and use their voice for the greater good. As a cheerleader, Laura took risks by using her imagination to create on-demand cheerleading drills to support the basketball team's defense. Later in the series, she became the squad's captain, which allowed the show to demonstrate Laura working to be a problem solver, to delegate tasks, and to partner with others to fundraise and serve as a peer model.

Although Laura is an important character, one cannot forget the show's primary protagonist, Steven Q. Urkel, a young man who consistently uses his imagination to create various inventions that could alter one's location (the Winslow's traveling from Chicago to Paris), weight (Aunt Una from Altuna losing weight), and physical and genetic makeup (Steven becoming Stephan). Steven's skills and scientific knowledge may have happened in class; however, he used his imagination and creativity outside of school to build inventions that would better himself and his community.

If you notice, there is a clear argument here: nontraditional educational spaces are crucial to the development of holistic young people. These outside-of-the-classroom spaces further the leadership, collaboration, problem-solving skills, and the ability to take risks. Furthermore, young people should experience the beauty of intergenerational relationships between themselves and adults who serve as facilitators or mentors. Lastly, these spaces helped them to nurture their career interests, connect with various young people from different identities and ethnicities, and begin finding themselves on their terms.

A Walk down Memory Lane

LaMar's Story

I cannot help but reflect on my experience as a young person and how educators and spaces curated outside of traditional schooling cultivated and enriched my mind. As a young person, I participated in various out-of-school programs; those experiences were the most crucial and supportive of my overall development into a critical and justice-oriented human being, who uses my voice to advocate for others. Participating in an extended-day after-school program and joining the step team shaped who I became and my lens of the world. These experiences rooted in me the conviction that thinking and writing about spaces beyond conventional school settings can have lasting, positive effects and provide young people with the capacity to explore their interests and skills in their personal and academic lives.

The after-school program helped us with academics and provided the means to engage with our peers socially. I received support in my academic courses, such as mathematics and English; however, the most memorable and impactful experience was participating in clubs. I was active in two clubs throughout my youth: the writing club and the step team, both of which greatly impacted my character and skill sets.

While I was participating in the writing club, our instructor encouraged us to dream big, to learn, and to use our writing voices to advocate for those in need. I wrote stories that reflected my experience as a young Black man living in an urban neighborhood, different issues that negatively impacted my community, and experiences that made my community wonderful. As a writer, I learned to be precise with my diction when advocating for others and to become a problem solver. Before I knew about the specific concepts of civics, equity, and justice in education, I practiced pondering topics and ideas that mattered to my local community and writing about them. I learned that I had a good eye and ear for storytelling, was critical, and questioned policies in schools and local government that did not fit my peers and me. I learned that my voice and words were a tool to bring awareness to my community. In addition, the writing club taught me to interrogate everything that I now teach my students every year, even to interrogate me, their teacher, and my thinking, demonstrating the power of our community: to question and think of possible solutions to disrupt situations that do not help humanity evolve and also to think of potential solutions to benefit all walks of life, especially those in Black and Latine communities.

Performing with my step team was an unforgettable experience. Together, we created routines for our favorite songs on urban radio. Stepping was another way I learned to use my skills and gifts to bring awareness to and reach the pathos of viewers. Whether it was working collaboratively to create routines, using precision, and developing and/or leading the group as an executive board member, I used my imagination to create step routines and facilitate meetings with the executive board to lead the group to greatness. We could step at rallies and protests using stepping as a demonstration to make our voices known. Participating in the writing club and the step team were the media through which I could dream, play, question, imagine, and create. Having facilitators who saw my peers and me as valuable young people and leaders who guided us always to use our skills for the betterment of humanity was life changing. Although I have had phenomenal teachers, there was something special about the nontraditional academic space that was liberating. There were no boundaries because it created unlimited possibilities for who I could become.

Nicole and Antero's Story

Even though we can each recall formative learning experiences in our youth that took place in community learning settings, it is sometimes difficult to hold on to them and remember their value when we ourselves become teachers. Both of us spent years in the high school English classroom, which understandably led us to focus our energies largely on developing powerful formal curriculum and instruction as we became comfortable with the rhythms and logics of the school day. When the two of us met as new graduate students in our doctoral program at UCLA, we bonded over our classroom experiences; while Antero was still teaching, Nicole was feeling a bit unmoored when it came to finding a place for herself without the familiar structures of the classroom. Who were we as educators, if not teachers?

The answer came in the form of a learning community called the UCLA Council of Youth Research. Our mentors developed a program that took place during summers and after school hours in which students from South and East Los Angeles gathered with us and teacher mentors to discuss the community issues that mattered most to them and to develop research projects that they conducted with their peers. While this inquiry model has a formal name in the scholarly literature—youth participatory action research (YPAR)—in practice, it felt like a regular family gathering. We discussed intellectual topics often covered in school, but now did so in a more casual atmosphere. The hierarchies between teachers and students dissipated a bit as we laughed together, ate together, and cared for each other. As trust grew between us, the barriers that sometimes keep formal learning from feeling immediate and authentic began to fall away, which allowed us to delve into serious topics from a stance of joy and resistance.

One of our roles as graduate students involved driving students home after our summer sessions. We listened to music, chatted, and decompressed—and when we reflected on these times afterward, we came to realize that they were just as crucial as our research sessions as spaces of learning. Our group recognized that this "carpool pedagogy" accessed our affective development and served as the gateway to playful dreaming about the futures we wanted to create together through our research. While our attention was directed toward the students, we soon realized that we were transformed as educators as well; this experience broadened our horizons of what kinds of learning were possible both inside and outside the classroom and reminded us to think beyond narrow conceptions of academic instruction.

Dream the Impossible

Any time the words *dream* and *imagination* are mentioned, we immediately think of the author Octavia Butler. She was a prolific thinker and writer grounded in speculation, (re)framing, (re) imagining, and (re)defining the ability to dream, to be creative, and to be critical. Through her words, she communicated the beauty and complexity of unlimited possibility and the use of the imagination. She is our muse, reminding us to take risks, use our imagination, and dream of various worlds. Her work is rooted in the idea and purpose of civics and speculation as she created characters, experiences, and communities opposite of the "norm." Civics in literacy spaces can break down barriers outside of content and remind us of the importance of inclusiveness in moving society forward.

The idea of civic education is typically associated with history classes. This is where young people learn about their rights and responsibilities as people in our society. However, the idea that civics only happens within historical content is outdated. Civics has a firm place in English and literacy spaces; young people can use their ideas and learn from civics to create a just, equitable, and inclusive world for all. As educators, our job is to provide a means for young people to engage in this work. Often, traditional schooling is restricted, focusing on state standards, learning goals, and assessment. When beyond-the-classroom spaces are created, students can operate at a higher vibration because they can utilize their personal, social, and academic skills outside of the confinements of school. As such, the possibility for young people to partake in civics, critical thinking, and problem-solving is limitless; they simultaneously imagine while engaging in acts of literacy skills such as reading, writing, speaking, and listening.

As the proud editors of this volume, we pose a few questions: How does your space impact young people in a positive light? How do you create a space grounded in liberation, dreaming, and imagination? And in what ways do you curate experiences for young people and adults to work collaboratively for the greater good of humanity?

Throughout this volume, each author presents how out-of-school clubs, organizations, activities, youth programs, partnerships, and experiences cater to the development of young people. These writers present theory and practice curated to demonstrate how nontraditional educational settings are essential. The beauty of this collection is that you have a plethora of knowledge and activities provided for educators by educators to utilize immediately. Each essay is particular because of the unique perspectives presented. This collection calls for educators and facilitators to give and nurture nontraditional school settings where young people can dream, create, and use their words, skills, and actions to move humanity forward to infinity and beyond.

Our current educational system can significantly harm young people, yet educators and facilitators operate with hope (Mirra & Garcia, 2020). Students face many barriers. Issues such as funding, preparation for state examinations as a way to demonstrate learning, the fight against antiracist education, and the banning of books have flooded onto our social media timelines and into the crevices of school. We want students to think critically about our world, become socially aware of issues facing humanity, and become solution-oriented. In addition, the students can be creative and critical, engage in debate and argumentation, and use their imagination to create a just society for all. However, due to legislation within various states, what sounds great to teach may be difficult for some teachers to have students engage with, such as diverse books (Dahlen, 2020), antiracism education (German, 2020; Paris & Alim, 2017), and LGBTQ+ inclusivity (Dodge & Crutcher, 2015), as well as considering multiple and missing perspectives. Therefore, spaces beyond the classroom are essential and needed for all. Students can use their imaginations to dream the impossible and engage in ways they may not typically engage with each other in their academic classes. Perhaps that may be the goal of speculative nontraditional educational spaces. The work between young people and educators/facilitators may demonstrate why these spaces are necessary. Out-of-school spaces define a speculative educational experience grounded in liberation, freedom, learning, fun, imagination, and all growth. Throughout the collection, we have one common goal: to disrupt the concept of traditional learning space and provide moments for students to work collaboratively and shape their academic, personal, and social skills.

We, the editors and contributing writers, have curated thirteen examples that provide educators working with youth in out-of-school spaces and ideas of what speculative approaches can look like today. These approaches are intentional and reflect the environment and communities we work in; the multitude of voices throughout this collection speaks of various environments of school grade levels, ethnicities, and cultural and socioeconomic backgrounds. Furthermore, these voices speak to the unlimited possibilities of working with young people.

Structure of This Book

This volume speaks to educators, expanding our understanding of what is possible in nontraditional educational environments. It offers concrete examples of various ways people can cultivate an impactful space working with youth to support their dreams, skills, and goals. Each essay is strategic and presents ideas and concepts that can be utilized instantly.

First, Francisco L. Torres and Astrid N. Sambolín Morales present findings from a two-year summer literacy program for Black children and youth in Ohio. They examine how comic storytelling can be used to explore local injustices, highlighting participants' civic engagement potential. The authors argue that combining imagination and critical pedagogy enables students to develop civic literacies that address injustices and empower them as change agents. The essay concludes with practical recommendations for educators to foster critical/creative storytelling and radical healing in their classrooms.

Next, Neisha Terry examines the impact of misrepresentational narratives on Black immigrant youth (BIY) in academic settings. She introduces podcasting as civically engaged story-telling (PACES) to amplify authentic BIY narratives. Drawing from a design-based research study, the author demonstrates how PACES enables BIY to challenge dominant discourses about their identities. The essay proposes PACES as an innovative approach for marginalized youth to craft critical identity narratives, contributing to discussions on inclusive educational practices.

The following essay by Jen Scott Curwood advocates for a broader conception of youth activism and civic engagement rooted in creative expression and critical reflection. She explores storytelling as a lens for understanding youth activism and its civic role. She then applies this framework to her research on spoken word poetry in Australia, demonstrating how creativity and criticality are shaping new avenues for youth civic participation.

Throughout the fourth essay, Michael Dando explores how Black youth use speculative design and Afrofuturism as tools for civic engagement and social justice. He examines the role of freedom dreaming, critical speculative design, and counterstorying in critiquing injustice and envisioning equitable futures. He also argues that creating spaces for marginalized communities to engage in speculative thinking is crucial for critical literacy and social justice efforts, challenging systems that undermine nondominant narratives across time.

Next, Dominique Skye McDaniel examines how youth of color utilize social media for civic literacy and social justice activism. She analyzes cases from 2021, exploring how these youth employ multimodal literacies across various digital platforms to engage in social movements. Through interviews, artifact analysis, and online observations, she investigates the experiences and identities of these young activists. The study emphasizes the role of digital literacies in empowering youth to confront systemic racism and to advocate for change. The section concludes by discussing the implications for educators to incorporate these digital civic literacy practices into classroom settings, highlighting the importance of recognizing marginalized youth's contributions in digital spaces.

As a team, Julia Lynch and Beth Gafford next present an arts-based literacy project examining how Black boys develop literacy skills to affirm their identity, build agency, and reclaim their futures. They describe how Black*Mother* scholars employed critical arts-based teaching as a culturally sustaining literacy method. Lynch and Gafford's findings reveal that Black boys learn to read the world early, experience tension between identity and intellect, and pivot societal stereotypes to access joy. They argue that culturally sustaining literacy practices can empower youth to explore their identities and challenge social and political structures through activism.

In the seventh essay, Megan Heise and Meg Booth challenge the narrow framing of civic engagement solely in terms of citizenship, particularly in relation to forcibly displaced people. The authors present a more expansive view of civic education by facilitating and listening to refugee-background youths' multimodal counterstories to prefigure a more inclusive civic society. Drawing on their work with the Alliance for Refugee Youth Support and Education (ARYSE), Heise and Booth share content from student interviews and their own reflections about two multimodal projects: a zine-making workshop and a collaborative book-making project. Using a counterstory framework, the essay elaborates on four core themes: expanding civic perspectives, crafting counterstories, leveraging multimodal tools, and fostering counter-publics. The authors argue that these approaches can help us work alongside and center refugee-background youth in reimagining new and more socially just civic realities.

Next, Emily Plummer Catena unpacks elements of a journalism summer writing camp curriculum designed to foster civic engagement through both the creation and critical consumption of journalistic media. By analyzing how headlines position youth activists, Catena demonstrates how students can deconstruct representations in journalistic media. Additionally, the essay explores how the camp reconstructed journalistic practices, emphasizing the role of a journalistic mentor in guiding students to transform news articles into dramatic monologues. This approach exemplifies how literacy educators can engage students in speculative civic literacy learning by approaching journalism as a personal and creative endeavor while critically attuning to the power and dynamics within youth writing.

Fabio C. Campos takes the reader on a domestic and international journey in the next essay, discussing the implementation of civic imagination workshops in Santa Ana, California, US, and Rio de Janeiro, Brazil. Through rich narratives, participants used their historicity and identity to learn about social issues and develop their agency and voice. Storytelling served as a tool for self-discovery and empowerment, enabling participants to challenge dominant narratives, address structural inequalities, and bring attention to social issues. The essay contributes to understanding the balance between criticality and imagination required for meaningful civic learning in ELA environments.

In the next essay, Ankhi G. Thakurta presents a transnational practitioner study exploring how India and US-based urban migrant girls developed their civic identities and perspectives within two separate virtual out-of-school inquiry communities. Drawing on coalitional literacies and transnational girlhoods frameworks, the study examines how girls in each nation engaged with diverse texts to cultivate critical and empathetic meaning-making practices. She discusses how youths' literacies reflected their emerging capacities for cross-boundary collaboration, essential for imagining and striving toward more just civic futures. The essay concludes with recommendations for ELA educators to support youths' coalitional civic literacies and imaginations.

Then, Shanna Peeples demonstrates how educators can leverage local landscapes for creative, interdisciplinary civics learning. The author presents the 2892 Miles to Go project, a place-based, community-engaged learning program centered on Route 66, as a case study. This essay illustrates the methods of place-based learning and place consciousness by applying social justice-focused texts in out-of-school contexts, even in politically restrictive environments. Collaborating with diverse partners and utilizing accessible digital tools, Peeples demonstrates the potential of creating "living textbooks" to center marginalized experiences and knowledge.

The next essay centers on collaboration as authors Karis Jones, M'mah Cisse, Anais Santigo, and Kimonye Mays explore how youth can navigate and resist toxic practices in participatory fandom discourses and exclusionary trends in the media industry. By changing their individual media consumption and engagement practices, youth can contribute to shifting larger structures of social inequalities toward more just futures. The essay presents takeaways from the "Meaningful Media" course, a virtual seminar series focused on developing critical media skills in youth-selected contexts, culminating in field trips to local anime and comic conventions. The essay considers implications for civic engagement through youth participation at in-person fan events, sharing speculative civic literacies practices for before, during, and after place-based conventions.

Our collection ends with Grace MyHyun Kim, who explores how digital literacy practices can cultivate empathy and action for global issues, particularly among youth. She examines the transnational fan activism of Korean popular music (K-pop) fans as an example of an online community that disrupts traditional civic learning paradigms. The essay centers on globally diverse youth as social change agents, highlighting examples of K-pop fans practicing civic engagement through their digital literacy practices. Additionally, she documents the joy and transnational relationality in civic literacy learning in out-of-school environments. The essay concludes by discussing the implications of these examples for teacher education and English language arts, proposing an expanded perspective of civic learning that supports the creative digital literacy practices of youth and the development of global civic futures.

We hope the readers of this book will gain a deeper understanding of the power of educators collaborating with young people and imagining radical, fun, engaging, and critically curated spaces to cultivate the minds and skills of all children and youth outside of our traditional school buildings.

Works Cited

Bickley, W., Boyett, R. L., Miller, T. L., Warren, M., & Duclon, D. (Executive Producers). (1989–1998). *Family matters* [TV series]. Miller-Boyett Productions; Bickley-Warren Productions.

Dahlen, S. P. (2020). "We need diverse books": Diversity, activism, and children's literature. In N. op de Beeck (Ed.), *Literary cultures and twenty-first-century childhoods* (pp. 83–108). Springer.

Dodge, A. M., & Crutcher, P. A. (2015). Inclusive classrooms for LGBTQ students: Using linked text sets to challenge the hegemonic "single story." *Journal of Adolescent & Adult Literacy, 59*(1), 95–105.

Farquhar, R., Finney, S., Spears, V., Edmonds, J., Hutcherson, W., & Johnson, F. (Executive Producers). (1996–2001). *Moesha* [TV series]. Regan Jon Productions; Saradipity Productions; Jump at the Sun Productions; Big Ticket Television.

German, L. (2020). *The Anti racist teacher: Reading instruction workbook.* Multicultural Classroom.

Lasseter, J. (Director). (1995). *Toy story* [Film]. Pixar Animation Studios.

Mirra, N., & Garcia, A. (2020). "I hesitate but I do have hope": Youth speculative civic literacies for troubled times. *Harvard Educational Review, 90*(2), 295–321.

Paris, D., & Alim, H. S. (Eds.). (2017). *Culturally sustaining pedagogies: Teaching and learning for justice in a changing world.* Teachers College Press.

Drawing from/for Justice: Black Children and Youth as Activists in Literacy Spaces

FRANCISCO L. TORRES & ASTRID N. SAMBOLÍN MORALES

Stop gun violence
—Amy (middle school)

Little opportunity for people when Black and more opportunity for the whites
—Eli (elementary school)

Racism is bad for everybody. Young kids should not experience racism during school time
—Mia (high school)

Introduction

In this piece, we argue that civic engagement—active participation in a democracy for the betterment of communities and the pursuit of social justice (Youniss, 2011)—should be nurtured and sustained in children and youth of color, beginning with storytelling and imagining different forms of activism against injustice. When imagining civic engagement in the current sociopolitical context, many might be inclined to think of practices and contexts firmly within the domain of adulthood. There is good reason for this inclination. As Cohen (2005) argues, "children are excluded almost wholesale from the freedoms that compose the oldest category of rights associated with citizenship," like the right to protest and exercise their freedom of speech (p. 224) among other examples. Warnick's (2009) work explores youth's speech rights in the US public school system, and he concludes that several intersecting factors limit speech rights in schools, including age and safety considerations among others. As such, free speech, a cornerstone of civic engagement, is often positioned as a right reserved for those old enough to have "experienced the world," positioning age as a significant factor in justifying whether a practice or stance "counts" as civic engagement.

Currently, university student protests of the war in Gaza are being met with attacks on a variety of fronts, including from critics who claim that the adults protesting are acting "as children are prone to do" (Downey, 2024). This example illustrates how civic engagement is positioned as being within the realm of adulthood. Moreover, it implies that only certain practices and discourses are considered to be "appropriate" or "proper" civic engagement. However, in our work with children and young adults from marginalized communities, our experiences and findings refute this idea, highlighting how young individuals have the capacity for and interest in civic engagement. Children and youth want to have their voices heard for the betterment of their worlds and communities, and they engage in alternative forms of civic participation, including creative and artistic expression, to this end (Cammarota, 2008; Ginwright et al., 2006; Ginwright, 2010).

Our essay draws from data collected during the summers of 2022 and 2023 when Francisco partnered with a local nonprofit serving the Black community to provide children and youth with a summer literacy program. Over the two summers, the project invited 38 participating Black children and youth to explore local injustices that mattered to them through comic storytelling. The quotes introducing this essay are just a few examples illustrating how children and youth of different ages—children belonging to marginalized communities and creating comics to name and critically analyze issues affecting their communities—engage in advocacy. Their words illustrate their critical consciousness that society has to transform for the sake of themselves and other people of color. The children and youth in this project accepted the invitation to participate in this work, and their contributions show the possibilities literacy spaces can open for imaginative worlds in support of criticality, imagination, and healing.

The research questions guiding this work were:

- What themes/conflicts/issues do Black children and youth identify in their comics as affecting their daily lives?
- What lessons can we learn from the activism and civic participation of Black children and youth in their comics?

The Three C's of Civic Engagement: Criticality, Creativity, and Cultural Responsiveness

Research has captured how civic engagement can be particularly beneficial for members of marginalized communities (Kahne & Middaugh, 2008; Levinson, 2012). For example, Hope and Jagers (2014) discuss how civic education can develop Black youth's awareness of institutional discrimination, thus increasing the likelihood of civic engagement to address inequity. It is important to note that, according to Hope and Jagers (2014), a crucial component of civic engagement is critical analysis. This awareness of institutional inequity developed through critical analysis can open pathways for Black youth to engage in "alternative social change strategies such as . . . politically motivated cultural and artistic expression through poetry and hip-hop" (Hope & Jagers, 2014, p. 460). Moreover, research reflects how Black and Latine youth's understanding of systemic racism and inequity through civic education can promote wellness through their truth telling (Hart & Atkins, 2002; Watts et al., 2003).

Cammarota's (2008) work links civic engagement with the idea of cultural production or the creation of cultural artifacts (e.g., poems, texts, images, etc.) that reflect certain values and ideas (Willis, 1981). As such, Cammarota (2008) argues that children and youth can create cultural artifacts that reflect and challenge their position and their circumstances in their community. With this framing, we place the roles of criticality, creativity, and culturally responsive/sustaining pedagogy in spaces that foster and sustain cultural production and civic engagement with youth of color at the forefront.

What Drives Us: Criticality, Creativity/Imagination, and Healing

We echo existing research that centers on criticality in civic education and engagement. Developing critical consciousness through critical pedagogy (Freire, 2005) requires individuals from minoritized communities to reflect and act to understand systemic oppression and how its mechanisms affect how they navigate the world (Freire, 2005; Hope & Jagers, 2014). We argue that this awareness and critical analysis—critical consciousness—serve as the starting point for youth of color to engage in civic education creatively. Thus, we believe *all activism begins with creativity and imagination;* one needs to imagine beyond one's current situation to understand and visualize what is worth fighting for and the possible outcomes. Creativity and imagination can be tapped to engage children and youth in taking activist stances through critical analysis and imagination. For example, Francisco's previous work (Torres, 2021) highlights how Latine fifth graders are able to subvert norms of submissiveness that are applied to children by adults through superhero storytelling, pushing students to fight for social change in issues that mattered to them, like bilingual education. In that study, children showed they had the imaginative and activist potential to articulate what they want to see in the world. These ideas are often silenced by adults who think they know better because of age and education. Enciso (2017) argues that imagination "entails the effort to manage gaps in time between what is, what has been, and what might become within contexts of unequal histories and expectations for speaking and being heard" (p. 35). In this way, imagination allows children and youth to engage in societal change and civic engagement in spaces where they typically are not recognized or encouraged due to their positionality (including but not limited to their age). Medina and Wohlwend (2014) remind us that "imagination is the antithesis of control" (p. 112). By providing spaces where children and youth of color can critically reflect and express themselves "in the cultural, social, and online spaces where they already are" (Kuttner, 2016, p. 530), they have opportunities/possibilities to subvert the genuine societal constraints placed on them as young members of minoritized groups.

Phillips (2021) highlights the power of imaginaries and critical futurisms where "the conditions of the present can be reimagined and reconfigured in the future . . ." (p. 2). This work subverts an "age of impossibility" (Giroux, 2012) and *dis-possibility* (Phillips, 2021) created by the racist, white supremacist systems Black children and youth are forced to navigate daily because, as Greene (1995) states, imagination allows for "visions of what should be and what might be" (p. 5) The "what might be" in this work is a time and space founded on our shared freedom and justice. Only then do we arrive at radical healing, or "the capacity of young people to *create* the type of communities in which they want to live" (Ginwright, 2010; emphasis added).

Engaging in Civic Comic Storytelling

During the summers of 2022 and 2023, Francisco led two literacy programs for youth with a local nonprofit that serves the Black community in Northeast Ohio. Both authors are Latine scholars committed to antiracist work and naming/combating anti-Blackness. During his time in the program, Francisco focused on how children and youth made sense of and articulated issues of inequity within their communities and how they could address them in culturally responsive and sustaining ways. It is important to note that a key difference between the programs of 2022 and 2023 was that the former was superhero themed and the latter was focused on participants' schools and schooling in general. Both programs followed the same premise: centering comic storytelling as an alternative practice for justice and civic engagement. The summer sessions followed three phases: 1) creating and sustaining a community by sharing our identities and experiences in ways that acknowledged the spaces participants occupied, 2) developing a shared understanding of injustice and then applying what we learned/discussed to our community through the development of critical consciousness, and 3) creating individual comics that addressed the injustices each student identified and cared about through storytelling. Thus, the methodology of this research followed the tenets of critical pedagogy by foregrounding 1) relationships and care, 2) issues that matter to participants, and 3) a recursive process of reflection and action.

Throughout this work, students journaled about their experiences, responded to questions posed by Francisco regarding their work, lives, and community, and created storyboards for their comics. For example, in phase 1, Francisco asked students to write their names in the journal and draw/write things around the name that they were willing to share with others. These included their favorite music and what/who they loved most. In phase 2, Francisco asked students to name the injustices they experienced in their communities or have seen others experience. Some of the injustices students named included bullying, bomb threats, and school shootings. In phase 3, students created storyboards based on the injustice they wanted to focus on. The prompt was for students to tell a story illustrating how they would face that injustice as themselves, by themselves, and then with others as a community. Beyond the journaling activity, students also used their journals to create comics about issues that mattered to them, centering the forms of activism they would take on if they could. The objective of these exercises—exercises resulting from a critical pedagogy approach—was to focus students' critical analysis on their lives, experiences, and what they cared about, engaging in storytelling and other creative expressions to imagine worlds where they could/should challenge injustices that affected how they navigated the world. The hope was to offer a space and possibilities for students to experience radical healing through their capacity to imagine and create the communities they wish and deserve to live in.

Data Collection and Analysis

The data collected during these two summers includes field notes, journals, audio recordings from classroom discussions, and the comics created by students. This entry will focus on the comics to highlight the possibilities of civic engagement through the stories children and youth of color choose to tell. These comics were analyzed using Multimodal Critical Discourse Analysis (Machin and Mayr, 2012) to critically engage with the discourses and images created by participants. Through this analysis, we found that participants reflected on and articulated the injustices that mattered to them as Black individuals (e.g., racism, violence, etc.) and how these shaped their identities and experiences. Below, we share a few examples of students' comics to highlight how they choose to share stories of injustice and how they imagine challenging them to create more hopeful futures. Finally, we conclude this piece by discussing practices teachers and researchers can take up in their spaces.

Lessons on Children and Youth Civic Engagement

Darrel

Students were asked to create stories centered on who they are as young people, and Francisco did not micromanage students' storytelling, only asking participants that they engage with an injustice they cared about even if they didn't want to include themselves in their story. Darrel, a Black fifth grader, decided to exclude who he was from the story, instead choosing to imagine himself as a samurai fighting a villain who wanted to kill Black people. In Figures 1 and 2, Darrel introduces his hero, the samurai, and the unnamed villain of his story, who states that "Black lives don't deserve [to] live." In these two pages, it is clear that Darrel is deeply concerned with Black lives. This concern reflects the larger sociopolitical context; Jayland Walker was murdered by police only a ten-minute drive away from the site of our project. Participants frequently brought up the protests and the injustice of Jayland's death.

One of the elements that Francisco asked students to take up in their storytelling was a final message for the reader. This request intends to center participants' reflections rather than leaving the story's message to interpretation. For Darrel, his final message after finally defeating his villain was "we should stop killing Black people and end racism" (Figure 3). This message and the comic used to convey it illustrate how children and youth can and do respond to opportunities for civic engagement. Through artistic expression, students enact their speech rights, producing cultural artifacts that reflect how they actively participate in the work of voicing injustices. Moreover, they dream up challenges against these injustices to improve their communities and to pursue social justice. Critical pedagogy acknowledges that reflecting and voicing oppression is essential in developing a critical consciousness. Thus, *speaking up is activism.* In addition, by encouraging participants to end their stories with a message to the reader, Francisco created a space for possibilities, one where children and youth shared their sensemaking through creativity, imagination, and self-expression, thus subverting material societal constraints placed on them as young people of color. Darrel wants racism to end, and his work poses important questions: How are his readers challenging this injustice? How is/will he?

Figure 1.

Figure 2.

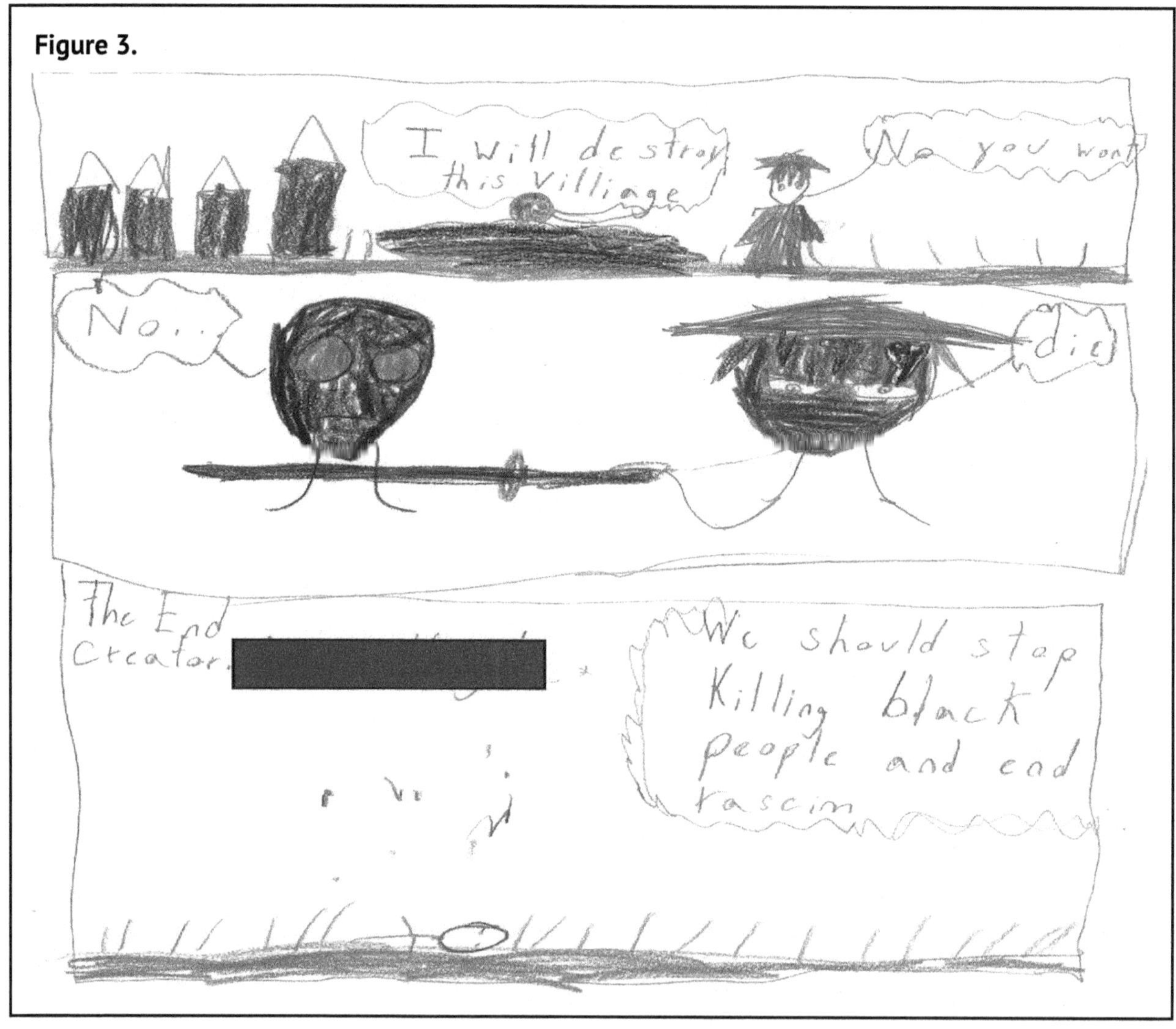

Figure 3.

Ren

Like Darrel, Ren, a Black sixth grader, focused on violence: he chose bullying as his topic. Ren's reflections and portrayal of death stood out to us. In the first four panels of his story (Figure 4), he imagines how he gets his powers, protects his identity, and lives as a hero. Across these initial panels, we also see two stories of death arise: his friend's and his family's. Unfortunately, we do not have data that might explain why he focused on death in the first section of his story. Perhaps he was merely following the trope of superhero narratives, where a death catalyzes the acquisition of superpowers, providing the superhero with the drive/rationale to fight crime. As the story progresses, Ren introduces his villain, a typical bully who is permanently "angry" and attacks others. Interestingly, Ren imagines the bully as someone who eventually becomes his friend after they resolve their issues through discussion.

In the final part of his story (Figure 5), Ren writes, "hey guys, I just want to tell you that don't be heartless, mean or bully. Its bad and a lot of people has been commiting suicides because of bullys." Here, Ren argues that injustice leads to violence, even death. Other deaths in Ren's comic seem unrelated to this message, but he connects death and bullying in his final message to readers. What stands out to us

Hi my name
is
I have Powers
I got powers from this explosion
It took my eyes out too but
somehow I can still
see.
I was with my best friend when it
happened but he died I thought
I moved in this house to keep my secret
identity
I captured all the bad guys and put them in Jail.
I lived alone because my family died in a car accident. I was so sad.
I had to learn that every body dies one day.
When I in my House I just play video games on my Xbox Like 2K and
Madden.
Thats my dresser xbox and TV
Da Goat
Xbox
when I'm Bored I go to Sleep
thats my bed and pillow covers
I have telekenisis powers. and I can be invisible.
I was watching the news today and I saw this bad guy who had Super strength, and Super Speed I said this was impossible because I thought I was the only one
They were saying on the news that he was so angry.
I came to the seen and punched me 10 Blocks away. When I came back I finally used my powers right and beat him he had a mask on so I took it off.
It was my best friend we vowed to never argue again and he became good too

Figure 4.

Figure 5.

about this image, beyond his message, is how Ren places his character at the center to tell the message without distractions from other characters or objects. He is addressing the audience earnestly, using comic storytelling and creative decisions—decisions available through this medium and resulting from his participation in a space guided by critical pedagogy—to convey his sensemaking regarding bullying and its impact. More importantly, Ren demonstrates confidence in the worth of his perspective. It might signal the beginning of radical healing or the capacity to dream up and *create* the community he deserves.

Brant

In Brant's narrative, we step away from the superhero genre to discuss how he views injustices as a student. The first page of his story highlights the issue Brant, a Black fourth grader, is most concerned about: school shootings. In his comic, he uses images and words to create a cultural artifact conveying the anxiety of being in a lockdown, the feeling of being trapped within the school while fearing for one's life, and the ensuing chaos once the police arrive (Figure 6). As previously mentioned, school shootings are a significant concern for students in our K–12 schools. At the time Brant was writing his story, the Uvalde school shooting and its twenty-one victims, nineteen of whom were children, dominated the news. As readers, we are left to wonder whether students have the opportunity to talk about the fear and anxiety regarding school safety and active shooter situations. As Brant's work illustrates, children and youth of color take up the opportunity to grapple with issues affecting their communities when given the space to express themselves.

Figure 6.

In the final section of Brant's story, he depicts the different forms of activism he would enact if an active shooter were at his school. Brant states in the first two panels that he would call the police and protest. These actions adhere to typical forms of civic engagement against this form of violence, but we are taken aback by the third panel (Figure 7), where he writes "I will tell the shooter don't do it then I will award him if he don't do it." What stands out to us here is Brant's decision to humanize the villain in his story, engaging in dialogue and extending an olive branch. In his comic storytelling, Brant suggests that offering a space for dialogue rather than attacking the villain of his story would lead to the best outcome. There

Figure 7.

is a restorative, healing component to Brant's proposed solution. His comic storytelling, an outlet for his criticality, creativity, and sense of justice, provides a space for this youth of color to voice his fears and to imagine better futures for the good of his community. Moreover, it opens pathways toward radical healing and dreaming through the development of critical consciousness.

Conclusion/Implication for Literacy Classrooms

Children and youth deserve opportunities to imagine and critically engage with systemic inequity. Moreover, educators and researchers must create spaces that center these voices and create/sustain practices that develop civic engagement for youth of color for critical reflection, activism, and healing. In the comic storytelling featured in this essay, Darrel, Ren, and Brant name and grapple with issues reflecting the systemic inequity that impacts their lives as well as the lives of their loved ones. They do so by drawing on what they see, hear, and interact with when navigating the world as young Black people: school shootings, police brutality, and bullying among others. The stories in this essay capture the criticality, imagining, and dreaming that can surface when we support and believe in children and young adults' ability to meaningfully explore issues that matter to them. In the section below, we highlight moves teachers and researchers alike can take to center student voices and activism in their practice.

Storying in Your Space

Identity: When using superhero comics or graphic novels, it is natural to want to have students become a character they aren't, like the Hulk, Black Panther, etc. Instead, teachers can encourage students to center who they are as young people whose voices and actions matter. We all deserve to find joy, peace, and strength in our perceptions of ourselves in the present. Thus, encouraging students to remember that who they are matters and should be included in the storytelling process is key.

Criticality: Injustice is all around us. When trying to get students to develop critical consciousness that leads to action, we can begin by listening to their concerns, wants, and needs. In our work, we begin listening to our students and then creating presentations based on data and research about issues they mentioned or are reflective of their experience, like the Black Lives Matter movement. This shift from naming a concern to engaging in research is meant to signal that students are not alone or misguided in relation to these fears. In addition, it helps develop tools they can use to ask questions about systemic inequity (like the steps the US can take to prevent school shootings) and then work toward a solution.

Creativity: The heart of this work is creativity and our ability as adults to nurture or stifle children and youth's creativity. To imagine more hopeful and activist futures/selves, we need imagination. In our work, we get students to see themselves as powerful, to research and engage in issues of injustice, and to imagine narratives that center their lives in powerful ways for better, brighter futures. You need creativity to civically engage and imagine new ways of resisting, thus enacting a powerful tool for change. In short, literacy spaces must center critical thinking/consciousness, the self, and imagination as they encourage students to see themselves as agents of change who can and will make a difference.

Works Cited

Cammarota, J. (2008). The cultural organizing of youth ethnographers: Formalizing a praxis-based pedagogy. *Anthropology & Education Quarterly*, *39*(1), 45–58.

Cohen, E. F. (2005). Neither seen nor heard: Children's citizenship in contemporary democracies. *Citizenship Studies*, *9*(2), 221–240.https://doi.org/10.1080/13621020500069687

Downey, C. (2024, May 8). *If students are children, ban them from life-ruining activism. The Telegraph.* www.telegraph.co.uk/us/comment/2024/05/08/student-protests-palestine-gaza-columbia-nypd-activism/

Enciso, P. E. (2017). Stories lost and found: Mobilizing imagination in literacy research and practice. *Literacy Research: Theory, Method, and Practice*, *66*(1), 29–52. https://doi.org/10.1177/2381336917718813

Freire, P. (2005). *Education for critical consciousness*. Continuum.

Ginwright, S. (2010). Peace out to revolution! Activism among African American youth: An argument for radical healing. *Young: Nordic Journal of Youth Research*, *18*(1), 77–96.

Ginwright, S., Noguera, P., & Cammarota, J. (Eds.). (2006). *Beyond resistance! Youth activism and community change: New democratic possibilities for practice and policy for America's youth*. Routledge.

Giroux, H. (2012). *Twilight of the social: Resurgent politics in an age of disposability*. Routledge.

Greene, M. (1995). *Releasing the imagination: Essays on education, the arts, and social change.* Jossey-Bass.

Hart, D., & Atkins, R. (2002). Civic competence in urban youth. *Applied Developmental Science*, *6*(4), 227–236.

Hope, E. C., & Jagers, R. J. (2014). The role of sociopolitical attitudes and civic education in the civic engagement of Black youth. *Journal of Research on Adolescence*, *24*(3), 460–470.

Kuttner, P.J. (2016). Hip-hop citizens: Arts-based, culturally sustaining civic engagement pedagogy. *Harvard Educational Review*, *86*(4), 527–555.

Levinson, M. (2012). *No citizen left behind*. Harvard University Press.

Machin, D., & Mayr, A. (2012). *How to do critical discourse analysis: A multimodal introduction.* SAGE.

Medina, C. L., & Wohlwend, K. (2014). *Literacy, play and globalization: Converging imaginaries in children's critical and cultural performances*. Routledge

Phillips, P. (2021). Critical Black futurism: Affecting affinities within curriculum studies. *Journal of the American Association for the Advancement of Curriculum Studies*, *14*(2), 1–23.

Torres, F. L. (2022). "It's our job as people to make others feel valued": Children imagining more caring and just worlds through superhero stories. *Research in the Teaching of English*, *56*(4), 360–384.

Warnick, B. R. (2009). Student speech rights and the special characteristics of the school environment. *Educational Researcher*, *38*(3), 200–215.

Watts, R. J., Williams, N. C., & Jagers, R. J. (2003). Sociopolitical development. *American Journal of Community Psychology*, *31*(1–2), 185–194.

Willis, P. (1981). Cultural production is different from cultural reproduction is different from social reproduction is different from reproduction. *Interchange: A Quarterly Review of Education*, *12*(2–3), 48–67.

Youniss, J. (2011). Civic education: What schools can do to encourage civic identity and action. *Applied Developmental Science*, *15*(2), 98–103.

Podcasting as Civically Engaged Storytelling with Black Immigrant Youth

NEISHA TERRY

"Ms. Neisha! Ms. Neisha! Let me tell you my story."

It was a warm summer day, and I was standing in a small classroom with seventeen Black immigrant youth (BIY) from West Africa. They were part of my research study, and we were engaged in the first of three podcast workshops exploring BIY identities in the US. Somewhere along the way, the discussion took an unexpected turn. The youth, eager to have their stories heard, began sharing stories of their schooling experiences before migrating.

I was initially concerned that the conversation was off track from crafting identity narratives in response to societal discourses. However, upon reflection, I discovered that these seemingly tangential stories were powerful identity narratives that offered a critical and enlightening counterpoint to the dominant societal discourses about BIY in the US. This realization underscores podcasting's transformative potential to amplify BIY voices. It also highlights how podcasting as civically engaged storytelling (PACES) can support BIY in navigating their identities in the US.

In this essay, I share insights from a larger design-based research study on how PACES can support BIY identity navigation. The study involved a podcasting program that was implemented with seventeen middle and high school youth from West Africa, most of whom had lived in the US for fewer than five years. The program featured three identity workshops in which participants discussed and recorded podcasts addressing dominant discourses about Black immigrants. After each workshop, I held focus groups and interviews to solicit feedback and suggestions for improvement. At the end of the program, participants published selected podcast episodes on our website.

Theoretical Frameworks

BIY's intersectional identities of being both Black and immigrant expose them to layered discrimination. Anti-Black and anti-immigrant discourses in the US affect societal views, educational policies, and practices, making BIY's identities nearly invisible in US K–12 education (Smith, 2023). This impacts BIY's academic experiences and trajectories (Terry, 2023; Vázquez Baur, 2022). As a Black immigrant, I have felt the trauma of migrating to an anti-Black, anti-immigrant country; as an educator, I have witnessed the symbolic violence against BIY in classrooms

(Kholi et al., 2017; Kiramba et al., 2023) through a lack of representation and the presence of stereotypical and derogatory narratives.

Critical Race Theory and BIY Identity Representations

Critical race theory (CRT) illuminates the experiences of marginalized peoples and suggests ways to combat their oppression. This study is based on three CRT tenets: racism is pervasive in US society, intersectional identities intensify oppression, and counter-storytelling can empower marginalized groups in liberatory ways (Delgado & Stefancic, 2017).

The importance of counter-storytelling is reflected in the call to center BIY's voices in their academic experiences via culturally responsive pedagogies (Skerrett, 2020; Smith, 2023). In response to this call, educators and researchers have diversified curricula and expanded their frameworks to offer more diverse representation and identity support (Skerrett, 2020; Smith, 2023). We are making progress.

However, learning spaces can still be places of identity negation and (mis)representation for BIY (Jones-Young, 2016). Linguistic hegemony exposes BIY to transraciolinguistic discrimination (Smith, 2023), and our mirrors and windows sometimes inadvertently offer stereotypical or discriminatory representations (Young, 2024) that do not truly reflect BIY. Moreover, authentic representation of BIY is challenging due to their diverse and evolving identities. BIY come from various regions and cultures (Tamir & Anderson, 2022), and their identities are constantly shifting (Hall, 1990; Young, 2024). Thus, it is difficult to define what authentic BIY mirrors should be.

Despite the challenges of accurately capturing and reflecting BIY's identities, our learning sites must provide spaces of belonging for BIY. BIY must see themselves and their stories in our work with them. We must also offer other learners authentic insights into BIY identities. Bishop (1990) argued that when we engage in pedagogical practices that do not accurately represent our students' identities, we send a message that our students are not valued.

Counter-storytelling is a crucial tool that empowers BIY to author their narratives in response to dominant discourses. When we provide spaces for BIY to engage in counter-storytelling, we create opportunities to dispel stereotypes, thereby fostering a more authentic representation of identity. We are also creating spaces of belonging and recognition.

Multiliteracies and Amplifying BIY Narratives

The challenge of authentically representing BIY identities underscores the need to nurture strategies for them to tell their own stories. This conviction led me to the second theoretical framework for this study. The theory of multiliteracies (Cazden et al., 1996) argues that existing discourses often misrepresent identities, creating a disconnect between self-perception and societal positioning. It emphasizes the need to redesign discourses through critical interrogation that can agentively transform identity positioning. This approach includes four elements: situated practice, overt instruction, critical framing, and transformed practice. I used these elements in my identity workshops to amplify BIY voices in reshaping dominant discourses.

I utilized podcasting as a vital aspect of the program because the platform is a one-stop-shop that facilitates discourse interrogation, authentic response, and dissemination of participants' narratives. Table 1 provides a broad overview of the program. In the next section, I will discuss how podcasting supported BIY's critical civic engagement with dominant discourses.

Table 1. Table providing a broad overview of the podcasting program.

Program Elements	Descriptive Overview
Opening Activities	Introduction to the program and initial focus group discussions
Workshop One	Focus: Exploring and responding to dominant narratives in society about Black immigrants
Workshop Two	Focus: Exploring and responding to dominant narratives in K–12 about Black immigrants
Workshop Three	Focus: Exploring and responding to dominant narratives in affinity spaces about Black immigrants
Closing Activities	Closing focus group discussions and interviews; podcast publication and celebration

Podcasting and Black Immigrant Youth

Research shows that podcasting is an effective learning tool. Teachers and researchers have used it to engage youth in text analysis, discourse interrogation, and voice amplification (Hamilton & Nguyen, 2008; Kassaie et al., 2021). Podcasting also helps students understand complex texts, improve their language and literacy skills, and enhance their writing abilities (Besser et al., 2022; Curlee & Singer Early, 2023; Young, 2024). Podcasting is established as an effective strategy for literacy education.

The affordances of podcasting for immigrant youth are also well documented. Podcasting benefits immigrant youth by helping them explore racialized experiences and enhancing their storytelling (Barner, 2021; Smith et al., 2021). However, while many podcasting programs amplify immigrant youth narratives, few focus specifically on BIY. To increase authentic representation and amplify BIY voices, podcasting should be expanded as a culturally responsive strategy with BIY. Considering the proliferation of stories that (mis)represent or stereotype their identities, podcasting programs for BIY should be civic focused to facilitate BIY engagement with and reframing of dominant discourses.

Podcasting as Civically Engaged Storytelling (PACES)

Podcasting as civically engaged storytelling (PACES) uses podcasting as both a process and a product (see Figure 1). It integrates a socially conscious focus into programs for BIY. It also centers marginalized voices in critically interrogating and repositioning identities within societal structures and systems.

PACES has two distinct features. First, it incorporates multiliteracies to help participants interrogate dominant discourses and critique how these discourses position their identities. This feature requires participants to authentically (re)position these discourses, fostering civic engagement and influencing policy transformation.

Situated practice is a key element of the "how" of multiliteracies pedagogy that emphasizes establishing a learning community (Cazden et al., 1996). PACES embeds participants in various learning community configurations by designing opportunities for them to engage in dialogue and collaboration via whole group and

Figure 1. PACES as process and product.

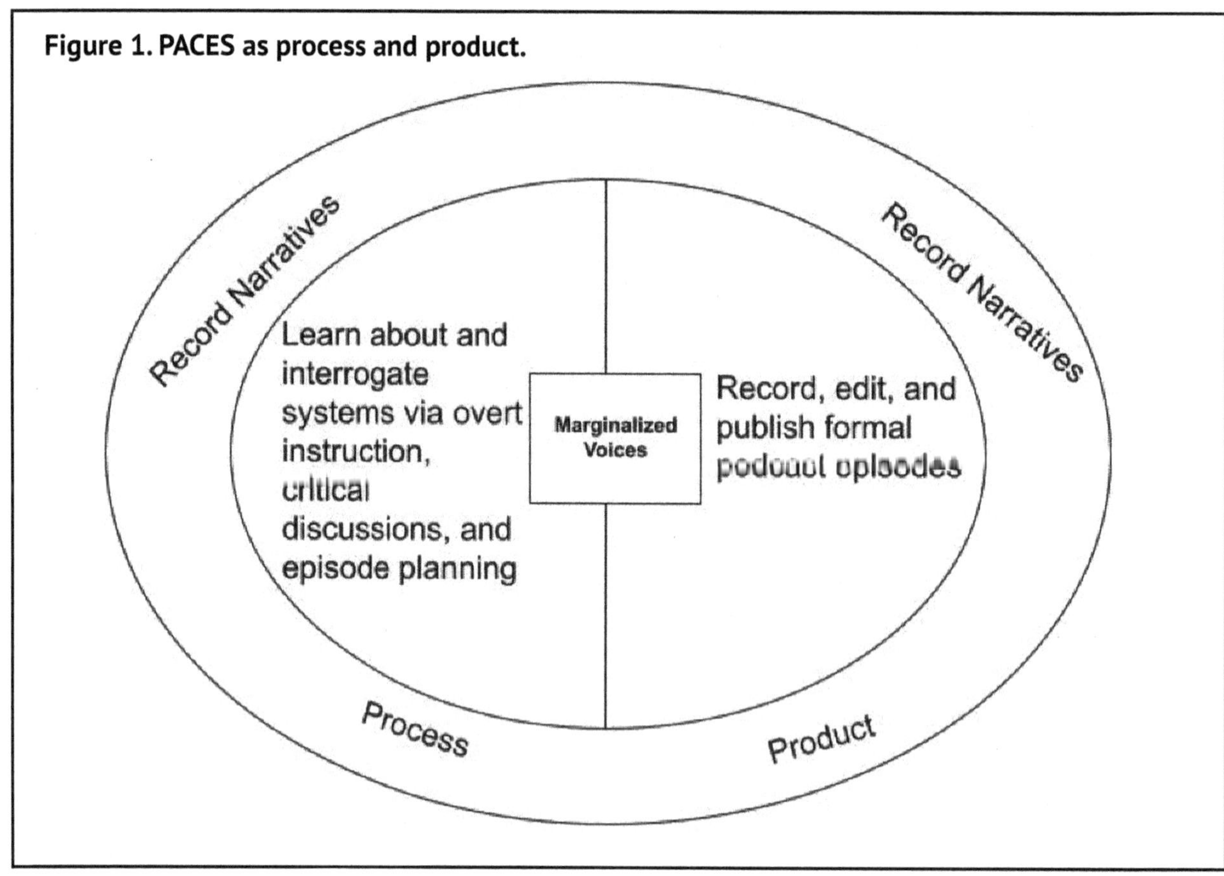

small-pod groups. Overt instruction and critical framing, other elements of multiliteracies pedagogy, are centered as symbiotic processes. Participants work with the instructional facilitator to expand their knowledge of dominant discourses, policies, and programs. While engaging in this knowledge building, participants collaborate in large and small groups to draw on their personal and collective experiences to interrogate these systems. These critical discussions allow participants to transform these discourses and (re)position their identities at various points throughout the workshop.

The second distinctive feature of PACES is acknowledgment that (re)positioning and transformation of discourse is an ongoing process and not just a culminating activity that occurs at the end of a workshop. PACES positions podcasting as both a process and a product in which the framing and planning discussions are just as crucial as the culminating recording. Participants' authoring of narratives is not limited to the formal recording sessions in which they engage toward the end of each workshop. Instead, participants respond to dominant discourses and author their identities at many different points throughout the workshops. With PACES, BIY are free to examine and respond to dominant discourses about their identities in ways and at points in time that come naturally to them, increasing their agency and authenticity in telling their stories.

The symbiotic relationship between discourse analysis and storytelling, fostered by the PACES approach, has profound implications. It underscores the necessity of creating numerous opportunities for learners to engage in dialogic encounters with each other. These conversations should be thought-provoking, student-centered discussions in which learners feel safe and

Table 2. Outline of PACES workshop.

Workshop Objectives: Examining and Responding to Institutional Discourses in K–12
Present BIY with clear information on systemic identity positioning in K–12. Engage BIY in critiquing the positioning of their intersectional identities. Create multiple opportunities for BIY to reflect on and redesign their identities. Provide space for BIY to express transformed opinions and share podcasts.
Workshop Flow
Day 1 Work with students to explore the Four Ps of school that shape their experiences: Policies, Programs, Pedagogy, and Perception. Examine the history of the ESSA and its provisions for immigrant youth. Examine federal, state, and district-level school funding policies. Critique academic programs and curricula employed to support BIY.
Days 1 and 2 Engage students in whole-group and small-group discussions of how their academic experiences have been influenced by the policies, programs, pedagogies, and perceptions of others. Have them explore how they have been positively and/or negatively influenced and invite them to explore if they would like to push back against any of the Four Ps and why.
Days 3 and 4 Participants work in their pod groups to determine what they wish to focus on in relation to K–12 discourses and plan their podcast narrative. They then record their episodes and edit the recordings for publication. Participants and the facilitator meet in small focus groups to review the aspects of the workshop that were effective and what could be improved before the next workshop.

empowered to voice their opinions. Additionally, since participants can interrogate discourses and author narratives at any point throughout the workshop, all discussions (whole group, small group, focus group) should be recorded as potential podcast episodes. Everything has transformative value. In Table 2, I present an outline of one of my program's workshops to demonstrate PACES implementation.

Civic Engagement through PACES: Examples from My Work with BIY

In this section, I share brief examples of how PACES allowed BIY to share their stories while critiquing societal structures and stereotypes. The examples I share underscore the recognition that participants author narratives in various ways and at various times. In sharing these insights, I draw on data from several participants in my study. During the study, participants authored narratives of identity (re)construction that directly challenged injustices and (mis)representation in societal, institutional, and affinity contexts. They also told other stories that were seemingly simple on the surface but elucidated complex examinations of systemic oppression and identity navigation.

Critical Consciousness and Agency

PACES helped to raise BIY's critical consciousness by inviting learners to be skeptical when analyzing dominant discourses about Black immigrant identities. In doing this, PACES expanded participants' knowledge of the dominant discourses and the policies and attitudes that result from these discourses. This led to participants' increased awareness and agency in (re)positioning identity within these discourses. In a post-workshop interview, Jake shared

> Before, I didn't pay much attention because I just think everybody is the same thing. I know they got a rise in racism. But I didn't think it was a lot. But after everybody shared their story . . . now, I start paying attention to that. Before the program, I saw myself . . . like I was watching myself. Now, the way I see myself, the way I look at myself, my background, and how I describe myself to other people . . . that changed a lot.

Jake's professed change after engaging in PACES is a sign of agency, as he now feels empowered to author more authentic asset-based narratives of his identity. His narratives also demonstrate an increased critical awareness of the experiences of other Black immigrants in relation to navigating discourses.

During a focus-group discussion, Jabar likewise demonstrated an increase in his critical consciousness and agentive advocacy. He articulated that participating in the program helped to deepen his sense of self. He shared, "I think that the fact that the main focus of the podcast is to talk about our identity allows us to learn more about who we are . . . about our identity." He then agentively challenged essentializing discourses about his identity, declaring, "I am more than an African."

Pogba demonstrated an increase in his critical consciousness by challenging dominant discourses that foster an environment of unbelonging for Black immigrants. Pogba was born in the US but migrated to Senegal as a baby. He returned to the US as a French-speaking Black immigrant. During a pod-group discussion about ethnic identity positioning, Pogba declared, "I am African American." By stating this, he resisted being othered and claimed his right to citizenship, challenging the conceptualization of immigrant identity in the broader society.

(Re)Positioning Identity in Academic Experiences

During the second workshop, participants explored the systemic structures that shape their K–12 experiences. They critically examined provisions for immigrant youth in the Every Student Succeeds Act (ESSA) and interrogated school funding policies at all levels. They explored various immigrant-support programs in their school districts and discussed their teachers' pedagogy. As they learned, they questioned what they were learning and entered into dialogue with each other and the facilitator. This integrated examination, facilitated by the podcasting process, led to a rich critique of K–12 systems and discourses, as participants built off each other's questions and insights to share their own responses at different points throughout the workshop.

A key discourse participants examined during the workshop was the stereotypical representation of English language learners (ELL) as intellectually inferior. They continuously challenged this discourse by reiterating their intelligence at various points and in various ways throughout the workshop, demonstrating the value of podcasting as a process.

During her independent reflection, May addressed the stereotype of intellectual inferiority by critiquing her teacher's pedagogy. She shared:

> My teachers gave me an advantage on multiple-choice tests in elementary school. When there were more than three choices, they crossed out one to make it easier for me to get the correct answer. I didn't need help in the first place.

May's reflection critiques the assumptions and policies surrounding academic accommodations for ELL immigrant youth. In our focus-group discussion, Zer also challenged assumptions about ELL immigrant youth. He shared that he wanted people to know he was a smart boy. He emphasized that he had learned English in only two years and was an A student.

During our whole-group discussion, several participants critiqued the practice of grade repetition in the US. They shared that the practice is also present in Guinea. However, they argued that grade repetition in Guinea reflects the rigor and high standards of the education system, where students matriculate from one grade to the next only after they demonstrate mastery of their current learning objectives. Participants argued that how grade repetition is implemented in Guinea spurs academic excellence; students work hard to achieve learning milestones to avoid repeating a grade.

In contrast, participants argued that grade repetition in this country felt demeaning and was a demotivating setback for students. These narratives (re)position BIY academic identities by countering dominant stereotypes of the African education system. They also critique the efficacy of the policies governing grade repetition for immigrant youth in the US.

Embedded Narratives

> This story is when I went to France for the first time. In Africa, when a kid plays with you too much, you would just beat him, so I thought it was the same in France. The kid started talking lots of bad things. So, I beat him up. He went home crying. My cousin told me he would come back tomorrow with his family. I said, "I don't care," because I thought it was the same thing as in Africa. The next day, I saw him coming with his family. His parents explained everything to my aunt. I saw my aunt's face go from laughing to angry. I knew she was about to beat me. She grabbed me and asked me why I beat the kid. She said I don't get to do that. She beat me. After that day, I didn't beat any white kid . . . never again.
>
> —Jake's narrative

Jake shared a story of moving from Burkina Faso to France and being reprimanded by his aunt for fighting a white boy. He initially shared this story in a whole-group discussion, during which many other stories of fights were shared.

Though seemingly simple, Jake's story has an embedded narrative. It is a bildungsroman of sorts that recounts his journey of racialization. It is a poignantly painful narrative of his dawning consciousness of how he is positioned as a Black boy in a predominantly white society. It complicates our understanding of racialization by demonstrating his Black aunt's reification of the racial status quo, and it critiques the role that Black citizens play in upholding racial hegemony.

Reflexivity and Cultural Humility: The Teacher's Stance

Like the two-headed Janus of ancient myth, civic-minded pedagogy is most effective when it directs its gaze both ways. In our work with BIY to examine how they are positioned by dominant discourses, we must also engage in critical reflexivity to continuously monitor our presence and biases in the learning space. Critical reflexivity is paramount when engaging BIY in PACES.

Through my responses to my participants' stories, I noted the importance of self-awareness and critical self-interrogation. I was surprised when some of my participants shared that they had not experienced oppression in the US. Upon reflection, I realized that my assumptions about my participants had influenced my incredulity. My participants and I have a shared ethno-racial identity. As a result, I assumed knowledge of who they were and what they would share. This culturally situated (mis)representation was also evident in the foci and content I initially designed in the identity workshops. I assumed that participants would want to discuss their post-immigration experiences in the US. However, participants were more eager to tell their pre-immigration narratives.

The disconnect between my assumptions and what participants wanted to share highlights the danger of a single story (Adichie, 2009). For BIY, essentializing discourses are not just perpetuated outside the Black diaspora or by forces of hegemony and discrimination. It is just as possible for other members of the Black diaspora and social justice, equity-minded scholars to act in ways that reinforce stereotypes and delimit BIY's narrative authoring (Young, 2024). Considering this, educators and researchers who utilize PACES must practice cultural humility. They must be willing to release their assumptions and make room for BIY to help craft the pedagogical efforts to support their identity navigation. Below, I share additional guidelines for educators and researchers who wish to utilize PACES in their work with BIY and other immigrant youth.

- Programs designed with PACES should allow their participants to examine and critique the systems with which they interact on a daily basis. This will enable participants to draw on their experiences as they interrogate structures.
- When using PACES, it is essential to remember that participants will author their individual narratives at different points and in varying ways throughout the workshop. All discussions can and should be recorded and assessed, as profound narratives may be embedded in the seemingly mundane.

Conclusion

In this essay, I shared insights from a podcasting program with BIY. The insights point to the benefits of designing podcasting as a civically engaged storytelling platform (PACES) for work with BIY. For centuries, stories have been used to (mis)represent Black identity and reify racialized oppression. Thus, the work we do via podcasting to support BIY as they tell their own stories must engage with and (re)position those narratives. For members of the Black diaspora, stories are not neutral; therefore, BIY storytelling via podcasting cannot be neutral. When working with BIY to tell their stories via podcasting, we should strive to enact podcasting as civically engaged storytelling.

Works Cited

Adichie, C. N. (2009, July). *The danger of a single story* [Video]. TED. www.ted.com/talks/chimamanda_ngozi_adichie_the_danger_of_a_single_story

Barner, B. N. (2021). *The last place they thought of: Black podcasts and the performance of marginalization* [Doctoral dissertation, University of Texas at Austin]. https://doi.org/10.26153/tsw/14735

Besser, E. D., Blackwell, L. E., & Saenz, M. (2022). Engaging students through educational podcasting: Three stories of implementation. *Technology, Knowledge and Learning, 27*(3), 749–764. https://doi.org/10.1007/s10758-021-09503-8

Bishop, R. S. (1990). Mirrors, windows, and sliding glass doors. *Perspectives: Choosing and Using Books for the Classroom, 6*(3), ix–xi.

Cazden, C., Cope, B., Fairclough, N., Gee, J., Kalantzis, M., Kress, G., Luke, A., Luke, C., Michaels, S., & Nakata, M. (1996). A pedagogy of multiliteracies: Designing social futures. *Harvard Educational Review, 66*(1), 60–92.

Curlee, A., & Early, J. S. (2023). Teaching the podcast: Using a genre approach to secondary writing instruction. In B. L. Hott (Ed.), *Quality instruction and intervention strategies for secondary educators* (pp. 87–107). Rowman & Littlefield.

Delgado, R., & Stefancic, J. (2017). *Critical race theory: An introduction* (3rd ed.). New York University Press.

Gravemeijer, K., & Cobb, P. (2006). Design research from a learning design perspective. In J. van den Akker, K. Gravemeijer, S. McKenney, & N. Nieveen (Eds.), *Educational design research* (pp. 17–51). Routledge.

Hall, S. (1990). Cultural identity and diaspora. In J. Rutherford (Ed.), *Identity: Community, culture, difference* (pp. 222–237). Lawrence & Wishart. https://muse.jhu.edu/book/34784

Hamilton, M., & Nguyen, T. (2008). Podcasting in middle school: A case study and implications for teacher education. *Proceedings of the Technology, Colleges and Community Worldwide Online Conference, 2008*(1), 50–60. www.learntechlib.org/p/43818/

Jones-Young, N. (2016). *Immigration, identity, and the Caribbean immigrant student in the English language arts classroom* [Masters thesis, Southern New Hampshire University]. ProQuest Dissertations and Theses Global. www.proquest.com/docview/2628512453/abstract/56D14F7973C44364PQ/1

Kassaie, L., Shairi, H. R., & Gashmardi, M. R. (2021). Integrating MALL into the classroom: The cultural and pedagogical impact of authentic podcasts on FFL learners' listening and speaking skills. *International Journal of Society, Culture & Language, 9*(1), 69–85.

Kiramba, L. K., Kumi-Yeboah, A., & Sallar, A. M. (2023). "It's like they don't recognize what I bring to the classroom": African immigrant youths' multilingual and multicultural navigation in United States schools. *Journal of Language, Identity & Education, 22*(1), 83–98. https://doi.org/10.1080/15348458.2020.1832499

Kohli, R., Pizarro, M., & Nevárez, A. (2017). The "new racism" of K–12 schools: Centering critical research on racism. *Review of Research in Education, 41*(1), 182–202. https://doi.org/10.3102/0091732X16686949

Marsh, V. L. (2022). (Re)Active praxis: Disrupting segregated knowledge flows: Reflections from an evolving abolitionist. *English Education, 54*(4), 341–350.

Skerrett, A. (2020). Investing in the learning of transnational youth: Considerations for English/literacy educators and researchers. *Research in the Teaching of English, 54*(3), 287–290.

Smith, P. (2023). *Black immigrant literacies: Intersections of race, language, and culture in the classroom.* Teachers College Press.

Smith, R., Danford, M., Darnell, S. C., Larrazabal, M. J. L., & Abdellatif, M. (2021). "Like, what even is a podcast?" Approaching sport-for-development youth participatory action research through digital methodologies. *Qualitative Research in Sport, Exercise and Health, 13*(1), 128–145. https://doi.org/10.1080/2159676X.2020.1836515

Tamir, C., & Anderson, M. (2022, January 20). *The Caribbean is the largest origin source of Black immigrants, but fastest growth is among African immigrants.* Pew Research Center. www.pewresearch.org/race-ethnicity/2022/01/20/the-caribbean-is-the-largest-origin-source-of-black-immigrants-but-fastest-growth-is-among-african-immigrants/

Terry, N. (2023). Multicultural education and the ESEA: The ebbs and flows of policy alignment between 1965–2015. *Multicultural Education Review, 14*(4), 211–227. https://doi.org/10.1080/2005615X.2023.2164964

Vázquez Baur, A. (2022). *How to ensure Title III funds reach every newcomer student.* Next100. https://thenext100.org/how-to-ensure-title-iii-funds-reach-every-newcomer-student/

Young, N. T. (2024). *I get to tell my story: A design-based research study exploring the affordances of multiliteracies in supporting Black immigrant youth identity navigation* (Publication No. 31301808) [Doctoral dissertation, Drexel University]. ProQuest Dissertations & Theses Global. www.proquest.com/dissertations-theses/i-get-tell-my-story-design-based-research-study/docview/3066232752/se-2

"The Stories We Live By": Creativity, Criticality, and Civic Futures

JEN SCOTT CURWOOD

In a fractured age,
when cynicism is god,
here is a possibly heresy:
we live by stories,
we also live in them.
One way or another we are living the
stories
planted in us early or along the way,
or we are also living the stories we
planted—
knowingly or unknowingly—in ourselves
We live stories that either give our lives
meaning
or negate it with meaninglessness.
If we change the stories we live by,
Quite possibly we change our lives.
(Okri, 1997)

Introduction

Stories are woven into the fabric of our being. From our earliest moments, we are told stories—of ourselves and of the world around us—and they shape our identities and our interactions. As we repeat or reinvent or subvert these same stories, we strive to give meaning and purpose to our lives, locating ourselves "amongst the networks of relationships that comprise our realities" (Kwaymullina, 2018, p. 140). This is how the act of storytelling allows us to grapple with history, exert agency, construct identity, and imagine more sustainable and equitable futures. Storytelling gives young people the opportunity to share their experiences and push back against inequities and injustices. Particularly for youth whose voices have historically been marginalized or silenced, storytelling encourages them to critically reflect on their lived experiences, to bear witness to others' stories, and to see themselves as change agents.

"Let us begin by telling our own stories, for one way we understand culture is through the stories we tell of ourselves: stories of belonging, of embodiment, of place," proclaim Christos Tsiolkas and Clare Wright in *Revive*, Australia's new National Cultural Policy (Australian Government, 2023, p. 11). The act of storying involves how stories are shaped and told over time, and it is inherently connected to power, including who can tell stories, when, and under what conditions (Adichie, 2009). *Restorying* sits at the intersection of creativity and criticality and offers an opportunity to reorient youth activism by leveraging young people's contexts and experiences to create opportunities for engagement, inclusion, and action. It involves imagining alternative narratives, "and by extension feelings" (Coleman, 2023, p. 4), through changing narrative elements, including identity, time, mode, metanarrative, perspective, and place (Thomas & Stornaiuolo, 2016).

Responding to Cohen's (2010) call to interrogate what counts as civic engagement today, Mirra and Garcia (2017) reconceptualize civic learning by focusing on initiatives that amplify youth voices through new channels. This innovative vision invites youth to actively engage in civic life in new ways that are often creative, collaborative, and performative. It is through storytelling—within schools, communities, and online contexts—that young people can challenge systemic inequalities and resist deficit narratives. By situating "struggle as just as powerful a catalyst for civic action as patriotism" (Mirra & Garcia, 2017, p. 153), storytelling offers young people a way to understand and express their own struggles while witnessing and empathizing with the struggle of others.

I begin this essay by arguing for an expanded understanding of youth activism and civic engagement that is rooted in creative expression and forged through critical reflection. I then consider how storytelling offers a way to conceptualize youth activism and its role in, for, and as civic participation. Finally, I situate this framework within my research on spoken word poetry in Australia to explore how creativity and criticality are carving a new path forward for young people's civic futures.

Youth Activism and Civic Engagement

The ways in which we conceptualize youth impact how we understand the capacity for their activism to enact meaningful change. While youth is often conceived socially, Tuck and Yang (2014) argue that such a reductive view obscures how youth is a "legally, materially, and always raced/gendered/classed/sexualized category around which social institutions are built, disciplinary sciences created, and legal apparatuses mounted" (p. 4). By attending to the structural, historical, generational, and political positioning of young people, they highlight the power and capacity for youth resistance.

The very idea of youth recognizes "the power of young people not as 'kids' to be controlled and 'children' to be quieted but as growing adults who possess the capacity to be leaders in the present" (Bishop, 2015, p. 2). Narrow definitions of youth lead to restrictive conceptualizations of youth activism that fail to recognize the powerful contributions young people can make. More than providing a platform for young people, "giving voice to children is not simply or only about letting children speak" (James, 2007, p. 262). Rather, it involves understanding and valuing their unique perspectives and insights while respecting that youth voices may emerge through new channels and offer disparate narratives.

When youth are perceived as "citizens-in-the-making but not yet 'finished' citizens" (Gordon, 2007, p. 636), it can undermine their work as activists in their own right and function to discredit their capacity to lead local initiatives or enact global change. Their resistance might circumvent established political institutions or defy adults' expectations of what it means to be a "good citizen." Youth resistance may not look like traditional notions of civic engagement—when young people are not legally allowed to vote or they feel like elected officials don't represent their interests and views, they may take to the streets in protest, camp out in public spaces, perform spoken word poems, make art, or take up hashtags—all in an effort to engage in democracy.

The dynamic, creative, and often unpredictable nature of youth resistance can be an asset rather than a hindrance. It is often designed to disrupt, whether that disruption is to the status quo or to daily routines. However, resistance is "not just something that under-resourced youth do toward justice, but also is what over-resourced youth do to secure the longevity of their privilege" (Tuck & Yang, 2011, p. 526). For this reason, the motivations, material realities, and effects of youth activism can vary greatly, resisting any monolithic, reductive conceptualization of how, when, and under what circumstances young people can shape their civic futures.

As young people wield voice and authority, they come to understand their own complex identities and see themselves as activists who can resist socioeconomic, gendered, racial, and linguistic inequities. Not only can this prompt them to critically reflect on their own lives, it encourages them to bear witness to the lives of others as well, which may cultivate empathy. In this respect, modern-day civic engagement extends beyond explicitly political acts to embrace a "different" kind of politics that "builds the commonwealth" (Boyte, 2003, p. 9) among people from diverse backgrounds, belief systems, and lived experiences. Mirra and Garcia (2017) argue that youth practices offer tremendous promise for "challenging systemic inequalities in civic life and for challenging deficit narratives of youth of color in the public sphere" by situating "struggle as just as powerful a catalyst for civic action as patriotism" (p. 153) and expanding our conceptualization of civic agency. This expansion occurs through decentering formal institutions and engaging in dialogic practices (Mirra & Garcia, 2022), which invariably involves making sense of contradictions and reconciling differences in the quest for just, equitable futures.

A new approach to civic engagement is needed that centers informal collective affiliations and networks rather than governments as driving forces in democratic education and civic action. Speculative civic literacies foreground young people's creativity in (re)storying their engagement in modern democracy to promote equity and empathy (Mirra & Garcia, 2020). The speculative turn in civics highlights the power of youth practices and radical imaginaries in shaping how they engage with and create ideational and material artifacts, tools, and stories to generate civic futures that are sustainable and equitable. It also highlights the global "shift in civics scholarship that takes a bottom-up rather than top-down approach" (Mirra & Garcia, 2022, p. 6). Young people's creative endeavors are a powerful way for them to engage in civic life beyond formal electoral politics. The following section grounds youth creativity and criticality within story.

Youth Storytelling as Activism

By focusing on young people's civic engagement through storytelling, a new understanding of civics can leverage their intersectional identities and creative capacities. Stories are our way of entering, interacting with, and changing the world, and we may use multiple modes, diverse channels, and digital tools to craft and disseminate them. "People shape their daily lives by stories of who they and others are and as they interpret their past in terms of these stories" (Connelly & Clandinin, 2006, p. 477), and stories are also the medium through which we build our futures. If storytelling is situated at the heart of culture, the process of creating, sharing, and witnessing stories allows young people to express their creativity and to cultivate civic literacy. Moving beyond the idea that "stories are lived before they are told" (MacIntyre, 1981, p. 197), futures also need to be imagined before they can be lived.

When young people gather to share their stories in out-of-school contexts, including poetry slams, arts festivals, neighborhood centers, and social media channels, there is a powerful opportunity to grapple with inequities and injustices and to participate in visible activism (Curwood & Jones, 2022). Storytelling is not monolithic, unidirectional, or even individual, as shown through Indigenous storying which reflects "generations of storytellers who told tales in words, painted them in art, and sang and danced them in rhythm with the seasons and the sun and the stars" (Kwaymullina, 2014). Stories told in the present are our way of reconfiguring the past, imbuing it with salience and relevance, and then carving out a way forward. In this process, we may come to reject the stories that society has told of our family or even the stories that our family has told of us. Emotions and stories are inextricably linked together, pulling one another through space and time. It is through stories—the ones told to us, the ones told of us, the ones we tell others, and the ones we tell ourselves—that we make sense of our complex emotions and lived experiences.

(Re)storying is a powerful way for young people to reclaim their voices and depict themselves fully and fairly while engaging in the ongoing, dialectical, and reflective process of identity construction. "When people only have access to a single story—one that simplifies and flattens the complexity of human experience and excludes many perspectives from being represented—they can become constrained in what they imagine to be possible" (Thomas & Stornaiuolo, 2016, pp. 313–314). Coleman (2023) highlights the power of the narrative repair process in allowing individuals to put emotions into words: "storying your pain is an explicit presencing of history and the sticky emotions attached to it" (p. 7). The act of storytelling involves a witnessing (Dutro, 2019) of our own, as well as others', histories and emotions. We move from a damage-centered to a desire-based (Tuck, 2009) framework when we honor the spaces, channels, and tools through which young people tell their stories in an effort to reconcile their emotions and experiences while forging more equitable, sustainable futures.

Young people develop their creativity and criticality through storying and restorying. Because stories can be expressed through diverse modes and mediums, storytelling can cultivate creativity. Criticality serves to amplify creative work within civic contexts by encouraging the interrogation of power and oppression, particularly regarding their impacts on historically marginalized peoples. Muhammad (2018) argues that criticality is also "related to seeing, naming, and interrogating the world not only to make sense of injustice but also to work toward social transformation" (p. 138). Criticality, much like creativity, is an active, dialectical, and often collaborative process, one that can be embodied in and expressed through storytelling.

If creativity and criticality are inherent in storytelling, then the act of storying is how young people can generate their civic futures. Drawing from narrative inquiry, Clandinin and Connelly (2000) posit that "wherever one positions oneself in that continuum—the imagined now, some imagined past, or some imagined future—each point has a past experiential base and leads to an experiential future" (p. 2). Stories exist on a continuum, and they connect disparate temporal states and lived realities. For communities that have been historically subjected to systemic oppression, their members' stories have often been silenced, repurposed, or maligned. When young people engage in storytelling, they can leverage their creativity and criticality in order to imagine and enact new civic futures.

Youth Storytelling and Civic Engagement in Australia

Turning to the Australian context, the disconnect between young people's capacity as activists and positioning as active citizens becomes apparent. The Melbourne Declaration articulates civic and citizenship goals for young Australians, arguing that "all young Australians should become successful learners, creative and confident individuals and active and informed citizens" (MCEETYA, 2008). However, the very same government that trumpets these goals and values also limits young people's activism.

In relation to the Schools Strike for Climate, Australian Prime Minister Scott Morrison called for "more learning in schools and less activism in schools" (*The Guardian*, 2018), and teachers were accused of "politically correct" bias that served to indoctrinate students (Sutton, 2019). This is not an isolated incident; most school-based civic learning avoids critical discussion of what citizenship means (Vickery, 2017), which can feel disingenuous to young Australians growing up in a country that recently voted against an Indigenous Voice to Parliament.

Recent Australian research focuses on creative agency, arguing for a globalized, networked approach to promoting youth creativity (Harris, 2017). A 2022 survey found that 43 percent of young Australians participated in arts, cultural, and music activities in the past year (Mission Australia, 2022), indicating that creative endeavors are a critical component in the everyday lives of many Australian youth. Consequently, there is an opportunity to leverage creative expression for the purposes of civic engagement.

Australia's new National Cultural Policy argues, "It is not the role of governments to create culture. Let's leave that to the artists, makers, and storytellers—the creative practitioners. The government's role is to invest in our creative infrastructure" (Australian Government, 2023, p. 11). What is unknown is how such substantial investments in infrastructure can encourage the country's 3.2 million young people between the ages of 15 and 24 (Australian Government, 2021) to leverage their creative endeavors in order to meaningfully and impactfully engage in civic life. Storytelling is the focus of Australia's National Cultural Policy, and storytelling offers a compelling, accessible, and multidisciplinary lens to examine the intersections of creativity and civic literacy.

As a literacy scholar and teacher educator, I have a commitment to following the "contours of a problem" (Donovan & Snow, 2018). This has led me to explore how young people are engaging in storytelling within school, community, and online contexts and to consider how (re)storying offers a way to amplify the voices of historically marginalized communities. I am interested in how we can understand and account for young people's civic participation through creative expression and understand its role within the Australian curriculum and its impact on Australian society.

I have led extensive research to understand how Australian youth engage with spoken word poetry in school and community contexts (see Curwood, 2024; Curwood & Bull, 2023; Curwood & Jones, 2022; D'Netto & Curwood, 2022; Jones & Curwood, 2020; Kim-Rich & Curwood, 2023). Through my research-practice partnership with the Bankstown Poetry Slam, I have examined young people's engagement in storytelling through spoken word poetry and how their craft as storytellers is supported through the work of mentor poets. Situated in one of the most culturally and linguistically diverse community in Australia, this partnership has advanced research on modern storytelling within schools and communities, particularly with immigrant and refugee youth.

The Bankstown Poetry Slam was highlighted in a recent article in the *Sydney Morning Herald*, which proclaimed, "Against the odds, western Sydney is fostering an authentic, organic, and truly global arts groundswell. Sydney's most culturally and linguistically diverse region is giving rise to vibrant arts practitioners. It is also home to Australia's largest Indigenous population" (Marks, 2022). The Slam is now the largest in the country and hosts monthly poetry slams and the school-based Real Talk workshops, as well as other initiatives like the Brave New Word Poetry Festival and the National Youth Poetry Slam. Along with the Slam's social media channels combined 6,000 followers, young people have new platforms to make their voices heard. Notably, these are the same voices that are often silenced in the civic arena.

Conservative politician Mark Latham launched an attack on the Slam in 2018, the largest in the southern hemisphere, deeming it an "Islamic political group ranting hatred towards Australia and our institutions, especially the police, soldiers, and even the ANZACs [Australia and New Zealand Army Corps during the First World War]" (Knaus, 2018). Such inflammatory comments prompted the Bankstown Poetry Slam to require undercover police and hire private security guards. This incident highlights how a redefined vision of civic participation that involves creativity and criticality can be deeply unsettling to the status quo. It emphasizes the power of storytelling in a world rocked by crises and conflicts: "The power to narrate, or to block other narratives from forming and emerging, is very important to culture and imperialism, and constitutes one of the main connections between them" (Said, 1994, p. xiii).

Storytelling through spoken word poetry encourages youth poets to critically reflect on their lives, bear witness to inequities, and see themselves as change agents. Consequently, poetry can be a transformative tool for generating new civic futures. The intersection of creativity and criticality through spoken word poetry offers an opportunity to reorient civic learning by using young people's contexts and experiences to create opportunities for engagement, inclusion, and action.

Crafting New Civic Futures

How can storytelling inform the cultivation of civic futures in out-of-school learning environments?

1. Appreciate how today's youth move between and across school, community, and online environments. In Australia, youth storytelling often sits at the intersection of these, such as the Bankstown Poetry Slam's Real Talk workshops in Sydney schools or 100 Story Building's innovative School Hub initiative in Melbourne. Look for opportunities and synergies to build young people's creative and civic capacities.
2. Model the practice of storytelling. When young people have the opportunity to learn alongside arts practitioners, youth workers, or other mentors, they can see how other people tell their stories, engage in empathetic witnessing, and use story as a vehicle to build community and enhance solidarity.

3. Consider how storytelling can occur within and across different modes and media. Young people may tell their stories through photos, artwork, poems, videos, or the dramatic arts, and their engagement in storytelling within out-of-school contexts can encourage them to conceptualize the diverse forms of storying and prompt them to advance their own storytelling practices.
4. Directly link storytelling to activism. In order to dispel any narrow definitions of activism, it is critical that young people appreciate that they can take part in the civic arena beyond formal institutions and traditional avenues.
5. Encourage civic imagination through restorying. Through playful yet critical engagement with storytelling, young people can consider how identity, time, place, and perspective shape what stories are told, by whom, and to what effect.
6. Collaborate with young people to explore ways to amplify their stories. Whether they use a hashtag to reach a new online audience, take part in an art exhibition, get on stage at a poetry slam, or attend a protest, youth can be encouraged to share their stories more widely—and impactfully.

To build a future that is more sustainable, equitable, and just, we must begin by imagining it through our stories—of resilience, of struggle, and of hope.

Works Cited

Adichie, C. (2009, July). *The danger of a single story* [Video]. TED. www.ted.com/talks/chimamanda_ngozi_adichie_the_danger_of_a_single_story?subtitle=en

Australia's youth. (2021). Australian Institute of Health and Welfare. www.aihw.gov.au/reports/children-youth/australias-youth/contents/demographics

Australian government. (2023). *Revive: Australia's national cultural policy.* Commonwealth of Australia.

Barr, A., Gillard, J., Firth, V., Scrymgour, M., Welford, R., Lomax-Smith, J., Bartlett, D., Pike, B., & Constable, E. (2008). *Melbourne declaration on educational goals for young Australians.* Ministerial Council on Education, Employment, Training and Youth Affairs.

Bishop, E. (2015). *Becoming activist: Critical literacy and youth organizing.* Peter Lang.

Boyte, H. (2003). A different kind of politics: John Dewey and the meaning of citizenship in the 21st century. *The Good Society, 12*(2), 1–15.

Clandinin, D. J., & Connelly, F. M. (2000). *Narrative inquiry: Experience and story in qualitative research.* Jossey-Bass.

Cohen, C., Kahne, J., & Marshall, J. (2018). *Let's go there: Making a case for race, ethnicity and a lived civics approach to civics education.* University of Chicago.

Coleman, J. J. (2023). Narrative repair in teacher education: Restorying painful histories and "damaged" queer teacher identity. *Teaching and Teacher Education, 124,* Article 104031. https://doi. org/10.1016/j.tate.2023.104031

Connelly, F. M., & Clandinin, D. J. (2006). Narrative inquiry. In J. Green, G. Camilli, & P. Elmore (Eds.), *Handbook of complementary methods in education research* (pp. 477–488). Lawrence Erlbaum.

Curwood, J. S. (2024). "My beating and bleeding heart for all of you": Enacting culturally sustaining pedagogy through spoken word poetry. *Journal of Adolescent & Adult Literacy, 68*(2), 152–161. http://doi.org/10.1002/jaal.1374

Curwood, J. S., & Bull, K. (2023). In their own words: Amplifying critical literacy and social justice pedagogy through spoken word poetry. *English in Education, 57*(3), 154–168. https://doi.org/10.1080/04250494.2023.2183837

Curwood, J. S., & Jones, K. (2022). A bridge across our fears: Understanding spoken word poetry in troubled times. *Literacy, 56*(1), 50–58. https://doi.org/10.1111/lit.12270

D'Netto, G., & Curwood, J. S. (2022). Slam the exam: Spoken word poetry in the context of high stakes assessment. *English in Australia, 57*(3), 38–46.

Donovan, M. S., & Snow, C. E. (2018). Sustaining research-practice partnerships: Benefits and challenges of a long-term research and development agenda. In B. Bevan & W. R. Penuel (Eds.), *Connecting research and practice for educational improvement: Ethical and equitable approaches* (pp. 33–50). Routledge.

Dutro, E. (2019). *The vulnerable heart of literacy: Centering trauma as powerful pedagogy.* Teachers College Press.

Gordon, H. R. (2007). Allies within and without: How adolescent activists conceptualize ageism and navigate adult power in youth social movements. *Journal of Contemporary Ethnography, 36*(6), 631–668.

The Guardian. (2018, November 27). Scott Morrison tells kids going on climate strike to get back to school. www.theguardian.com/global/video/2018/nov/27/scott-morrison-tells-kids-going-on-climate-strike-to-get-back-to-school-video

Harris, A. (2016). *Creativity and education.* Palgrave Macmillan.

James, A. (2007). Giving voice to children's voices: Practices and problems, pitfalls and potentials. *American Anthropologist, 109*(2), 261–272.

Jones, K., & Curwood, J. S. (2020). Tell the story, speak the truth: Creating a third space through spoken word poetry. *Journal of Adolescent & Adult Literacy, 64*(3), 281–289. https://doi.org/10.1002/jaal.1080

Kim-Rich, E., & Curwood, J. S. (2023). Literacies, language, and schooling: Exploring writing pedagogy for English language learners. In R. J. Tierney, F. Rizvi, & K. Ercikan (Eds.), *International encyclopedia of education* (4th ed., pp. 65–75). Elsevier. https://doi.org/10.1016/B978-0-12-818630-5.07057-3

Knaus, C. (2018, March 8). Poetry slam hires security after Mark Latham calls it "Islamic political ranting." *The Guardian.* www.theguardian.com/australia-news/2018/mar/09/poetry-slam-hires-security-after-mark-latham-calls-it-islamic-political-ranting

Kwaymullina, A. (2014). *Walking many worlds: Aboriginal storytelling and writing for the young.* Wheeler Centre.

Kwaymullina, A. (2018). Literature, resistance, and First Nations futures: Storytelling from an Australian Indigenous women's standpoint in the twenty-first century and beyond. *Westerly, 63(2*), 140–153.

MacIntyre, A. C. (1981). *After virtue: A study in moral theory.* University of Notre Dame Press.

Mirra, N., & Garcia, A. (2017). Civic participation reimagined: Youth interrogation and innovation in the multimodal public sphere. *Review of Research in Education, 41*(1), 136–158. https://doi.org/10.3102/0091732X17690121

Mirra, N., & Garcia, A. (2020). "I hesitate but I do have hope": Speculative civic literacies for troubled times. *Harvard Educational Review, 90*(2), 295–321. https://doi.org/10.17763/1943-5045-90.2.295

Mirra, N., & Garcia, A. (2022). Guns, schools, and democracy: Adolescents imagining social futures through speculative civic literacies. *American Educational Research Journal, 59*(2), 345–380.

Mission Australia. (2022). *Annual youth survey.* www.missionaustralia.com.au/what-we-do/research-impact-policy-advocacy/youth-survey

Muhammad, G. (2018). A plea for identity and criticality: Reframing literacy learning standards through a four-layered equity model. *Journal of Adolescent & Adult Literacy, 62*(2), 137–142. https://doi.org/10.1002/jaal.869

Okri, B. (1997). *A way of being free.* Phoenix House.

Said, E.W. (1994). *Culture and imperialism.* Vintage.

Sutton, M. (2019, March 13). *Climate change student strike inspired by politically correct teaching, academic says.* ABC News. www.abc.net.au/news/2019-03-14/politicallycorrect-teaching-to-blame-for-climate-change-strike/10897682

Thomas, E. E., & Stornaiuolo, A. (2016). Restorying the self: Bending toward textual justice. *Harvard Educational Review, 86*(3), 313–338.

Tuck, E. (2009). Suspending damage: A letter to communities. *Harvard Education Review, 79*(3), 409–427.

Tuck, E., & Yang, K. W. (2011). Youth resistance revisited: New theories of youth negotiations of educational injustices. *International Journal of Qualitative Studies in Education, 24*(5), 521–530. https://doi.org/10.1080/09518398.2011.600274

Tuck, E., & Yang, K. W. (Eds.). (2014). *Youth resistance research and theories of change.* Routledge.

Vickery, A. (2017). "You excluded us for so long and now you want us to be patriotic?": African American women teachers navigating the quandary of citizenship. *Theory & Research in Social Education, 45*(3), 318–348.

Dreamwalk with Me: Engaging Civic Literacy and Critical Speculative Design Praxis

MICHAEL DANDO

Introduction

To re-vision oppressive approaches to curricula, instruction, and pedagogy, it has recently become vogue to quote Octavia Butler (1990) and the concept of "new suns" as a shorthand for innovative approaches to education that recognize traditional avenues for formal education have been insufficient at best and oppressive at worst. Additionally, since the pandemic, many have understandably taken up Roy's approach that "Historically, pandemics have forced humans to break with the past and imagine their world anew. This one is no different. It is a portal, a gateway between one world and the next" (Roy, 2020). These well-intentioned and understandable ideological positions provide valuable perspectives; however, it is essential to understand that these are deeply political statements and imaginative approaches. These new suns and portals are necessarily borne out of ideological commitments from the communities that engage them.

Imarisha (2015) states, "All organizing is science fiction." It is this position that is the springboard for this chronicle of a "critical speculative design" workshop and one Black girl's creation of a deeply political, deeply personal counternarrative that explicitly speaks back to the ways she has been misrepresented, overlooked, and otherwise and unseen by dominant social, political, and cultural institutions. Speculative refers here to a broad category of genres of thought and fiction (including fantasy, mythology, and science fiction) that reach beyond or into realities other than the everyday in ways that inform and inspire the present day.

Her creation—a teenage superhero with mystical, ancestral connections—creates a literal counternarrative that describes the contours of an actualized and articulated sense of sociopolitical, creative, and civic self as authentic as it is speculative. This form of civic consciousness development requires that we engage in imaginative processes grounded in but not confined by current realities. Science fiction, here the future biography of a superhuman girl gifted with a form of second sight, allows for this form of civic-minded imagination. Her story invites readers and communities to envision worlds that do not (yet) exist while keeping the real world in mind.

Developing civic literacy is a crucial step toward freedom because, as Hall (2016) reminds us:

"People have to have a language to speak about where they are and what other possible futures are available to them . . . what is real, is the possibility of being someone else, of being in some other social space from the one in which you have already been placed" (p. 205).

This study posits that creating critical opportunities for the formation and mobilization of a civically oriented knowledge of self through speculative fiction can serve as an avenue for developing the meaningful, multimodal (verbal, visual, etc.) forms of hegemonic resistance.

To that end, I take up the following research questions:

- To what extent might speculative thinking serve as a space for civic literacy practice?
- How might Black and Brown youth mobilize speculative design and storying as an avenue for critical identity formation?

These questions and the chronicle that follows aim to provide a generative conceptual framework that centers and examines the possibilities of speculative design for critical civic engagement. I begin by reviewing speculative design as a counternarrative practice. I follow with a case study chronicling one participant's (Riley) development of a speculative fiction artifact and accompanying narrative as an avenue for self-expression, critical resistance, and civic literacy formation. Following this is an analysis through the lens of speculative storytelling drawing from the freedom-dreaming tradition, highlighting how Riley's speculative narrative acts as a counterstory and trajectory toward a more just future.

Theoretical Grounding

The theoretical work on storying and counternarrative can be a powerful approach to challenging dominant narratives and amplifying marginalized voices, particularly in race, education, and social justice. Recent academic research has explored the concept of Radical Black Imagination and its role in civic literacy development, particularly in the context of education and social movements (Benjamin, 2024). This research emphasizes the salience of cultivating radical imagination, particularly from nondominant communities, to challenge systemic racism and promote social transformation. This entry draws from two distinct frameworks, the Black Radical Imagination and civic literacy, to frame the discussion.

Black Radical Imagination

Freedom dreaming is definitionally unrealistic. Consequently, Kelley's (2002) conceptualization of the "Black Radical Imagination" is critical to reclaim, recover, and re-vision transformative paths toward resisting and disrupting hegemonic oppression. For Kelley, the Radical Black Imagination requires actively dismantling the violent status quo and imagining and constructing visions of what those communities wish to see. Civic transformation is revolution and, consequently, a "process that can and must transform us" (p. 1), rather than a set of discrete actions. The Black Radical Imagination here is significant, as it requires a particular set of ideological commitments theoretically situated with the intent of radical change that, as Davis (1988) notes, engages "[g]rasping at the root" (p. 353). This process requires changing how we think about ourselves, our history, and our societal role, which may have yet to be clearly expressed. This is the ancestral legacy of Black revolutionaries who envisioned a freedom that quite literally did not exist.

The Black Radical Imagination explicitly mobilizes imagination as a liberatory technology.

As Jennings theorizes, race is one of the original technologies and "can be hacked into, decoded, and made to function for a new agenda" (Chambliss, 2014). This article centers on Afrofuturism as a speculative design practice precisely because it positions imagination as an integral component of Black liberation (Anderson, 2016). Historically, Afrofuturism has served as an explicit pathway for Black artists, such as Sun Ra, Du Bois, or Rammelzee, to conjure new realities drawing from ancestral traditions while simultaneously fashioning visions of better, Blacker futures. In centering the speculative, particularly Afrofuturism, as integral to social justice work, activists can make specific educational and community organizing moves to seek out those proverbial other suns and do so with intentionality set on freedom.

Dreaming, particularly in education, is not simply reform but imagining other options that accomplish the same goals or re-inscribe the status quo. Instead of dreaming, in this instance, Afrofuturism invites interested communities to rethink education down to its very source code. Freedom dreaming requires abolition, as Love (2020) rightly suggests, and pathways that reach beyond traditional horizons and trajectories, as articulated by Mirra and Garcia (2023). These horizonings are necessarily rooted in liberatory forms of ideological creativity and imagination. They extend beyond the pragmatic, realizing that, as Sun Ra put it, "space is the place," meaning that current physical and geographic boundaries as they are understood today hold little promise for liberation. Mobilizing Afrofuturism through design thinking, as conceptualized by Dunne and Raby (2024), affords the space-time to evaluate the present, reflect on the past, and dream of what can be. The identities and literacies developed by speculative making through a Black Radical Imagination lens can be a powerful weapon against injustice, as participants can "real-ize": render tangible their freedom dreams while creating a space for collective competence, confidence, and collaboration.

Civic Literacy

A truly democratic and free society requires a civically literate public. For those mis- or underrepresented within a society to advocate for freedom, these communities must have a defined sense of civic identity and disposition. This was made explicit, for example, in the Civil Rights Movement of the late 1960s, when civic dispositions were front and center in the form of lunch counter sit-ins and signs that read "I AM A MAN." These actions were not solely borne out of righteous anger and frustration but also through civic literacy in the form of self-identity and understanding of what should be in the face of everyday life. Civic literacy might be broadly defined as the knowledge and set of skills that active citizens need to be able to effectively participate in a society (Milner, 2002). This includes knowing how politics and government function and operate and advocating for citizens' rights, roles, and responsibilities.

Furthermore, it involves the capacity to question media messages effectively and critically as a part of the decision-making process in a participatory democracy. A critical civic literacy is deeply rooted in our ability to engage meaningfully and make critical choices as participatory members of a democratic society. In other words, critical civic literacy is neither inert nor apolitical but a future-oriented form of radical hope. As Zinn (2018) reminds us, "We don't have to wait for some grand utopian future. The future is an infinite succession of presents, and to live now as we think human beings should live" (p. 208).

There are many conceptions regarding what civic literacy might involve or entail. Civic knowledge, abilities, and dispositions are some of the fundamental elements of civic literacy (Komalasari, 2012). Understanding governmental procedures, structures, and citizen rights and obligations is an essential component of civic knowledge. The capacities essential for participation in civic life effectively are often referred to as civic skills. These consist of the ability to think critically, communicate, and collaborate. Mutual understanding, empathy for others, and a sense of civic responsibility underpin the beliefs and principles that drive democratic practices that have been incorporated into the notion of civic disposition. All these issues connect to both Afrofuturism and speculative design.

I take inspiration from research and literature that explicitly connect the development of civic literacy with emancipation (hooks, Collins, Ladson-Billings, and Toliver). Collins's (1990) intersectionality theory, for instance, examines how overlapping social identities—such as gender, race, and class—directly affect people's experiences and possibilities to participate in civic life. Likewise, by advocating an inclusive, participatory, and revolutionary educational approach, hooks's focus on education as a means of liberation is in keeping with civic literacy's explicit goals (hooks, 2000). Finally, by validating students' identities and urging them to engage in community-related challenges, culturally sustaining and relevant pedagogies advocate civic engagement (Ladson-Billings, 1995) once again, a key facet of civic literacy.

These are all salient factors in approaching the construction and navigation of speculative forms of design and liberation. As Mirra and Garcia (2020) note, civic literacy development, understood as a complex process, is essential in fostering democratic engagement and a well-informed citizenry that must go beyond the popular understanding of the voting booth or naming the branches of government. By incorporating a more nuanced perspective, educators can co-power opportunities for more inclusive and effective strategies for cultivating the knowledge, skills, and dispositions necessary for active and informed civic participation. Riley's story is an excellent example of how this can be achieved.

Method

People make sense of and organize their worlds, "mainly in the form of narrative—stories, excuses, myths, reasons for doing and not doing, and so on" (Bruner, 1991, p. 4). Consequently, I used a narrative inquiry methodology to understand better Riley's speculative artifact and how she could use it for self-actualization and civic resistance. Her speculative story, her future-myth, actualized her present conceptions of reality and the requisite interventions needed to pursue equity and make legible possible pathways to liberation. Narrative inquiry's emphasis on participant voices is significant because this approach is based on the idea that individuals shape their identities and understand their lives through storytelling. Rather than other equally exciting perspectives, such as portraiture, the story here is "-etic" rather than "-emic" because it comes directly from the most insider perspective possible. As such, a narrative inquiry approach seemed appropriate for uncovering Riley's insights' nuanced and deeply personal tone and perspective.

As Clandinin and Connelly (2000) note, narrative inquiry is "about stories lived and told," which affords a deeper, contextualized understanding of participants' experiences by holding space for their voices and acknowledging their perspectives. This is particularly significant in a contemporary context for Black and Brown youth, where their voices are both tacitly and explicitly silenced. This method also facilitates the exploration of identity, personal and cultural meaning making, and how individuals navigate and interpret their worlds. This article draws from a larger, iterative design project (Holbert et al., 2019) to determine how Black and Brown youth might leverage speculative design structures centered on speculative thought (Afrofuturism) to reflect, discuss, and critique experiences with social in/justice to create provocative and resistive frameworks for action. Highlighted here are short prose sketches, transcribed oral drafts, and iterative designs of one participant (Riley) that aim to uncover ways speculative design can foster speculative, civically oriented epistemologies and ways educators might transform their pedagogical practices and approaches in response to students' radical imaginations.

This study utilized a series of eight ninety-minute maker workshops designed in collaboration with a community outreach organization that occurred in an after-school setting at a community youth nonprofit organization. The series explicitly focused on inviting BIPOC (Black, Indigenous, and People of Color) youth into co-powering a culturally sustaining, speculative design process to think about their futures for themselves and their community. To that end, the end-of-experience objective was to facilitate the participants' ideation, design, iteration, and fabrication of an ARTifact that represented their visions for their community's future, specifically responding to the question, "What do you want your community to be like in twenty-five years?"

Research Context

This out-of-school workshop series hosted twenty-five participants, five organizational mentors, and three community artists. We selected and provided mentor texts (Laminack, 2017) written by Black and Brown authors, mainly but not solely from the comics medium. These included artists and writers of color, including Denys Cowan, Vita Ayala, and Eve Ewing among others. The intent was multifaceted: These resources were intended to present these mentor texts as both support and inspiration for participants to develop their ideas, to understand the features of speculative storytelling and design, and to create an artifact with the explicit intention of addressing a civic concern.

The mentor texts included *Ironheart* by Eve Ewing and the *Marvel Voices* anthology, which solely included stories by BIPOC writers, including Vita Ayala, Cody Ziglar, and Adam Serwer. Additional mentor texts were explicitly created for this project by Eisner Award-nominated creatives John Jennings and David Brame for participants to study, review, and enjoy. Additionally, multimodal artifacts were made available in wearables, pre-fabricated costumes, toys, textiles, and fabrics that served as artistic expressions of cultures. For example, we had a variety of batik-printed fabrics, leatherworks, and beadworks available for students.

Workshop Structure

Each workshop session was structured to foster a creative and inclusive environment that invited participants to reflect upon, research, and draw from their cultural and personal backgrounds. This included a series of Socratic discussions centered on a variety of open-ended questions that the research team developed ahead of time (Figure 1). These discussion provocations were created with an explicit focus on future-oriented, civic, and community engagement, which had no expected response but were designed to invite students to bring their expertise and experiences to bear on considering what a desirable future could and indeed should entail.

Participants wrote their responses on whiteboards and shared their thoughts with the group, creating a sense of solidarity and requiring each member to trust and to be vulnerable. Following these responses, we discussed what stories, objects, and narratives could best represent their ideas for a hopeful future. The subsequent sessions were divided into the following distinct phases to provide structure to the process.

Introduction and Ideation

The facilitators introduced the workshop participants to speculative design features, Afrofuturism's tenets, and how these can help visualize future communities. They also introduced the end goal of creating an artifact that told the story of the future that participants wished to see. Everyone in the workshop participated in collective discussions about civic futures, discussions led by participants and facilitated by community organization partners who responded to questions such as "What are your superpowers?" "What assets do you have in your community?" and "What are the challenges in your community?" The purpose of this phase was to inspire creative ideas and increase the diversity of views expressed.

Design and Planning

Alongside community artists, mentors, and teachers, participants began to brainstorm, design, and ideate objects. Some designed technologies while others began work on cityscapes. Others created superhero characters with identities and background narratives they felt addressed the

Figure 1. Array of open-ended, civic-oriented provocations used for community discussion and speculative thinking.

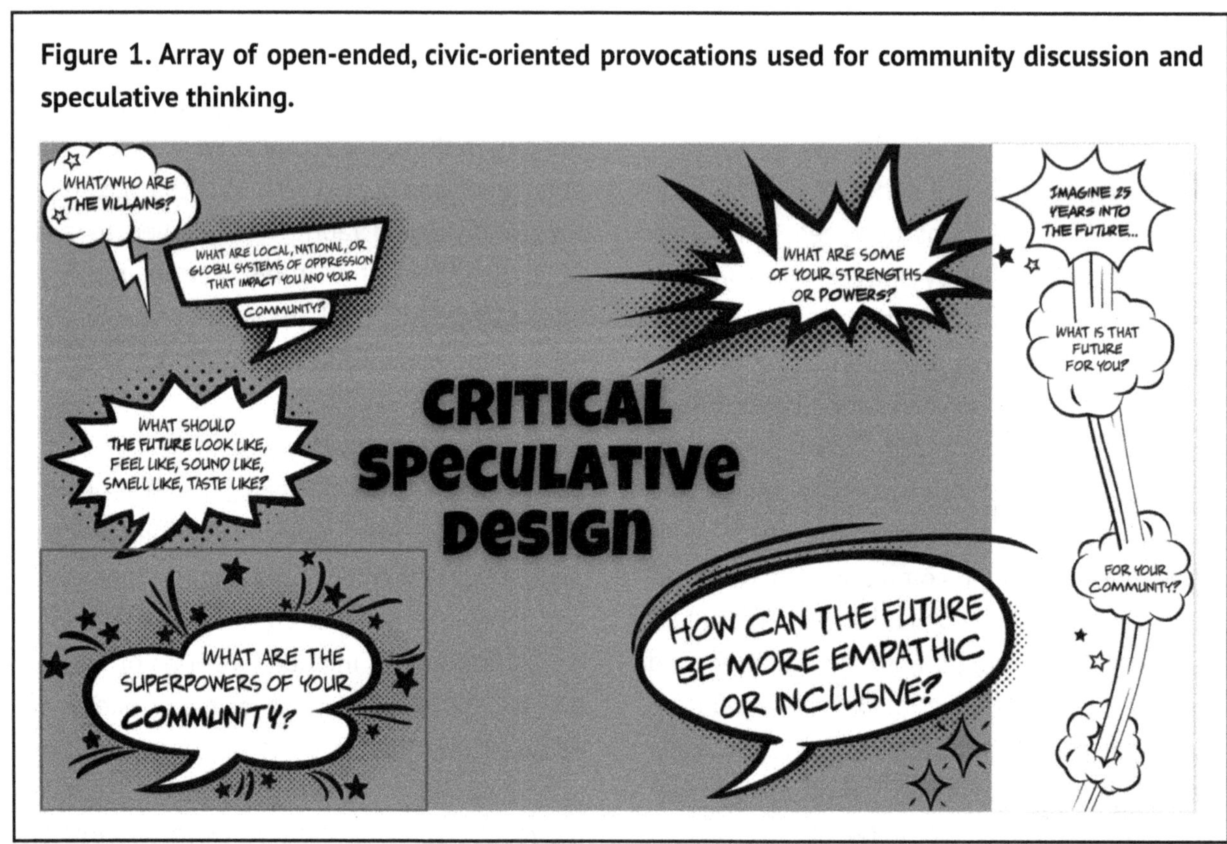

topics raised during the discussion responses. Facilitators organized discussions around design principles and methodologies in order to help participants adequately articulate their ideas.

Iteration and Feedback

After participants presented their designs to one another and the facilitators, they received critical feedback, which guided them through the honing process. Through collaborating and understanding the perspectives of others, this iterative approach motivated participants to refine their ideas based on group feedback.

Fabrication

In the final phase, participants transformed their designs into tangible artifacts. They visualized the future in comic book art or as physical models to dream their futures using tools and materials from sewing machines to pen and paper to create a physical representation of their desired future. This iterative, hands-on learning phase invited participants to hone various cognitive and technical skills to move from abstract ideas to specific products, which supported their articulation of the world they wished to see. Figure 2 shows a flowchart of the speculative design process.

The object lessons, speculative design instruction, and creative tasks were grounded in the Afrofuturist perspective. They included written excerpts and videos by Ruha Benjamin, Octavia Butler, Ytasha Womack, and Alondra Nelson. I drew from Auger's work (2013) and the concept of the "perceptual bridge" as a strategy for connecting a desired future and critiquing a challenging present as well as from a few of Toliver and Miller's (2019) thought experiment phases.

Augur's concepts are appropriate as they primarily deal with technology and the democratization of imagination. We also worked to develop a framework of questions and guideposts that attended to "the sociopolitical values and purposes of making" (Vossoughi et al., 2016, p. 227). We took guidance from Toliver

Figure 2. Flowchart of speculative design process utilized by this workshop series.

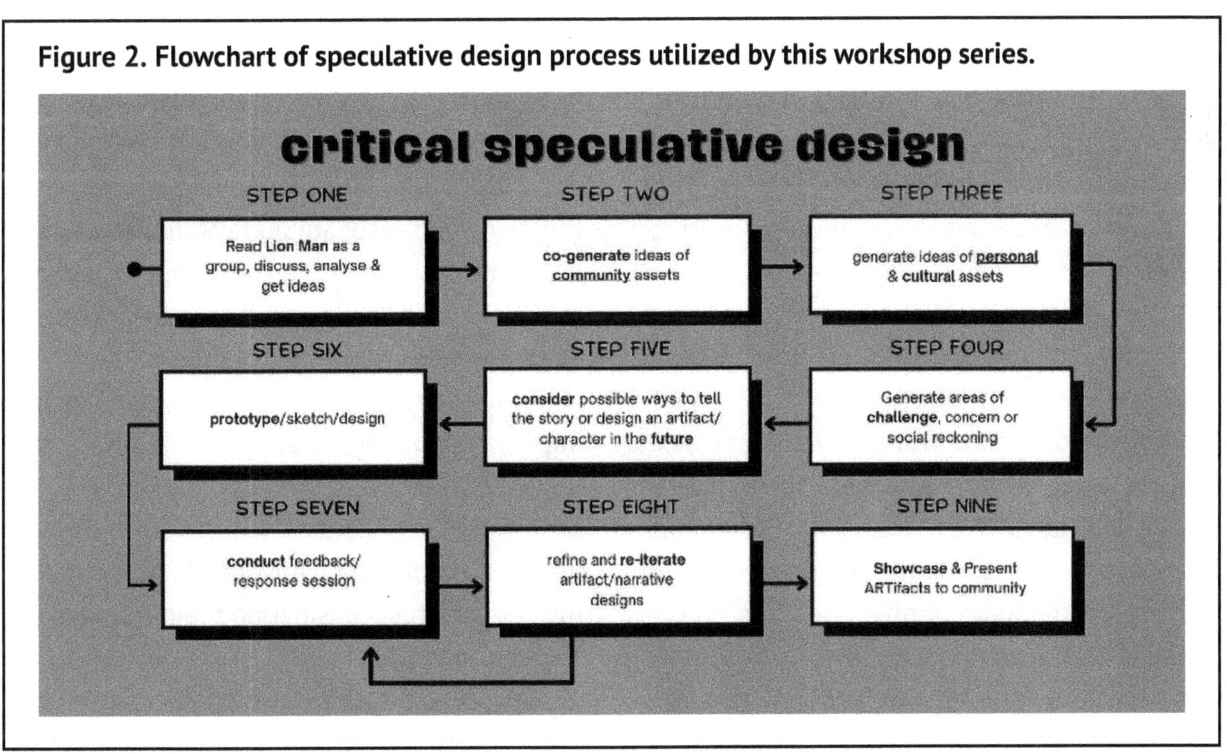

and Miller (2019) and the reminder to center science fiction, or fiction, to "interrogate identity positions and analyze oppressive hierarchies" (p. 58).

Researcher's Positionality

I self-identify as white, cisgender, nerd, researcher, and educator. As a white, adult, cis-male and self-professed comics aficionado, I was situated as both insider and outsider in this study and often in conflicting ways. I was an insider in that I shared an interest in speculative fiction, comic books, science fiction, and other cultural touchstones such as hip-hop music. Regardless of my intent and ideological commitments, my gender, race, education, and other positionalities required constant participant checks and reflection with other community members about perception, purpose, and intent.

We aimed to cocreate an imaginative, active, and supportive environment in which Black and Brown youth, historically under-respected in nearly every official space, could build a creative, critical, making community. To that end, we both participated in and facilitated the workshop by creating alongside, and sharing resources and making strategies with, the participants. We took part in every generative experience (including writing, brainstorming, etc.).

The group intentionally co-constructed space for and participated in conversations around various topics, including racism, comics, hip-hop, K-pop, police brutality, and heterosexism. We designed and told our stories during the latter phases of the workshop. Facilitators only gave direction that the designs be speculative. Participants were given free rein on the artifacts' forms, content, and focus. Facilitators were encouraged to adopt a "yes/and" approach to ideation so that participants could exist in a free space, one in opposition to a space telling them to edit or revise or dream smaller. This was a space for big dreams and big ideas built in solidarity and community.

Standards and Assessments

Students in the Afrofuturist Speculative Design Workshop are invited to produce artifacts that envision a future based on African and diasporic histories, cultural practices, and sociopolitical commitments. These artifacts could be comic strips, short speculative tales, or physical objects. Through the integration of Afrofuturist concepts with speculative fiction, students investigate topics including cultural resilience, technological innovation, and freedom.

In considering the implications for ELA instruction and pedagogy, we found multiple areas of alignment and synergy regarding standards and assessments. For example, the NCTE/IRA Standard 5, which emphasizes the need for students to use a variety of writing strategies and process aspects to communicate with varied audiences for multiple objectives, is clearly addressed in the participants' creative work. Learners are encouraged to think deeply about how their design and storytelling techniques in the workshop resonate and communicate their vision to their peers, teachers, and community members of a more just society. Participants have the opportunity to navigate multiple creative literacy and compositional stages including brainstorming, drafting, reiterating, and publishing while simultaneously considering both the messages they wish to send through designing their speculative artifacts, worlds, or futures, all while considering their intended audiences carefully.

Furthermore, the multimodal approach of the Afrofuturist workshop is in line with NCTE

Standards' emphasis on employing a variety of communication techniques. To that end, participants explore creating narratives and ideas across multiple media by combining spoken word, visual design, and written composition.

This project also holds interdisciplinary and adaptive potential. With the use of the rhetorical devices and narrative structure that this workshop engages, students studying English language arts concentrate on speculative storytelling, composition, and narrative worldbuilding. Simultaneously, they might incorporate social studies by working with historical topics and research methods, constructing other histories and futures with different sociopolitical paths.

This workshop also holds possibilities for STEM education. For example, the workshop can engage students in computational thinking processes as well as skill development such as coding. The workshop might invite students to dream across disciplines about technological and cultural possibilities that aim toward equitable societal transformation.

Thoughts about Practical Implementation

Culturally responsive and sustaining pedagogic approaches are essential for educators wishing to conduct an Afrofuturist speculative design workshop. In addition to providing a safe, structured, and supportive environment for peer review, ideation, and collaboration, teachers should invite students to explore topics of identity, race, and social justice in their writing and dreaming. To support students in perceiving their work as a part of a larger discussion on equality and justice, teachers can make connections between their speculative designs and contemporary social movements. How has dreaming and the speculative always been a part of civic life and forward progress?

The workshop facilitators should offer scaffolding to students that enables them to comprehend design thinking as well as Afrofuturist ideas. Educators should guide students through conversations about subjects including dystopia, utopia, social organizing, cultural histories, and the possible futures of Black communities to support the compositional and design process. It is important to incorporate iterative cycles and peer involvement into the process so that students may improve their writing, designing, and thinking, both in and with a community.

To support learners' facility with ways speculative futures can be conceived, created, and communicated through various media, it is also critical to present vibrant models of Afrofuturist literature and art, such as Octavia Butler's writings, music from artists like Janelle Monae, or Wangechi Mutu's visual designs. Students can explore integrative strategies to their work that include spoken, written, and visual languages and rhetorics for a range of objectives, including information exchange, enjoyment, and persuasion, by engaging with the representations and frameworks offered by this workshop.

Participant Engagement and Cultural Responsiveness

Throughout the workshops, we intentionally employed a culturally sustaining pedagogic framework (Alim & Paris, 2017), taking time to engage not only intellectual skill sets but affective domains as well as issues of social justice. Still, we consistently reflected on ways these designs honored the past and pointed toward a more desirable future. We did this by engaging twin perspectives rooted in African diasporic traditions. The first was *ubuntu*, or the concept of "I am because we are," which directly opposes individualistic, Enlightenment-era thinking that often focuses on the salience of the individual over the collective. The second is the concept of *sankofa*, an Akan (Ghanaian) term roughly meaning "it is not wrong to return to take something if you forget it" (Opoku-Agyemang, 2017). *Sankofa*, often depicted by a bird looking behind itself at an egg on its back, holds particular significance, as Adinkra symbols originate from African oral and folkloric traditions.

To ensure the cultural assets and lived experiences of BIPOC youth were explicitly foregrounded in the iterative and design process, facilitators, including award-winning artists and educators, were selected based on their expertise and commitment to culturally responsive teaching practices. They provided mentorship and support, fostering an environment where participants felt valued and understood.

Data Collection and Analysis

I collected data through various methods, including participant observations, interviews, and artifact analysis. These data sources included eight audio-recorded and transcribed workshop sessions. Interviews were conducted during and immediately following Riley's creative process and centered on her design processes, innovative tools, and storytelling. Additional data included workshop artifacts and one brief orally relayed (and transcribed) narrative. Participant observations focused on collaborative interactions and the iterations of their designs. Insights into participant thought processes, motivations, and reflections on the workshops' impact were provided through interviews. At the same time, artifact analysis examined the final fabrications, assessing to what extent participants felt they achieved their visions and cultural narratives. I used thematic analysis (Braun & Clarke, 2006), focusing on storytelling and the iterative process. I also identified recurring themes and patterns related to participants' experiences, cultural expressions, and the self-described effectiveness of the speculative design process regarding accomplishing their chosen narrative and critical objectives. I focused on Riley's design process in tandem with her storytelling and iterative process.

Designing Misty Walker: Contextualizing the Narratives—Speculative Fiction as Testimony and Counterstory

There were many artifacts that emerged from this workshop, including the development of a futuristic language system, transportation technology, and the development of a biotechnical city that had no need to mine fossil fuels for power. All of these were testaments to the brilliance and creativity of the participants. This section focuses on one participant, Riley, and her creativity via the details of a step-by-step process (Peppler, 2021) to centralize her knowledge and experiences and their influence on approaches to her final iteration. During this process, Riley drew from history, real-life experience, knowledge of civic self, and critical imagination to create her statement of resistance through her original character, Misty Walker. I end with discussing the connections between the fictional story and Riley's writing and civic disposition and engagement.

Biography of Misty Walker

Note: *The following passage is a "biography" of Misty Walker. It was transcribed from the story* *told orally firsthand by Riley to the group using notes she had written. It was edited for clarity and length by the transcribers.*

Misty Walker was born in a big city to immigrant parents. She is a first-generation American with ties to her West African cultural background. At a young age, Misty discovered she had a heritage and talent that transcended physical boundaries. Her parents, who worked long hours to provide for her, told the old tales with a reverence that inspired Misty's curiosity and pride.

At twelve years old, Misty experienced what her doctors called a "maladaptive dream state" but what she called "the Dreaming." These were not daydreams or blackouts but trips into realms in which she could talk with her ancestors and different past incarnations of herself. At first, these events were random and involuntary. She would trip out in class or on the bus or while talking with friends. She would return feeling confused and weak and sore. Misty eventually accepted the challenge of this ability because she was also aware that her gift could tap into long-forgotten knowledge from her history.

After a while, Misty realized that she could transmit the wisdom and emotions of these "dream-dark" ages into melodies, beats, and music. Her lyrics were words from conversations with ancestors. Those sacred conversations were sometimes encouragements, sometimes warnings, and sometimes legends, but they always landed in Misty's journal, a book she maintained like it was top-secret information.

Her journal was a permanent reminder and record of her newfound wisdom and the pathways by which she now conversed with her mystical relations, particularly Aunt Angela. At any time, she would keep bits and phrases such as "what is good and right" in her mind to ask the ancestors on the next trip. The issues Misty began to address within the Dreaming revealed a duality in herself. Every moment she spent in the dream world made her more potent within, but there was a toll. The longer she stayed in the Dreaming, the more her corporeal self weakens. However, Misty eventually got good at balancing the two worlds through practice, training, and research. Misty's extraordinary power was her ability to fight evil through an African Talking Drum that could produce and control soundwaves. This became a unique weapon against the global onslaught by those who would harm her people or take over their city. Thanks to the "juju" in her drum, she could emit soundwaves that paralyzed adversaries and protected those less able. It was not simply a vehicle for expression but an agent of resistance and transformation.

All her life, Misty had to combat doubts and harsh criticisms. Surprisingly, and to the chagrin of some, she appeared frivolous: a young woman with talent going to waste on what they saw as flights from reality. Nevertheless, Misty was unyielding. Her city, community, and self would benefit significantly from her unique talents and perspective, but only time will tell how.

The story of Misty Walker is a story of resilience and empowerment. Using her ancestors' wisdom as her guiding light in the physical realm, she closes the divide between past and present by storytelling ancient and future wisdom.

As a carrier of this ancient knowledge, her medium is music. Through Aunt Angela's melodies, she shows the raw truth and inspires those who listen. Soon, Misty's formerly derided skills serve as the foundation for her legacy and reveal that what was thought of as a fault was an incredible gift for herself and her family.

Designing Misty Walker

Riley designed her character, Misty Walker, throughout five separate sessions. The initial phase of Riley's project involved concept design, in which she engaged in brainstorming sessions to generate ideas for her character. During these sessions, Riley considered various attributes of Misty Walker (Figure 1), such as her background, personality, and the unique abilities she would possess. Misty initially knew she wanted to create a character who was a young girl with "special powers." Furthermore, she brought a few ideas to the initial design that expressed her desire for something she hadn't seen or done before. "I wanted to try something different because I know many people do actual waterpower or firepower, but I wanted to do something different. So, that's why I went with music and historical things, and I just started writing notes and actually the main story." Drawing inspiration from her cultural heritage and personal experiences, Riley envisioned Misty Walker as a resilient and resourceful young girl from a futuristic urban environment. Misty's primary ability would be to "daydream and communicate with her ancestors and other lives."

Following the conceptualization, Riley conducted thorough research to deepen her understanding of speculative fiction and character development. In so doing, she incorporated the West African concept of "juju" into Misty's character. She explored existing characters in literature and media, analyzing their traits, backstories, and the sociocultural contexts they represented. This research phase was crucial for Riley to ensure that Misty Walker would be a unique and compelling character, distinct from existing archetypes yet resonant with cultural themes.

To further develop Misty Walker's character, Riley created story notes that mapped out critical scenes and interactions within Misty's world. This narrative development phase involved crafting detailed story arcs and character interactions highlighting Misty's abilities and personality traits. Riley focused on how Misty's cultural background influenced her worldview and actions, ensuring the narrative was engaging and culturally authentic.

Riley proceeded to the sketching phase using Midjourney AI technology as visualization support. She created initial drafts of Misty Walker, focusing on visual elements such as her attire, physical appearance, and distinguishing features. Riley employed various drawing techniques to capture Misty's essence, experimenting with different styles and expressions to convey her character's depth and complexity. This iterative sketching process allowed Riley to refine Misty's design, ensuring each element aligned with Riley's envisioned narrative.

She then presented her sketches and storyboards to peers and mentors within the workshop for feedback. This collaborative critique session provided Riley with diverse perspectives and constructive suggestions, enabling her to identify areas for improvement. She iterated on Misty's design and story, incorporating feedback to enhance the character's coherence and appeal. This iterative process underscored the importance of collaboration and revision in speculative design.

In Misty's design and story, Riley blends the real world with the speculative, highlighting the United States' legacy of physical, emotional, and mental policing, all intentionally used to enforce submission and situate young Black women as deficient and problematic. Furthermore, Misty's power-set and personality are a thinly veiled metaphor for the ways in which Riley feels (un)seen and (dis)regarded by many of the official structures and institutions she deals with in the everyday. These are the embedded responses to the provocations in the brainstorming sessions. What superpowers do you have? What are the challenges in your community? These responses show up in the worlds and characters Riley constructs.

By connecting the actions of Misty's speculative design to the genuine actions, structures, and institutions that engage in everyday forms of oppression, surveillance, and subjugation, she explicitly embeds the realistic into her fictional tale. Ultimately, she uses her story to comprehend, analyze, and educate others regarding injustice, and through her character's story, she makes a case for fundamental change, an essential facet of counter-storytelling.

Riley makes her real-life experiences and desires an essential part of the story. She made specific moves to incorporate her everyday existence when crafting Misty's character and look. She recounted putting her personality into the narrative itself.

> ***Riley:*** *I based this off of my own self, actually.*
>
> ***Mike:*** *Oh really? How so?*
>
> ***Riley:*** *Misty, she's like, she's bubbly. And I'm really bubbly, but I know when to get serious when I need. I try to express that. And I really like fashion.*

Riley cares deeply for her family, community, and other people and wants the world to be a place of support born out in her design and creation. As with the grown-ups in Misty's narrative, Riley disclosed that she often gets told to "pay more attention" when she is deep in thought. She has a deep-seated desire for mutual understanding, liberty, and equality for all and holds a profound desire to communicate with people through art with the goal that they will work together toward collective social uplift.

As Riley blends her personal and social worlds into her speculative creation, the story makes the injustices she has experienced visible, affirms her humanity and sense of creative and civic self, and invites the audience into an empathetic conversation. Through Misty, Riley's creative narrative operates as a critical pathway to articulate her sense of civic and social self, to testify to her struggles, and to challenge oppression.

Riley's artifact and the speculative backstory reveal how she critically examines her world. Drawing from her experiences, community, and research into cultural traditions and lifeways, she is invited to think meaningfully through structural injustices. She carefully considers how dominant structures position young people, in this case a Black girl, as problematic or deficient. For example, Black girls' mental health has been mishandled or ignored, being called a crisis "hiding in plain sight" (Alessandrini, 2021). This includes, among other things, an under-diagnosis of ADHD, which often results in over-punishment, such as suspension, which can result in over-representation in incarceration (NBWJI, 2021).

For Riley, if the public does not alter its deficit perspectives, that is, to see Misty's "maladaptive" state as a gift and a benefit rather than a problem, then a dystopian reality and perhaps a worse future is not a fantasy or a genuine possibility. Rather than focusing solely on oppression, though, Riley includes an emancipating response in the form of art (music) as resistance and the salience of ancestral wisdom as a perspective to persuade readers to become active civic participants by reengaging with and rethinking ways they consider youth and the powerful positive potential youth can hold in their community. Riley uses her story both to describe the contours of structural injustices and to articulate how speculatively constructed knowledge of self, situated in community, family, and culture, renders civic engagement and social change both desirable and possible.

Misty Walker focuses on the specifics of a singular character as a speculative artifact, but the individual's power is centered explicitly in, by, and through her community itself. Misty Walker's intentional historical and cultural design, which draws on past and present in ways that speak to the future, explicitly articulates how collective civic dispositions can be liberatory, how collective action can be a catalyst for meaningful and lasting change, and how a culturally sustaining and historical sense of self can serve as a countermeasure to forms of sociocultural oppression. Riley's design articulates a pathway for civic literacy and engagement through counterstory for people on a mission for intergenerational, co-powered equity.

Often, counterstories are positioned in the present and are declarations of defiance that oppose the grand narratives proffered by dominant ideologies. Nevertheless, there is a deep, speculative tradition among Afrofuturist thought dating back to literary luminaries, including Phillis Wheatley's poetry, which envisions new futures for Black people, Pauline Hopkins's 1902 novel *Of One Blood* (2022), and W. E. B. Du Bois's short story "The Comet" (1920). As Toliver (2019) powerfully reminds us, this speculative tradition is alive and well in the spirit of Black women and girls today.

It is this tradition that Riley engages in through self-affirmation, forged through the design process and Black joy, by literally writing her into a space of activism and social change. She engages her community by creating her own story in her own space, on her own terms explicitly intended for her community to review, rethink, and re-story the meanings of civic dispositions and community engagement for just futures. Through Misty's story, Riley engages in radical, hopeful truth telling, conjuring a future she wishes to see, even though it may be challenging. Riley's engagement in speculative design and storytelling about what she wishes and desires acknowledges Davis's (2016) reminder that imaginative, optimistic work is necessary "even though we don't yet see a glimmer on the horizon that it's actually going to be possible" (p. 29). Riley highlights situations in the real world through her culturally situated design and narrative. Misty's surreal story of juju, ancestral dream walking, and music as resistance is, in reality, an extended metaphor that incorporates Riley's authentic personal and social experiences as a strategy of resistance to catalyze conversations about the need for social justice.

Conclusion

Riley's story affirms that "Every black neighborhood in every city in the United States comes equipped with its own storytellers" (Smitherman, 1986, p. 148). Riley is one such storyteller, a young Black girl who used her imagination to condense broad, theoretical observations about life, love, and people into a speculative narrative. Riley's narrative is an alternative reality wherein she provides a brilliant instance of ways those often pushed out of design spaces, particularly Black girls, think about their lived experience and engage in deeply intellectual creative pursuits to draw from their communal past in order to build a future, regardless of stereotypical expectations or what is traditionally considered plausible. Speculative design and thinking, mainly through Afrofuturism, has been historically deployed to tell stories of survival. It has invited diasporic communities—whose collective pasts have been erased or destroyed—opportunities to construct new visions of possibility and a means to safeguard lifeways amid institutional, symbolic, and physical destruction. Speculative design and storying, manifested by Riley in the form of Misty Walker, tell stories that create worlds beyond the one we currently inhabit and imagine more just futures. Through her story, Riley shared her understanding and experiences of the world, allowing readers to listen and respond.

The Radical Black Imagination articulated through Riley's artifact is inherently radical because it refuses to accept an existent, unjust world that disregards hopes, dreams, and lives while simultaneously dreaming of a world to come. Through this dreamed articulation, realities can be re-formed, and spaces for subaltern communities to confront and resist white supremacy and imagine brave new voices and worlds are paramount. A flourishing, vibrant democracy requires myriad paths forward. The Radical Black Imagination has often been at the center of these movements, from Harriet Tubman to Bayard Rustin to the Black Panther Party for Self-Defense. In an era of specifically anti-Black, anti-democratic mobilization by extraordinarily imaginative white nationalists and supremacists, it is perhaps more critical now more than ever for teachers and learners to cultivate radical imaginations in every space possible as a means of civic defense and resistance.

Ultimately, the Speculative Design Workshop engages participants in ideation, iteration, and fabrication that invites them to draw from their lived experiences and cultural backgrounds to envision critical speculative futures through original worldbuilding, artifact design, and character creation. Through this workshop, learners both engage and develop capacities to question established social systems and to envision possible horizons where justice, equity, and inclusion are foregrounded. By inviting participants to actively and intentionally build the skills necessary to create and influence futures that reflect their intellectual and affective wants, needs, and desires, this approach cultivates a critical consciousness. It affords opportunities to investigate intersections of race, technology, and culture that question their construction and reiteration as well as what other possibilities might be realized. Through the integration of critical thinking and speculative design, the workshop prepares students to articulate their visions for social change and supports them in building the social and interpersonal skills needed to take concrete steps in bringing those visions to life through cooperative problem solving, critical community conversations, and socially oriented creation. Rather than a simple exercise in imagination, this workshop supports students intellectually, interculturally, and interpersonally to become change agents in their communities.

Works Cited

Alessandrini, K. A. (2021, May 11). Suicide among Black girls is a mental health crisis hiding in plain sight. *Time.* https://time.com/6046773/black-teenage-girls-suicide/

Alim, H. S., & Paris, D. (2017). What is culturally sustaining pedagogy and why does it matter? In D. Paris & H. S. Alim (Eds.), *Culturally sustaining pedagogies: Teaching and learning for justice in a changing world* (pp. 1–23). Teachers College Press.

Anderson, R. (2016). Afrofuturism 2.0 & the Black speculative arts movement: Notes on a manifesto. *Obsidian, 42*(1–2), 228–236.

Auger, G. A. (2013). Fostering democracy through social media: Evaluating diametrically opposed nonprofit advocacy organizations' use of Facebook, Twitter, and YouTube. *Public Relations Review, 39*(4), 369–376.

Benjamin, R. (2024). *Imagination: A manifesto.* W. W. Norton & Company.

Braun, V., & Clarke, V. (2006). Using thematic analysis in psychology. *Qualitative Research in Psychology, 3*(2), 77–101.

Bruner, J. (1991). The narrative construction of reality. *Critical Inquiry, 18*(1), 1–21.

Chambliss, J. (2014, February 20). *Black Kirby now: An interview with John Jennings.* PopMatters. www.popmatters.com/179294-black-kirby-now-an-interview-with-john-jennings-2495685683.html

Christian Aid. (n.d.). *Christian aid in Bangladesh.* www.christianaid.ie/our-work/where-we-work/bangladesh

Connelly, F. M., & Clandinin, D. J. (1990). Stories of experience and narrative inquiry. *Educational Researcher, 19*(5), 2–14.

Davis, A. (1988). Radical perspectives on the empowerment of Afro-American women: Lessons for the 1980s. *Harvard Educational Review, 58*(3), 348–354.

Davis, A. Y. (2016). *Freedom is a constant struggle: Ferguson, Palestine, and the foundations of a movement.* Haymarket Books.

Delgado, R. (1989). Storytelling for oppositionists and others: A plea for narrative. *Michigan Law Review, 87*(8), 2411–2441.

Du Bois, W. E. B. (2021). *The Comet.* Mint Editions. (Original work published 1920.)

Dunne, A., & Raby, F. (2024). Speculative everything: Design, fiction, and social dreaming. The MIT Press.

Collins, P. H. (2000). Black feminist thought: Knowledge, consciousness, and the politics of empowerment (2nd ed.). Routledge.

Garcia, A., & Mirra, N. (2023). Other suns: Designing for racial equity through speculative education. *Journal of the Learning Sciences, 32*(1), 1–20.

Hall, S. (2016). Culture, resistance, and struggle. In J. D. Slack & L. Grossberg (Eds.), *Cultural studies 1983: A theoretical history* (pp. 180–206). Duke University Press.

Holbert, N., Dando, M., & Correa, I. (2020). Afrofuturism as critical constructionist design: Building futures from the past and present. *Learning, Media and Technology, 45*(4), 328–344.

hooks, b. (2000). *Feminism is for everybody: Passionate politics.* Pluto Press.

Hopkins, P. E. (2022). *Of one blood: Or, the hidden self.* Broadview Press.

Imarisha, W. (2015). Introduction. In A. Brown & W. Imarisha (Eds.), *Octavia's brood: Science fiction stories from social justice movements* (pp. 3–6). AK Press.

Kelley, R. D. G. (2002). *Freedom dreams: The Black radical imagination.* Beacon Press.

Kinloch, V. (2009). *Harlem on our Minds: Place, race, and the literacies of urban youth.* Teachers College Press.

Komalasari, K. (2012). The effect of contextual

learning in civic education on students' civic skills. *EDUCARE: International Journal for Educational Studies*, *4*(2), 179–190.

Ladson-Billings, G. (2014). Culturally relevant pedagogy 2.0: a.k.a. the remix. *Harvard Educational Review*, *84*(1), 74–84.

Laminack, L. (2017). Mentors and mentor texts: What, why, and how? *The Reading Teacher*, *70*(6), 753–755.

Love, B. L. (2019). *We want to do more than survive: Abolitionist teaching and the pursuit of educational freedom*. Beacon press.

Milner, H. (2002). *Civic literacy: How informed citizens make democracy work*. University Press of New England.

Mirra, N., & Garcia, A. (2020). "I hesitate but I do have hope": Youth speculative civic literacies for troubled times. *Harvard Educational Review*, *90*(2), 295–321.

National Black Women's Justice Institute. (2021, June 7). *The case for focusing on Black girls' mental health*. www.nbwji.org/post/the-case-for-focusing-on-black-girls-mental-health

Opoku-Agyemang, K. (2017). Looking back while moving forward: The case of concrete poetry and *Sankofa*. *Hyperrhiz: New Media Cultures*, *16*. https://doi:10.20415/hyp/016.e07

Peppler, K. (2022). *Creativity and innovation*. Routledge.

Roschelle, J., Penuel, W., & Shechtman, N. (2006). Co-design of innovations with teachers: Definition and dynamics. In S. Barab, K. Hay, & D. Hickey (Eds.), *Proceedings of ICLS 2006* (Vol. 2, pp. 606–612). International Society of the Learning Sciences.

Roy, A. (2020, April 3). Arundhati Roy: "The pandemic is a portal." *Financial Times*. www.ft.com content/10d8f5e8-74eb-11ea-95fe-fcd274e920ca

Smitherman, G. (1986). *Talkin and testifyin: The language of Black America*. Wayne State University Press.

Solórzano, D. G., & Yosso, T. J. (2002). Critical race methodology: Counter-storytelling as an analytical framework for education research. *Qualitative Inquiry*, *8*(1), 23–44.

Toliver, S. R. (2021). Freedom dreaming in a broken world: The Black radical imagination in Black girls' science fiction stories. *Research in the Teaching of English*, *56*(1), 85–106.

Vossoughi, S., Hooper, P. K., & Escudé, M. (2016). Making through the lens of culture and power: Toward transformative visions for educational equity. *Harvard Educational Review*, *86*(2), 206–232.

Westheimer, J., & Kahne, J. (2004). What kind of citizen? The politics of educating for democracy. *American Educational Research Journal*, *41*(2), 237–269.

Zinn, H. (2018). *You can't be neutral on a moving train: A personal history of our times*. Beacon Press.

Not Just Acting Like Activists: Youths' Civic-Focused Justice Work in Social Media Communities

DOMINIQUE SKYE MCDANIEL

"Come On America" —Johnavan

Instagram social media post by Johnavan, a fourteen-year-old Black boy, in reaction to the January 6, 2021, insurrection attack on the US Capitol in Washington, DC.

Youth's Civic Literacy Practices and Social Media

External communities, such as social media (Kelly, 2020; McDaniel, 2023; Shrodes, 2022), activism programs (Carey et al., 2021; Hadley et al., 2020), after-school programs (Anyiwo et al., 2021), and civic summer camps (Bauml et al., 2022), are valuable for youth of color. While literature addresses the intersection of civics and digital spaces like social media within K–12 classrooms (Chapman & Marich, 2021; Garcia & Mirra, 2021; Middaugh et al., 2022), there is also significant scholarship on youth engagement with civic literacies and digital ecologies (Hauge & Roswell, 2020) when focused on their activism practices on social media (Neag et al., 2024; Stornaiuolo & Thomas, 2017).

Leveraging technologies like social media helps better our understanding of how youth of color engage in civic literacy practices online (Garcia et al., 2020; Garcia et al., 2021). Scholars argue for reconsidering how these youth are positioned as civic agents through their engagement with social justice practices via digital media (Mirra & Garcia, 2017). They also emphasize the need to expand digital citizenship to address challenging issues like racism (Garcia et al., 2021; Mirra et al., 2022). To prepare students for future civic engagement, these scholars explore components of digital citizenship education that include student voice. As for what this entails for educators, leveraging digital literacies for equity and social justice could be taken up in justice-oriented teaching and learning within English language arts (ELA), positioning youth of color's unique civic work as sophisticated and worth interacting with.

The question of how to leverage digital literacies for equity and social justice has been widely debated in the critical digital literacies field and in our political and cultural realities. Scholars like Price-Dennis (2016), Price-Dennis and Carrion (2017), Price-Dennis and Muhammad (2021), and Price-Dennis et al. (2015, 2017) emphasize the need to better understand how youth, particularly youth of color, engage with twenty-first-century literacies. Furthermore, the literature emphasizes that youth digital advocacy is a new form of civic participation. As civic engagement intersects with digital citizenship (Garcia et al., 2021; Garcia & Mirra, 2021; Mirra & Garcia, 2022; Mirra et al., 2013; Mirra et al., 2022), insights into how young people participate in online activism enhance our comprehension of the intersection between civic engagement and youths' literacy practices.

About the Project: Youth of Color's Civic Literacy Practices on Social Media

This essay is based on a 2021 study examining how six youths of color—self-identifying as Black, Latina, and Latine—use literacy practices for social change through justice-oriented activism and civic engagement on social media. The study aimed to understand how these young activists and allies responded to the heightened social justice movements of 2020 and 2021. They utilized multimodal literacies to engage in civic-focused work across social media platforms such as Instagram, X (formerly Twitter), TikTok, and YouTube. This essay focuses on data from three of the participants (all names are pseudonyms): Dakari, a sixteen-year-old Black girl who prefers Instagram and YouTube; Laura, an eighteen-year-old Latine girl who prefers Instagram and X; and Tatum, an eighteen-year-old Black girl most active on Instagram and X.

I selected teens of color who were regular, but not well-known, social media users. This approach aimed to capture the genuine online experiences of everyday youth engaged in activist literacies and civic participation through social media while shaping their identities in the process. Recruitment involved youth of color who were using social media platforms like Instagram, X, TikTok, and YouTube, leveraging hashtags and social media algorithms to contact potential participants initially through direct messages or emails and later through virtual recruitment meetings. I aimed for a diverse selection of youth interests spanning intersectional climate justice, social change for LGBTQIA+ communities, advocacy for the Latine community, and addressing injustices around Black lives. My roles encompassed both observing and participating in social media. As an observer, I closely monitored participants' personal posts. As an active participant, I simultaneously used social media profiles created for the project to occupy the same spaces, engaging in social justice content and interacting with youths' content by liking, commenting on, and sharing their content.

To analyze the multiple case studies, or the youth in the study, I engaged in a two-phase process. Phase one focused on crafting individual narratives for each participant. This involved reviewing weekly analytic memos, unearthing emerging themes for each youth using single case-study analysis on data sources—interview transcripts, observation field notes, analytic memos, and digital artifacts. In addition, I composed individual case narratives of each teen. The second phase involved a cross-case analysis, identifying overarching patterns, commonalities, and shared meanings across the six cases. Here, I composed a cross-case analysis. For this reason, youth are sectioned individually in the essay, since a multicase study method was employed. Each youth was a single case—analyzed individually and collectively—in this cross-case study, where I looked at similarities, differences, and conundrums between the single cases.

This essay foregrounding youth voices, particularly the voices of youth of color, takes a compelling and necessary stance in our current political context. The recent surge in opposition to critical race theory (CRT) in schools and the enactment of legislation banning certain books have made censorship efforts increasingly politicized. In order to understand how new laws and regulations are restricting students' access to knowledge, it is important to connect the arguments presented in this piece with the broader cultural context. Given widespread anti-CRT and book-banning legislation, it is important to recognize how youths' online activism is a way for them to resist this work and gain access to what they cannot in schools. Over the past four years, we have experienced a global pandemic, civil unrest related to police and state-sanctioned violence, and the implementation of laws that restrict and censor content and texts. These events have disproportionately impacted certain communities, making it necessary to adapt teaching methods to address the new challenges.

To fully understand the affordances of multimodality in youth's civic lives, we must aim to understand the experiences and positionalities of social media as spaces for youth activism around social justice, racism, and sites of their civic engagement. Reflecting on semi-structured interviews with youth of color, data collected from their social media literacies, and observations of their online engagement, this essay suggests ways that multimodality and social media literacies are embodied. In conclusion, this project, by closely examining the ways youth of color use social media literacies to advocate for social justice, sheds new light on the rarely acknowledged perspectives and experiences of marginalized students within social media spaces.

Youth Changemakers, Social Media, and Civic Literacy Practices.

Young people on social media have found unique civic literacy practices for changemaking. Taking on an activist stance, Dakari confronted systemic racism by utilizing literacies for change as a content creator on social media. She frequently challenged the idea that age or adulthood is a prerequisite for making a difference in the world through her civic literacy practices (McDaniel, 2024) on social media (see Figures 1–3).

Online communities serve as a realm for youth changemakers to operate independent-

Figure 1. Instagram post by Dakari on systemic racism.

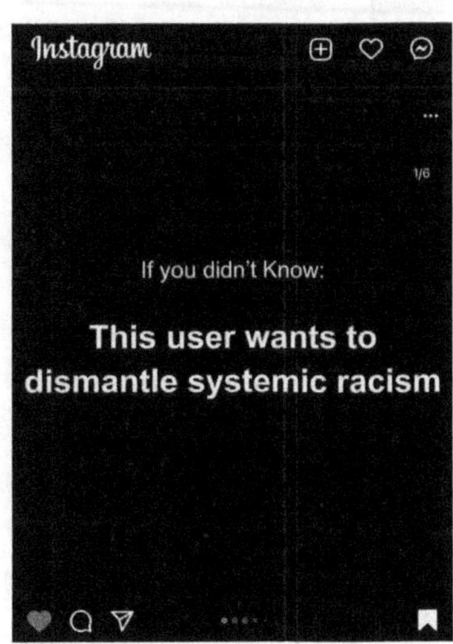

Figure 2. Instagram post by Dakari on systemic racism, continued.

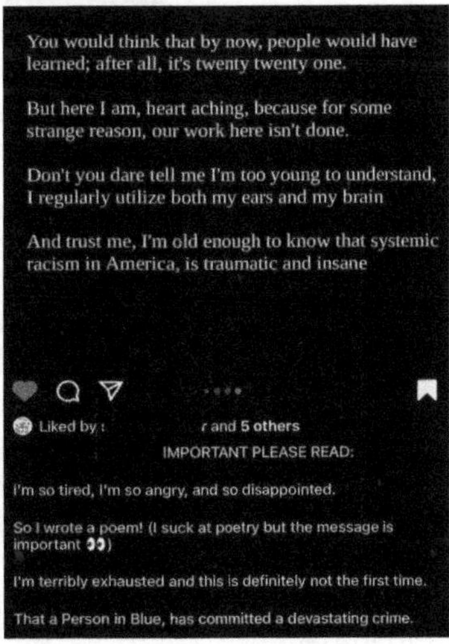

Figure 3. Instagram post by Dakari on social change.

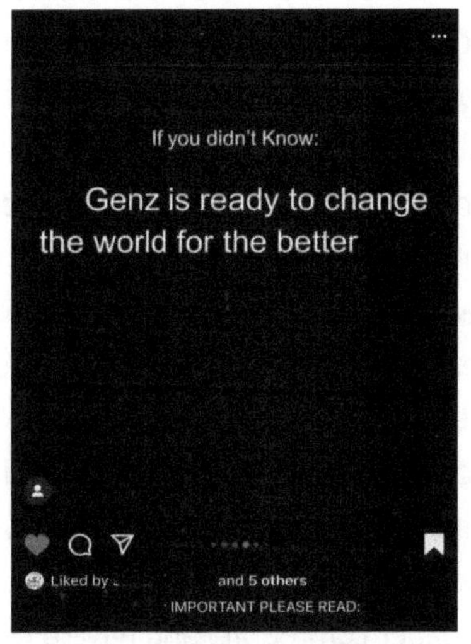

ly from the constraints of adult supervision such as parental or teacher surveillance, unless restricted by access limitations. In essence, social media offers a platform where many young people feel liberated to be open, vulnerable, and fearless, engaging in critical discussions about social change. On social media, youth can express their true civic selves or adopt identities aligned with such ideals. Educators may find value in exploring the aspects that make these online communities appealing to youth engaged in this activism, as well as identifying transferable assets to the classroom environment such as content creation, community, and other elements like choice and autonomy.

Considerations for Youth Changemakers

To support youth in developing action-oriented literacies, I offer several considerations to help teachers integrate advocacy into their classrooms. First, educators can foster opportunities for students to engage in action-oriented projects and assignments by utilizing their digital advocacy as a bridge to civic participation. Additionally, teachers can create assignments that leverage teens' action-oriented literacies (see Table 1 on page 67 for examples). It is also important for teachers to incorporate action-oriented topics to explore how young people advocate for social change, contribute as citizens, demonstrate social responsibility, impact communities positively, and use online literacies for diversity and inclusiveness. Adding to this, teachers can expand texts to include readings from youth activists, like informational texts, online magazine articles, social media stories, website news articles, or speeches by youth activists. Finally, teachers could involve community stakeholders as potential audiences for student work, ensuring that students' efforts reach a broader community and have a real-world impact.

Social Media as an Action-Oriented Space for Civic Literacy Practices

One teen, Laura, used social media, specifically Instagram and X, to engage in civic-related literacy practices focused on social justice issues. She encouraged her audience to participate in voting, signing petitions, calling legislators, and educating themselves (see Figure 4). In another post (see Figure 5), she expressed her allyship with the Black community, offering actionable steps in context with the notion that there is no excuse for inaction.

These posts demonstrate Laura's efforts to motivate her audiences to move beyond performative activism, which she views as superficial engagement without meaningful action. She advocates for taking tangible steps, such as signing petitions, making phone calls, engaging in conversations, and calling out injustice through social media posts. Laura emphasizes the importance of educating friends, family, and even strangers in

Figure 4. Instagram story by Laura on suggested advocacy.

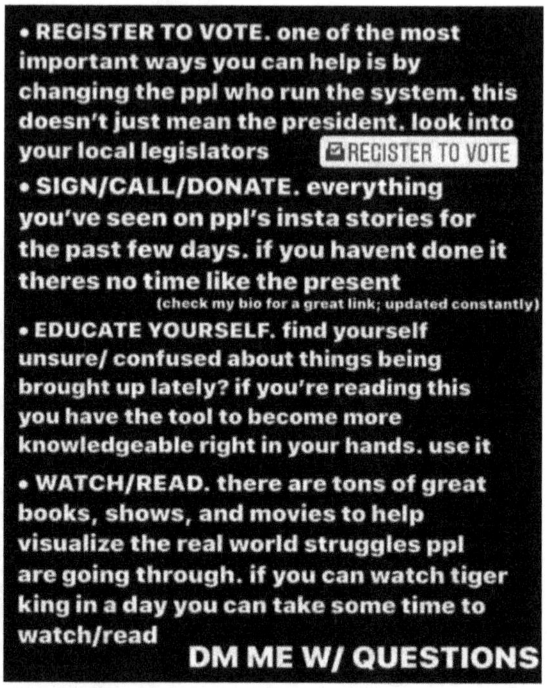

• REGISTER TO VOTE. one of the most important ways you can help is by changing the ppl who run the system. this doesn't just mean the president. look into your local legislators REGISTER TO VOTE
• SIGN/CALL/DONATE. everything you've seen on ppl's insta stories for the past few days. if you havent done it theres no time like the present (check my bio for a great link; updated constantly)
• EDUCATE YOURSELF. find yourself unsure/ confused about things being brought up lately? if you're reading this you have the tool to become more knowledgeable right in your hands. use it
• WATCH/READ. there are tons of great books, shows, and movies to help visualize the real world struggles ppl are going through. if you can watch tiger king in a day you can take some time to watch/read
DM ME W/ QUESTIONS

Figure 5. Instagram story by Laura on suggested advocacy, continued.

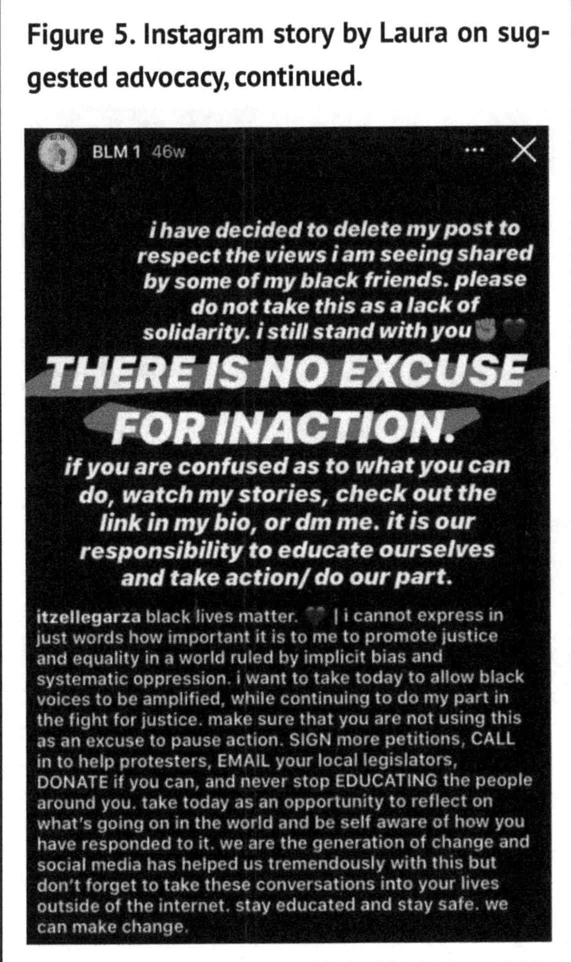

order to avoid complacency, and she urges her audience to never turn a blind eye to injustice.

Social media provides young people with opportunities to participate in action-oriented civic literacy practices. Utilizing this space could be advantageous for teachers aiming to cultivate justice-oriented education. For instance, educators could explore how young people utilize social media for social activism and practicing active citizenship. With recognition of social media as a space conducive to action-oriented civic literacy practices, educators can effectively integrate it into their curriculum and pedagogical approaches.

Considerations for Action-Oriented Online Spaces

Social media platforms are spaces where youth showcase their action-oriented work. Educators can use these platforms as models to highlight students' civic literacy and social justice activism. For example, educators can integrate YouTube into their classrooms by showcasing videos created by youth activists and allies, followed by critical discussions about these videos and related issues. Educators can also assign projects that promote civic literacy practices, such as challenging students to create TikTok videos focused on fostering change. Moreover, educators can offer assignments that integrate imagery with social justice on platforms like Instagram, offering students diverse opportunities to express themselves. In the next section, I focus on how two teens in the study used podcasting alongside social media compositions to uniquely engage in content creation to produce action-oriented work.

Podcasts as a Voice-Centered Space for Civic Literacy Practices

Some youth in the study, such as Tatum and Dakari, used social media platforms to reference podcasts (see Figures 6–8) as a means for using their voices for social justice activism. By doing so, their civic literacy practices are further amplified. In this context, online communities reinforce to young people, particularly youth of color, that their voices matter to the public. Furthermore, podcasting in addition to social media expands the possibilities for civic engagement among young people seeking digital platforms to practice activism and allyship. It further allows them to effectively leverage the impact of current technologies.

Those working with educators and youth can consider including podcasting in content area courses such as English language arts (ELA). This method offers a space for multimodal composing (Aleo et al., 2024), civic work (Garcia et al. 2021; Mirra & Garcia, 2017), voicing counternarratives (Greene, 2021), and justice-

Figure 6. Tweet shared on X by Tatum on podcasts.

Figure 7. Post shared on Instagram by Dakari on podcasts.

Figure 8. Post shared on Instagram by Tatum on podcasts.

oriented activism and allyship (Shelton & Macias, 2021). Using podcasts as a voice-centered space for youth, particularly youth of color, to engage in civic literacy practices provides another platform to highlight their action-oriented work. Those working with youth or teachers can also create opportunities for podcasting focused on social justice activism and civics.

Considerations for Justice-Oriented Podcasting

Introducing podcasts into the classroom is significant because it meets our youth where they are, offering a new form of literacy and social advocacy. For example, students can create podcasts to share different experiences and perspectives on social justice issues. Further, podcasting can be used in the classroom to foster critical conversations on social justice topics, centering youth voices as a teaching tool. Incorporating podcasting offers students a platform to write with their own voices. This form of social advocacy promotes awareness of important issues through outreach. Here, youth become both content creators and social media users.

Lesson Ideas: Blending Digital Spaces and Civics with ELA

Classrooms can benefit from incorporating external contexts, like digital media spaces and social media. Integrating critical learning experiences through civics, creating speciali-zed spaces for justice-oriented literacies, and using social media for literacy practices can serve as forms of digital capital. These approaches can help move youth from enacting change online to taking community action (McDaniel, 2023). This can be achieved by connecting with youth of color's activism for social change, their interests in social justice, and their civic engagement as active citizens in online communities. Those working in the field with youth and educators could use justice-oriented classroom resources for lesson ideas to include advocacy, activism, and teaching and learning for equity and justice. Below, I provide lesson plan ideas for teachers from Learning for Justice, a website that offers innovative and practical ideas and resources for classroom use.

Table 1. Learning for Justice website resources.

Justice-Oriented Resource	Lesson Title	About the Lesson	Suggested Grade Level
Learning for Justice Classroom Resources	Digital Activism Remixed: Hashtags for Voice, Visibility, and Visions of Social Justice	Students explore how young people create and use hashtags related to themes of identity, diversity, justice, and social action as tools to share digital content and develop awareness and agency related to social activism.	6–8
	Civic Engagement and Communication as Digital Community Members	Students learn how to communicate in internet groups and respond to bias online for more inclusive and safe spaces.	6–8
	Social Media for Social Action	Students learn about how people use technology and social media as tools for social activism and social change.	6–8, 9–12
	Digital Tools as a Mechanism for Active Citizenship	Students explore how technology can be used as a tool for active citizenship.	9–12

Teachers can incorporate the following essential questions, adapted from the lessons above, into their ELA standard curriculum:

- How can social media hashtags serve as tools for youth of color in creating and sharing digital content?
- In what ways can young people of color use social media hashtags to foster awareness of and agency in social activism?
- How do young people of color employ technology and social media in activism?
- What are the advantages of online social activism for youth of color?
- What role does digital technology and social media play in promoting the active citizenship of youth of color?

Youth activism toward social justice work will continue online as long as youth choose to engage in it. By expanding classroom contexts to include online spaces, such as social media platforms where students spend considerable time engaging in civic activities, we can better support a generation of learners committed to enacting social change through digital activism. Ignoring these spaces risks failing to recognize valuable civic engagement and learning that is happening in online spaces. In short, there is an imperative to extend digital citizenship education in ELA classrooms to address challenging issues through critical conversations and literacies (Mirra et al., 2022). This involves reimagining the landscape of teaching and learning to include the critical democracy work of young people engaging in digital civic participation (Mirra et al., 2013).

Possibilities for Civic-Focused Justice Work in Social Media Communities

Practitioners and community-engaged teacher educators can leverage the civic-focused activities of youth on social media. By doing so, they can expand literacy practices related to activism, advocacy, and allyship. To some, it may be surprising to see youth involved in extensive learning and teaching outside the classroom; however, in online communities, youth often become learners about society and its treatment of individuals.

It is essential to recognize young people's online engagement as a form of civic engagement. They are leveraging social media to educate themselves, peers, and strangers on political and social justice issues. Many young people have large followings and are heavily networked with their peers and communities. This enables them to disseminate information quickly and with ease. Social media is regularly used to share news and petitions, to provide political commentary, to share acts of injustice, and to motivate their audiences to take action. There are vast possibilities for continuing civic-focused work in these communities, as it is here that youth assume a level of autonomy over their literacy practices that is not always possible within the classroom.

Works Cited

Aleo, T., Jerasa, S., & Nash, B. (2024). "What would other Swifties think?": Multimodal composing with communities in mind. *English Journal, 113*(4), 27–36. https://doi.org/10.58680/ej2024113427

Anyiwo, N., Richards-Schuster, K., & Jerald, M. C. (2021). Using critical media literacy and youth-led research to promote the sociopolitical development of Black youth: Strategies from "our voices." *Applied Developmental Science, 25*(3), 201–216. https://doi.org/10.1080/10888691.2021.1906246

Bauml, M., Davis Smith, V., & Blevins, B. (2022). "Who cares?": Young adolescents' perceived barriers to civic action. *RMLE Online: Research in Middle Level Education*, *45*(3), 1–20. https://doi.org/10.1080/19404476.2022.2033069

Carey, R. L., Akiva, T., Abdellatif, H., & Daughtry, K. A. (2021). "And school won't teach me that!" Urban youth activism programs as transformative sites for critical adolescent learning. *Journal of Youth Studies*, *24*(7), 941–960. https://doi.org/10.1080/13676261.2020.1784400

Chapman, A. L., & Marich, H. (2021). Using Twitter for civic education in K–12 classrooms. *TechTrends: Linking Research and Practice to Improve Learning*, *65*(1), 51–61. https://doi.org/10.1007/s11528-020-00542-z

Garcia, A., McGrew, S., Mirra, N., Tynes, B., & Kahne, J. (2021). Rethinking digital citizenship: Learning about media, literacy, and race in turbulent times. In C. Lee, G. White, & D. Dong (Eds.), *Educating for civic reasoning and discourse* (pp. 319–352). National Academy of Education.

Garcia, A., & Mirra, N. (2021). Writing toward justice: Youth speculative civic literacies in online policy discourse. *Urban Education*, *56*(4), 640–669. https://doi.org/10.1177/0042085920953881

Garcia, P., Fernández, C., & Okonkwo, H. (2020). Leveraging technology: How Black girls enact critical digital literacies for social change. *Learning, Media and Technology*, *45*(4), 345–362.

Greene, D. (2021). (W)rites of passage: Black girls' journaling and podcast script writing as counternarratives. *Voices from the Middle*, *28*(4), 38–42. https://doi.org/10.58680/vm202131275

Hadley, H. L., Burke, K. J., & Wright, W. T. (2020). Opening spaces of restoration for youth through community-engaged critical literacy practices. *English Teaching: Practice & Critique*, *19*(1), 95–106. https://doi.org/10.1108/ETPC-05-2019-0068

Hauge, C., & Rowsell, J. (2020). Child and youth engagement: civic literacies and digital ecologies. *Discourse: Studies in the Cultural Politics of Education*, *41*(5), 667–672. https://doi.org/10.1080/01596306.2020.1769933

Kelly, L. L. (2020). Exploring Black girls' subversive literacies as acts of freedom. *Journal of Literacy Research*, *52*(4), 456–481. https://doi.org/10.1177/1086296X20966367

McDaniel, D. (2023). Supporting justice-oriented English instruction through teens' digital activist literacies. *English Journal*, *113*(1), 49–57. https://doi.org/10.58680/ej202332630

McDaniel, D. (2024). "Bold of them to assume I want to wait until I'm older to do what I love": One teen's activism and civic engagement online. *Journal of Adolescent & Adult Literacy*, *67*(6), 363–375. https://doi.org/10.1002/jaal.1343

Middaugh, E., Bell, S., & Kornbluh, M. (2022). Think before you share: Building a civic media literacy framework for everyday contexts. *Information and Learning Sciences*, *123*(7–8), 421–444. https://doi.org/10.1108/ILS-03-2022-0030

Mirra, N., & Garcia, A. (2017). Civic participation reimagined: Youth interrogation and innovation in the multimodal public sphere. *Review of Research in Education*, *41*, 136–158. http://www.jstor.org/stable/44668690

Mirra, N., McGrew, S., Kahne, J., Garcia, A., & Tynes, B. (2022). Expanding digital citizenship education to address tough issues. *Phi Delta Kappan*, *103*(5), 31–35.

Mirra, N., Morrell, E. D., Cain, E., Scorza, D., & Ford, A. (2013). Educating for a critical democracy: Civic participation reimagined in the Council of Youth Research. *Democracy & Education*, *21*(1), 1–10.

Neag, A., Supa, M., & Mihailidis, P. (2024). Researching social media and activism with children and youth: A scoping review. *International Journal of Communication*, *18*, 2107–2128.

Price-Dennis, D. (2016). Developing curriculum to support Black girls' literacies in digital spaces. *English Education*, *48*(4), 337–361.

Price-Dennis, D., & Carrion, S. (2017). Language arts lessons: Leveraging digital literacies for equity and social justice. *Language Arts*, *94*(3), 190–195. https://doi.org/10.58680/la201728912

Price-Dennis, D., Holmes, K. A., & Smith, E. (2015). Exploring digital literacy practices in an inclusive classroom. *The Reading Teacher*, *69*(2), 195–205. https://doi.org/10.1002/trtr.1398

Price-Dennis, D., & Muhammad, G. E. (Eds.). (2021). *Black girls' literacies: Transforming lives and literacy practices*. Routledge.

Price-Dennis, D., Muhammad, G. E., Womack, E., McArthur, S. A., & Haddix, M. (2017). The multiple identities and literacies of Black girlhood: A conversation about creating spaces for Black girl voices. *Journal of Language and Literacy Education*, *13*(2), 1–18.

Shelton, S., & Macias, H. (2021). Intersectional LGBTQ+ identities: Being an ally through podcast instruction. *English Journal*, *110*(4), 115–117. https://doi.org/10.58680/ej202131146

Shrodes, A. (2022). "SAME GURL": Political feeling in LGBTQ+ digital composing. *Journal of Literacy Research*, *54*(4), 434–457. https://doi.org/10.1177/1086296X221140862

Stornaiuolo, A., & Thomas, E. E. (2017). Disrupting educational inequalities through youth digital activism. *Review of Research in Education*, *41*(1), 337–357. https://doi.org/10.3102/0091732X16687973

An Afrofuturistic Hope for Literacy: Using Arts-Based Teaching to Cultivate Black Boy Literacy Genius

JULIA LYNCH & BETH W. GAFFORD

Introduction

There is a national educational apartheid happening with our Black youth, specifically our Black boys, within our communities. National studies reveal the interconnectedness between the academic health of Black boys and childhood traumas, noting the impact of these adverse experiences on their educational outcomes (Crumb et al., 2023; Wint et al., 2022). This research underscores that exposure to chronic trauma significantly increases the risk of mental health disorders and poor academic achievement among children and adolescents, particularly those from minority racial/ethnic groups and low-income backgrounds. The prevalence of adverse childhood experiences (ACEs) is notably high among Black men, with nearly 90 percent reporting at least one ACE, showcasing the urgent need for interventions that consider the influence of early adversity on mental and physical health outcomes. More pointedly, research suggests that the academic health of Black boys living in rural communities can indicate their civic contributions, or the lack thereof, to society as economically productive citizens (Smith et al., 2022). Adjacently, research also indicates that even with early academic intervention, Black youth nationally still perform significantly below grade level compared to their white peers (Flowers, 2016; Morrison, 2010; Roberts et al., 2005). The research noted above draws our attention to the ways structural and environmental injustices influence the educational outcomes of Black youth, specifically our males.

However, there is a stark divide in our literature where the experiences, voices, and counternarratives of our Black youth are lacking. That is, we see in literature the ways the pendulum can swing, placing blame on the home environment, on teachers, and on students. However, as Black*Mother* scholars, we ask: What do our boys have to say about this? This research aims to respond to the existing, though deficit, research and offer a safe space of counterstorytelling. We hope to add to a growing body of literature on the culturally sustaining literacy practices that center Black youth's past/lived experiences within society and education that offer educators a way to understand how those experiences are interconnected and interact with each other. With many urgent needs to address the academic and mental health of Black boys, we as Black*Mother* scholars were interested in the ways Black boys are understanding and evaluating their academic experiences. To do so, we used multiple access points (art, pictures, emails, etc.) to provoke critical thought that helped them make sense of themselves, their worlds, and their futures. In other words, how are Black boys reading the world through text (literature, social media, art, and beyond) and making sense of who they are? Then, how do educational scholars reimagine their culturally responsive critical literacy practices to reflect the Afrofuturistic perspectives of Black boys?

Situating Critical Literacy in a Rural Context

This project took place in the southeastern part of the United States, in an "urban" school district. However, we challenge the language and definitions of *urban* and *rural* in this project and beyond. Historically, Black, Indigenous, and other communities of color were excluded from access to schooling and, through structural racism, suppressed from traditional reading and writing (Anderson, 1988). Black communities were eager to gain proper literacy skills coming out of enslavement so that they were considered contributing members of their society, actively participating as a citizen, and contributing to the economy (Givens, 2021; Love, 2019). Being exempt from formal schooling, Black people established their own learning communities. They were also able to create and sustain formal schools known as the Freedom and Rosenwald schools during Reconstruction and had significant legislative milestones like the landmark Brown v. Board decision in 1954 (Anderson, 2010; Nieto & Bode, 2018). As Black*Mother* scholars, we posit that schools formed in formerly colonized states still perpetuate colonialistic ideologies and are therefore a rural *rurality*. We contend that, despite the formal legislative measures enacted to desegregate educational institutions, the phenomenon of de facto segregation, along with inequitable access and persistent inequalities, continues to prevail as a result of variables such as residential segregation and socioeconomic disparities. This creates a need for our Black youth to engage in critical literacies that foster a deeper understanding of their sociopolitical climate, allowing them to reclaim and rediscover their civic identity and position themselves as contributing citizens.

Centering the Black Experience in Civics

Political and civic participation is a fundamental aspect of schooling, and early on, youth are taught about citizenship, government structures, and the principles of democracy in a number of ways. However, Black experiences and discourse concerning political and civic participation are unique to our experiences (Bauml et al., 2023). Historically, conventional curriculum and teaching, particularly in elementary and middle school, often overlook and exclude Black youth's past/lived experiences, the historical trauma of civics within the Black community, and the societal discourses on who is entitled to democracy (Kahne & Sporte, 2008; Malin, 2011). Understanding these social foundations of education could help educators create a more culturally responsive literacy instruction that better understands how Black boys are making sense of who they are in civic society and then choosing how to participate and engage with the world. Additionally, it is crucial for educators to understand how to build a culturally sustaining literacy practice that inspires and sustains civic engagement within our Black youth community.

Black Boys' Civic Education

The goal of civics education is to equip youth with the necessary knowledge and skills that will enable them to actively participate in civic affairs as engaged and responsible citizens. The civic literacy of Black boys is a vital component of their development, often shaped by the interconnectedness of their contextual and societal understandings, along with their interactions with schools and the community. Some research underscores this positive impact of civic engagement on Black male youth, highlighting the necessity for a deeper understanding of their involvement in community spaces and extracurricular activities (Bauml et al., 2023; Johnson & Thomas, 2022). Participation in civic education is regarded as a liberating tool for Black youth, enabling them to overcome intersecting marginalizations and to have a voice in decisions affecting their lives. Unfortunately, oftentimes, Black boys' civic participation in civic classrooms may exclude issues related to an analysis of complex issues such as race, class, and gender or cultural differences leading them to making assumptions about how they define citizenship (Kahne & Sporte, 2008; Santau & Ritter, 2013). By elevating the voices of young Black boys and integrating their perspectives into curricula and pedagogy, educators and policymakers can advance meaningful civic objectives. These objectives and teaching should cultivate a sense of agency, power, and purpose as Black youth navigate the complexities of their intersectionalities.

Black Literacy Circles

In Black communities, informal learning environments were always neutral spaces that served as opportunities for reading the world, making connections, and fact checking. When reading and writing were prohibited, Black communities still found very ingenious ways to communicate with each other, therefore creating a set of Afrofuturistic literacy skills that have equipped them with the ability to make sense of things, themselves, and the world using their own semiotic rules (Perfetti & Stafura, 2014; Son & Morrison, 2010). This key piece of literary information is very important in understanding how Black people may comprehend text, interpret others, and the decision-making process because they are significantly influenced by semantics (Roberts et al., 2005). When Black communities take up storytelling, it is an implicit multidimensional learning experience in which students are able to listen (even through eavesdropping), engage, respond, and fact check while multiple things may be going on around them. This is important when understanding the ways Black boys may read the world and their educational experiences and make sense of their identity based on those understandings. They do this in informal learning environments and through implicit learning.

Informal Learning. Informal learning environments play a crucial role in the acquisition of vocabulary knowledge and reading skills outside traditional classroom settings (Collentine, 2004; Reese et al., 2008). Since the inception of studies focusing on basic reading skills, scholars have recognized a significant correlation between reading proficiency and vocabulary comprehension (Perfetti & Stafura, 2014). Nevertheless, the exact characteristics of this correlation, the processes through which vocabulary acquisition occurs, and the factors conducive to enhancing such acquisition remain largely ambiguous. Therefore, we used our understanding of the ways Black people congregate, take up reading, and engage in conversations within informal settings to create a safe literacy environment where students were able to enter and exit conversations informally. These environments provide opportunities for individuals to learn through everyday experiences, interactions with others, and self-directed exploration. Unlike formal settings, informal learning environments are often unstructured and spontaneous, allowing learners to pursue their interests and passions freely. This type of learning can take place in various settings such as museums, libraries, community centers, and even online platforms. In informal learning environments, individuals have the flexibility to learn at their own pace, focus on topics of personal interest, and engage in hands-on activities that promote active learning.

Implicit Learning. In a formal or informal setting, implicit learning can occur as learners acquire new knowledge through exposure to language in context, such as reading or listening to activities (Nezhad et al., 2015). In these ways, we as researchers were able to use art to investigate the relationship between children's text comprehension, their ability to acquire new word meanings, and the factors that influence vocabulary acquisition from visual contexts. Vocabulary is absorbed naturally through repeated exposure and usage in various contexts. Learners may infer word meanings through context clues, without direct instruction on definitions. This understanding of implicit learning within an informal learning environment helped us further understand the ways Black youth may be introduced to new knowledge, develop their understandings, and go back and forth with the new knowledge to fact check it. This implicit learning highlights how Black boys may develop vocabulary and language subconsciously through immersion in the language and dialogue.

Context and Purpose

With the state of Black education, the academic and mental health of Black boys, and the predicated outcomes within society, we as Black-*Mother* scholars framed this research to center the cultural literacies of Black boys located within a rural community. We used our understandings and experiences of Black literacy circles to help inform the ways we created an art-informed culturally sustaining literacy practice. Our understanding of culturally sustaining literary practices comes from within the diaspora of culturally responsive teaching and perspectives of Geneva Gay, Gloria Ladson-Billings, Gholdy Muhammad, Sammy Alim, and Django Paris. Additionally, we see this work intersecting with our abolitionist scholars like Farima Pour-Khorshid, Erica Mieners, Bettina Love, and others who have challenged educators to name and interrupt carceral logic by critically analyzing and changing the practices and policies that govern schooling in ways that mirror policing and prisons and by mobilizing alongside youth to struggle for the liberatory education we all deserve (Love et al., 2021).

Each of the authors is involved with a nonprofit organization located in a rural community within the southeastern part of the United States. The I Help U Collective (TIHUC) embodies a culturally responsive approach to fostering youth and family development, offering a holistic and integrated system of support aimed at addressing educational inequities. Through collaborative efforts, TIHUC curates opportunities that bolster social-emotional learning through art and sports, encourage civic engagement, foster leadership skills, create innovative teaching to propel academic mobility, and promote life sustainability, ensuring every individual has the resources and guidance needed to thrive. This organization serves as a hub to identify educational and opportunity gaps and to connect families to communities and schools in order to build a thread of support, access, and academic success for students.

In collaboration with this organization,we were able to build this project with some of the Black youth who attend their leadership academy after a few parents met with the director to get assistance on how to navigate their upcoming parent meetings. We, as frequent volunteers of the nonprofit, started speaking with the boys regarding their thoughts about their schooling experiences. Below, we describe in more detail the culturally sustaining literacy practice and the findings.

Culturally Sustaining Art-Informed Teaching to Evoke Critical Consciousness, Agency, and Activism

As Black*Mother* Scholars working with communities of color, we intentionally drew upon Black*Mothering* Scholarship (BMS) as a theoretical framework (Lynch and Atkinson, 2023), which helps frame the beliefs, practices, attitudes, knowledge, and behaviors of mothering that Blacks take up in rurality spaces as a way of cultural preservation and sustainability. In duet with BMS, the Black*Mother* scholars engaged with a quilting methodology as a form of arts-based research (Tian, 2023). Using pictures, music, media, text messages, and emails, students critically read and explored their identities in an identity-affirming environment that recognized students as knowledge producers.

With seemingly multi-urgent needs to address the reading gap in Black boys, we as Black*Mother* scholars were interested in the ways Black boys are accessing literacy through multiple access points and making sense of themselves, their worlds, and their futures, as well as how we can reimagine literacy instruction. In other words, how are Black boys reading the world through text (literature and beyond), and making sense of who they are? Then, how do educational scholars reimagine the teaching and evaluation of reading from an Afrofuturistic perspective using the genius of Black boy literacy?

To this end, we completed an arts-based participatory action project to demonstrate the ways Black boys take up literacy to (re)discover their agency, power, and well-being. As a way to engage with our Black boys, the researchers used an art-informed culturally sustaining literacy approach that 1) created a safe literacy environment that affirmed the lived experiences of the Black youth; 2) acknowledged students' literacy and language assets; and 3) made connections to their academic success and the world using transmedial text (pictures, text messages, emails, etc.) to cultivate their civic literacy skills. The practice of including art-informed teaching methods was imperative to create a critical literacy practice that drew upon the cultural backgrounds of the Black boys and illuminated the sociopolitical systemic barriers they faced. More importantly, this practice aimed to dismantle the pervasive stereotypes and prejudices that hindered their educational progress, promoting self-empowerment, identity development, and academic achievement. By addressing the unique challenges faced by Black boys, such as cultural dissonance, racial bias, and limited representation in curricula, these practices contribute to fostering a more inclusive and equitable educational environment. This art-inquiry teaching framework includes:

1. **Asset-Based Approach:** A proven set of culturally responsive strategies designed to develop deep literacy understandings through art that will work with any curriculum.
2. **Reflective Inquiring:** An inquiry-based learning approach that helps students

master larger literacy concepts through problem solving, dialogue, and critical thinking, providing them with the tools they need to succeed using art.

3. **Transmediation:** Translanguaging through art involves utilizing linguistic and semiotic resources in a dynamic and integrated manner to create a space for knowledge construction and meaning making.

There was one distinct finding from using this teaching approach: Black boys, from an early introduction to schooling and society, learn to read the world to know their place. Other themes that were illuminated with these two participants were that 1) Black boys were disassociating their identity from this idea of being "smart," and 2) Black boys pivot societal stereotypes to access Black boy joy. Overall, this work sheds light on the importance of creating a culturally sustaining literacy practice to center the experiences of Black youth in order to fully understand how educators should design civic education that is connected to the mental, social, and academic well-being of Black youth.

Mapping the Black Boy Literacy Identity

Cash's Story

Cash is a seventh grader who attends an inner-city Title I school located in the southeastern part of the United States that serves about 618 students; 65 percent of the students are considered economically disadvantaged; 23 percent of Black students are reading at proficient levels; and 80 percent of the teachers are on nonprovisional/emergency licenses. Cash recently had to be moved off of his original seventh-grade team and placed on a different team after several meetings between his parents and teachers and his parents and the administration. Cash, who does not receive any services (IEP, 504, AIG, etc.), was receiving zeros for not completing assignments, was testing poorly on assessments, and was failing to thrive on his current team due to ineffective community building and a lack of culturally responsive teaching practices. His mom requested a meeting with the principal, who went over Cash's reading and math scores from the previous year and said he did not need to move off the team and into the advanced math class because he might struggle, and those kids in that class were just "different." In other words, a) no Black kids were currently on that team, and Cash would stand out, and b) the state allowed homogenous grouping in that way based on state scores. The parents pushed against this idea of exclusion and requested Cash be moved to the other team. Over the course of a few days once Cash was moved, Author 1 tracked his progress and would check in on him when Cash visited the afterschool leadership program. Cash described his first few days of being on the new team by saying, "I think my math teacher goes to church," because she referred to him as Brother Cash. She would say, "Sister Kay [a white female student], make sure Brother Cash is on the screen on his Chromebook." On other days within the first few weeks, he quickly dissociated from his Black boy identity with intellectualism by saying, "All my friends are on the other team. I'm on the team with all the smart white kids, the kids that don't speak English, and the kids that bring their laptops to school." Cash spoke about this dissociation in other ways when asked about how other students interact with him on his new team. "Um . . . well, I noticed in our math groups, they wait for me to answer the questions and then say things like, 'Dang, how did you do that?' and I show them. The other day they showed me how they sneak into other screens on their Chromebooks because they took coding and knew how to erase or hide their computer history, it was crazy!"

To cultivate Cash's literacy genius, we employed the art inquiry teaching method, which required Cash to use pictures from his own life to help him self-actualize his identity, agency, and genius. Using art as inquiry in this context was a way to awaken Cash's critical consciousness, activate reflexivity through the critical-thinking dialogue, and provoke transformative learning and liberation. In a co-constructive process, we:

1. **Collected multimodal text.** We went through his email and phone to collect only pictures, text messages, and images of things that he felt represented or helped him draw conclusions about his Black boy identity.
2. **Incorporated reflexive inquiring.** Cash and Author 1 analyzed each picture by participating in a complex dialogic conversation in which Author 1 modeled inquiry-based critical thinking questions using prompts such as: "In what ways does this picture speak to your classroom?" or "Talk to me about what is happening in this picture" or "How does this picture represent who you are?" During this process, Cash had several moments when he paused during discussions to self-affirm his identity, make connections to his school experiences and inequities, and pivot the story to center the freedom and joy he felt in describing his pictures.
3. **Practiced transmediation.** Cash used his conversations and dialogue to patch together an interwoven story of Black boy identity. This quilting story (see Figure 1) was now an emancipatory gesture that allowed Cash to actualize and substantiate his Black boy agency, identity, and genius.

The authors were able to work with Cash and the other students once a week during the spring semester from January to April. Each week, the authors would spend about 15 minutes with the participants, discussing goals for the week, mastery of last week's goals, and overall check-in/check-out conversations.

Figure 1. Cash's quilting story.

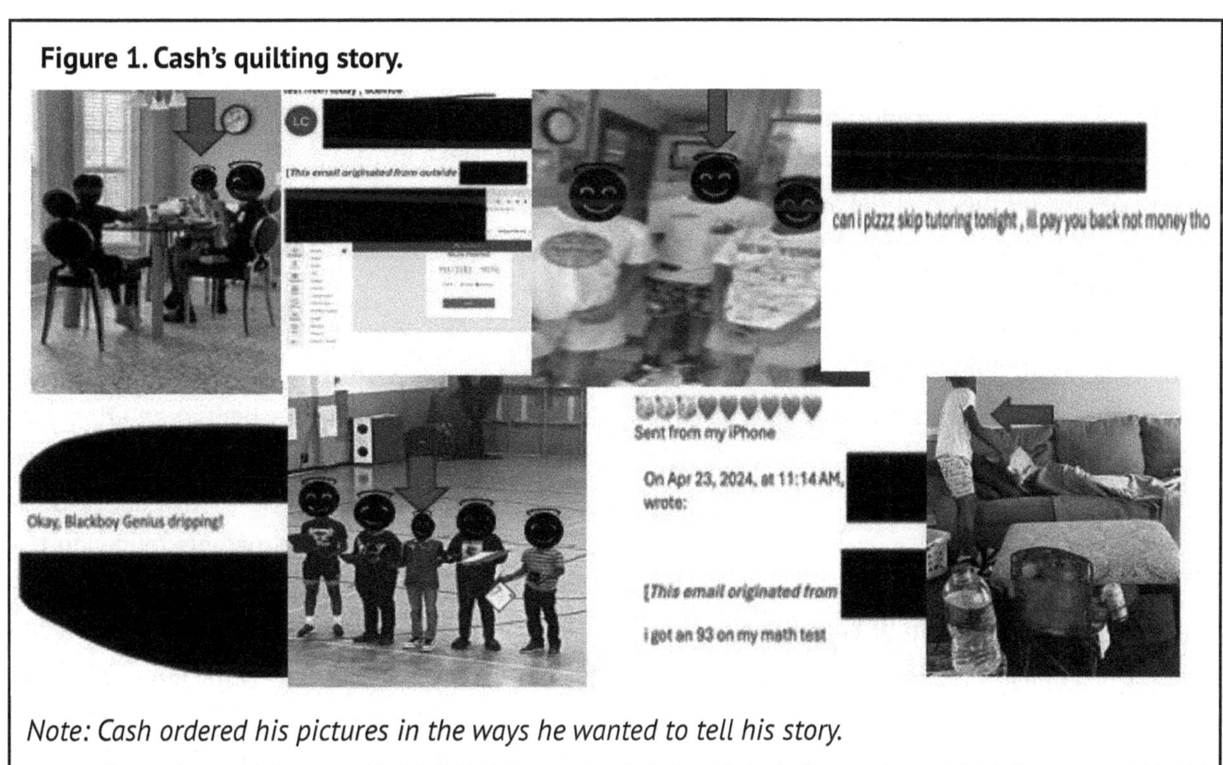

Note: Cash ordered his pictures in the ways he wanted to tell his story.

Living in the Dichotomy of Black Boy Genius and Intellectualism

The historical challenges encountered globally by Black individuals encompass issues such as enslavement, colonialism, racism, bias, and discrimination. The current challenges experienced by Black people in the United States, specifically Black males, including incidents of police harassment, violence, shootings, and fatalities, have contributed to the emergence of the "This class is for the White kids, they all bring their own laptops and keyboards to school" mindset. As Black boys enter our educational systems, they grapple with the tensions of who they are and what comprises their intellectualism. This dichotomy of Black Boy genius and whether genius can coexist with their Black boy identity involves an intricate interaction of societal elements that impact Black boys' educational and personal growth. Tony Sewell's research revealed a similar finding. Sewell's research sheds light on the need to address the intersecting influences of stereotypes, biases, and systemic barriers that shape Black boys' experiences in schools (Sewell, 1997). By comparison, Lewis and Diamond's work analyzes how even well-intentioned educational structures and practices can perpetuate racial inequalities, often undermining the potential and brilliance of Black students. Their research highlights the ways in which institutional policies, norms, and biases within schools contribute to unequal educational outcomes (2015). Both of these are important findings in understanding how Black boys take up their agency in schools, their perceptions of their schooling experiences, and how they are making meaning of their genius.

Reading the World to Know Your Place

Societal discursive practices on the belonging, affirming, protecting, and agency of Black individuals, and more specifically, Black males, have emphasized their place in society as nonhuman, disposable, and depleted. When white teachers engage with our Black boys, we notice two things they experience. Teachers either over-discipline and over-police their Black bodies or they avoid any type of correction that may cause a disruption or that may cause the teacher to look like a racist. We noticed this as we listened to the boys talk about the interactions they have with their teachers and noted a few comments below.

> *"She scared of us"*
> [Referring to not being able to hear] *"Every time I ask to be moved she just say, 'sit down, Cash!' She don't ever tell them kids to shut up. She just keep writing."*

Taking into account the historical lineage of societal dehumanization of Black males—from enslavement to post-colonial times—where they have faced lynching, police killings, and the school-to-prison pipeline, it becomes clear that systemic change is essential to address these injustices and promote equity. These historical and contemporary societal structures and traumas are implicitly passed down to our youth, causing Black boys to understand their place to be nonexistent in society, which overlaps with their place in the classrooms.

PJ's Story

PJ Jackson is a sixth grader who attends a predominately white private school in an urban district outside of his home district. He has attended his current school since the third grade, a decision that was made by his parents following the COVID-19 pandemic. PJ is one of two Black students in his entire grade; both students identify as Black males. However, he is the only one native to the United States. Prior to attending his current school, he attended a public school in his rural hometown district where he had an IEP under the IDEA disability category of autism. Despite academic assessment scores showing a positive gap in the two subjects, PJ's services always included direct support in reading and math. PJ's parents had several meetings with the IEP team to discuss placement in advanced coursework; however, he was consistently denied advanced coursework because of his disability. This was a stereotype that was hard to overcome, and even more so being a Black boy.

PJ's current school required admission testing prior to full acceptance. Following testing, PJ was placed on the regular academic track. However, following the start of his fifth-grade year, he was placed into an advanced math track and has continued in that curriculum. It was then that he started to talk about how he self-identifies in the classroom.

Similar to Cash, we were interested in the ways PJ could construct a counternarrative that evoked his literacy genius, which responded to his academic experiences. Using the art inquiry teaching approach required PJ to critically analyze the pictures, text messages, or emails from his own life to help him self-actualize his identity and agency. Again, in a co-constructive process, we

1. **Collected multimodal text.** We went through his email and phone to collect only pictures, text messages, and images of things that he felt represented or helped him draw conclusions about his Black boy identity. PJ also wanted to use comments from his report card.
2. **Incorporated reflexive inquiring.** PJ worked with us to analyze each picture by participating in a complex dialogic conversation in which we modeled inquiry-based critical thinking questions, using prompts such as: "In what ways does this picture speak to your classroom experiences?" or "Talk to me about what is happening in this picture?" or "In this picture you are . . . ? How does this picture represent who you are?"
3. **Practiced transmediation.** PJ used his conversations and dialogue to patch together an interwoven story of his own Black boy identity. This quilting story (see Figure 2) was now an emancipatory gesture that allowed PJ to actualize and substantiate his Black boy agency, identity, and genius.

Figure 2. PJ's quilting story.

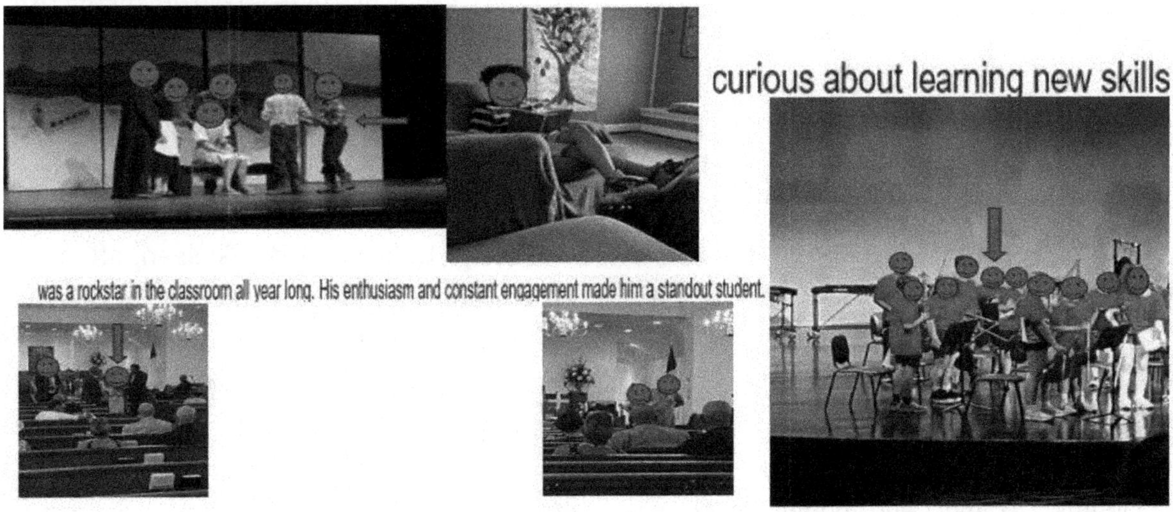

In the classroom, Black boys often face challenges when it comes to self-identification. Many of them struggle with stereotypes and biases that can impact their self-esteem and academic performance. These stereotypes can lead to feelings of inadequacy and a lack of belonging in the classroom.

In recent years, there has been a growing recognition of the importance of promoting positive self-identification among Black boys in the classroom. Although schools, educators, and policymakers are increasingly focused on creating culturally responsive and inclusive learning environments that affirm the cultural identities and experiences of all students, including Black boys (Kearl et al., 2023), these efforts should include critical literacy instruction that allows teachers to center the voices of their multiple-minoritized students.

"I'm always the only Black kid in my classes. I just go to school anyway." A continued feeling of isolation haunts the minds of Black boys and often hinders their ability to let their Black boy genius shine through. Instead of seeing themselves in a thriving space, they have to create their own safe space and ultimately stamp their place in the classroom. In these classrooms, they often see peers excelling and being recognized for achievements that they themselves either have no connection to or have already mastered that skill but lacked the recognition for it. So, where does that lead our Black boys? It leads to a numb feeling regarding the classroom and a self-made world where they self-recognize their own accomplishments or struggle with understanding their Black intellectualism.

Pivoting Societal Stereotypes to Access Black Boy Joy

Black boy genius further collaborates the idea that intellect, talent, and potential are not limited by race or gender. Black boys are not monolithic; they are creators, thinkers, innovators, and visionaries with unique perspectives and contributions to offer the world. By recognizing and celebrating the genius within every Black boy, we can cultivate a classroom that fosters the strengths of Black boys.

> *"Sometimes when I write my papers, I try to include stuff my mom talk about at home and what we learn about in church."*

To access Black boy joy and nurture the Black boy genius, we must first acknowledge and confront the stereotypes and biases that have historically marginalized Black boys. Education plays a crucial role in this process, as it provides a platform for young Black males to develop their talents, explore their interests, and realize their full potential. By creating culturally responsive literacy environments that prioritize the holistic well-being of Black boys, we can help them thrive academically, socially, and emotionally.

In addition to education, representation is key to dismantling stereotypes and expanding opportunities for Black boys. When Black boys see positive and multidimensional portrayals of themselves in media, literature, and popular culture, they are more likely to internalize positive self-perceptions and to envision a future filled with possibility. They don't feel forced to include parts of themselves in their work just to show their identity; their identity is seen all around them, and they are not solo authors. By highlighting the stories and achievements of Black boy geniuses, we can inspire the next generation of Black leaders, innovators, and changemakers. Black joy is after all, cultural (Lewis-Giggetts, 2022).

Implications for Building a Critical Literacy Practice

Key components of a critical literacy practice include the ability to analyze texts for social and political biases, engage in reflective dialogue, and connect reading to real-life contexts. Teachers can effectively integrate these components into their teaching practices through arts-based culturally sustaining literacy models, relationship building, and through creating a safe literacy environment (see Table 1). For instance, an arts-based culturally sustaining literacy practice has been shown to help students with analyzing power structures, questioning perspectives, and promoting social awareness. Additionally, relationship building can enrich school literacy programs by fostering a sense of care and concern with students and their families. This engagement is critical to the overall success of the students. Lastly, a super-safe literacy environment that combines a variety of structured and informal reading opportunities can neutralize testing dynamics that may threaten students' literacy skills.

Imagining Healthy Futurities

By acknowledging the historical, social, and political contexts, structural oppression, key figures, and impact, teachers and policymakers can strive toward fostering healthy academic and mental health outcomes for Black boys. The Center on the Developing Child at Harvard sheds light on our understanding of how these interconnected experiences affect our genes. In our novice understanding of epigenetics, this scientific research discovered that early experiences, particularly in development, may rearrange our epigenetic markers and positively or negatively impact our experiences (National Scientific Council on the Developing Child, 2010). It is crucial we address the specific needs of our marginalized communities in a culturally responsive way so that these signature epigenetic traits can be turned off or reversed to restore healthy brain function and reduce stress. As we noted earlier regarding the current research on the mental health and academic statuses of our Black males and combined with our findings that Black boys may also be suffering a Black intellectual death, we reiterate that we must become more critical in the ways we engage with our Black youth to center their experiences and work through their identities so that they themselves discover their identity and freedoms.

Relationship Building Is Trustworthy

Teachers can work to build trust and rapport with Black boys by incorporating culturally relevant texts, images, and material into their instruction and by using inclusive and affirming language. Additionally, providing flexible and student-centered learning environments that allow for autonomy and agency can help to foster a sense of ownership and motivation toward literacy. By adopting these strategies, educators can help to promote a love of reading and learning in Black boys and can ultimately support their academic success and personal growth.

By recognizing and celebrating the brilliance, creativity, and resilience of Black boys, we can create a more just, equitable, and prosperous society for all. The concept of the Black boy genius serves as a powerful reminder that diversity is a source of strength and that every individual has the potential to make a meaningful and lasting impact on the world. By embracing Black boy joy, we can unlock the limitless possibilities that exist within every Black boy and pave the way for brighter and more inclusive classrooms.

Table 1. Key components and guiding questions.

Suggested Practice	Implementation	Guiding Questions for Implementation
Building Relationships	Conversations that are student-led; it's okay for the teacher to be silent and let the student talk. (Students who do not feel connected to teachers will distance themselves more when teachers chime in with their "input" more than they listen.) Daily check-ins. (Remain in a conversational tone for deeper meaning and context.)	How often do I talk with my students? In what ways am I updated on community events? How have I built a classroom community with my students? How do I neutralize the power dynamics among teacher-student-family?
Culturally Sustaining Literacy	Multimodal representation within the product (ex: verbal song, written dialogue). Culturally Sustaining Literacy Practices (CSLP): Literacy Instruction that includes "L" and "l" literacy instruction. In this context, literacy goes beyond technical competencies to encompass a wide range of tools where students "read" art to analyze and question power dynamics inherent in all written works and embedded in society. Know and acknowledge your own implicit biases as a teacher. (You need to be uncomfortable with your intentions to overcome stereotypes.)	What cultural and linguistic strengths do my students and families have? How do my students acquire language and vocabulary? In what ways are students learning to read using nonconventional modalities (i.e. art)? How can I use visual art, poetry, or music to teach technical reading skills?
Safe Literacy Environment	Project-Based Learning This allows students to incorporate more than just cognitive abilities. Black youth have a rich social background that is rooted in their personal community (within the home or outside the home); project-based learning allows other aspects of development to be included. Reading spaces within the classroom environment. (Include current events, and displays directly from the students' communities.)	Have I established a safe literacy environment? Where: 1. Home culture and language is not threatened 2. Reading success is not threatened 3. Informal learning and implicit language and learning are welcomed. How have I created opportunities for learning using interdisciplinary skills and projects?

Works Cited

Anderson, J. D. (1988). *The education of blacks in the South, 1860–1935.* University of North Carolina Press.

Bauml, M., Quinn, B. P., Blevins, B., Magill, K. R., & LeCompte, K. (2023). "I really want to do something": How civic education activities promote thinking toward civic purpose among early adolescents. *Journal of Adolescent Research, 38*(1), 110–142. https://doi.org/10.1177/07435584211006785

Collentine, J. (2004). The effects of learning contexts on morphosyntactic and lexical development. *Studies in Second-Language Acquisition, 26*(2), 227–248. http://www.jstor.org/stable/44486770

Crumb, L., Matthews, J.C., Mingo, T. M., & Lynch, J. (2023). Introduction to special issue: Transformative trauma-informed practices in rural schools. *Theory & Practice in Rural Education, 13*(2).

Flowers, T. A. (2016) African American early literacy development: An integrative review of the research. *Journal of Research Initiatives, 2*(2), 1–10.

Gay, G. (2010). *Culturally responsive teaching: Theory, research, and practice.* Teachers College Press.

Givens, J. R. (2021). *Fugitive pedagogy: Carter G. Woodson and the art of Black teaching.* Harvard University Press.

Johnson, M., & Thomas, D. (2022). "For a good [civic] purpose?": Black immortal teachings of citizenship. *Education, Citizenship and Social Justice, 19*(2), 236–252. https://doi.org/10.1177/17461979221137895

Kahne J., & Sporte, S. E. (2008). Developing citizens: The impact of civic learning opportunities on students' commitment to civic participation. *American Educational Research Journal, 45*(3), 738–766. https://doi.org/10.3102/0002831208316951

Ladson-Billings, G. (1995). Toward a theory of culturally relevant pedagogy. *American Educational Research Journal, 32*(3), 465–491.

Ladson-Billings, G. (1998). Just what is critical race theory and what's it doing in a *nice* field like education? *International Journal of Qualitative Studies in Education, 11*(1), 7–24.

Larson, S., Chapman, S., Spetz, J., & Brindis, C. D. (2017). Chronic childhood trauma, mental health, academic achievement, and school-based health center mental health services. *Journal of School Health, 87*(9), 675–686. https://doi.org/10.1111/josh.12541

Lewis, A. E., & Diamond, J. B. (2015). *Despite the best intentions: How racial inequality thrives in good schools.* Oxford University Press.

Love, B. L. (2019). *We want to do more than survive: Abolitionist teaching and the pursuit of educational freedom.* Beacon Press.

Lynch, J., & Atkinson, M. (2023). Ataraxia and placemaking: Black *Mothering* in the academy. *Janus Unbound: Journal of Critical Studies, 3*(1), 20–27.

Malin, H. (2011). American identity development and citizenship education: A summary of perspectives and call for new research. *Applied Developmental Science, 15*(2), 111–116.

National Scientific Council on the Developing Child (2010). Early experiences can alter gene expression and affect long-term development: Working Paper No. 10. http://www.developingchild.net

Nezhad, A. N., Moghali, M., & Soori, A. (2015). Explicit and implicit learning in vocabulary acquisition. *Asian Journal of Education and e-Learning, 3*(1), 18–25.

Nieto, S., & Bode, P. (2018). *Affirming diversity: The sociopolitical context of multicultural education.* Pearson.

Perfetti, C., & Stafura, J. (2014). Word knowledge

in a theory of reading comprehension. *Scientific studies of Reading, 18*(1), 22–37.

Reese, E., Sparks, A., Kalia, V., Long, J., Suggate, S., & Shaughency, E. (2008). Oral narrative skills and reading ability: Implications for assessment. *Proceedings of the Nineteenth Congress of the International Association for the Study of Child Language,* Edinburgh, 28 July–1 August 2008.

Roberts, J., Jurgens, J., & Burchinal, M. (2005). The role of home literacy practices in preschool children's language and emergent literacy skills. *Journal of speech, language, and hearing research : JSLHR, 48*(2), 345–359. https://doi.org/10.1044/1092-4388(2005/024)

Santau, A. O., & Ritter, J. K. (2013). What to teach and how to teach it: Elementary teachers' views on teaching inquiry-based, interdisciplinary science and social studies in urban settings. *The New Educator, 9*(4), 255–286.

Sewell, T. (1997). *Black masculinities and schooling: How Black boys survive modern schooling.* Trentham Books.

Smith, C., Frerichs, L., Hoover, S., Robinson-Ezekwe, N., Khanna, A., Wynn, M., Ellerby, B., Joyner, L., Lindau, S. T., & Corbie, G. (2022). "If you're in a community together, then you're basically a family": Perceptions of community among a predominantly African-American/Black youth cohort in a semi-rural region in the southeastern United States. *Journal of Community Psychology, 51*(3), 880 905.

Tian, M. (2023). *Arts-based research methods for educational researchers.* Taylor & Francis.

Wint, K. M., Opara, I., Gordon, R., & Brooms, D. R. (2022). Countering Educational Disparities Among Black Boys and Black Adolescent Boys from Pre-K to High School: A Life Course-Intersectional Perspective. *The Urban review, 54*(2), 183–206. https://doi.org/10.1007/s11256-021-00616-z

Expanding Civics beyond Citizenship: Refugee Youths' Multimodal Counterstories

MEGAN HEISE & MEG BOOTH

Introduction

Civics is widely defined in relation to citizenship, but we take a broader view of civic education that includes non-citizens, such as refugees, with a focus on secondary-school-aged youth in out-of-school contexts. With forced migration at an all-time high—35.3 million refugees worldwide, nearly half of whom are children under the age of eighteen (UNHCR, 2024)—it's clear that citizens of a particular country are not the only members of the global community who desire to build a better world. For example, Kid Central Tennessee (2018) defines civic education as something that "empowers us to be well-informed, active citizens, and gives us the opportunity to change the world around us." If we replace the word "citizens" with "community members" to more inclusively reflect the makeup of our transnational communities, it becomes clear that *all* community members, regardless of citizenship status, have a stake in being well-informed, active changemakers. Indeed, as Guo-Brennan and Guo-Brennan (2018) assert, "As newcomers, immigrants and refugees contribute to social and cultural diversity, and play an important role in communities' social and economic development" (p. 31). When it comes to civic education, then, we argue that it is important to expand our view of what "civic" means into a realm that is inclusive of *all* community members.

While resettled refugees are important members of their new communities, "their talent, energy, and entrepreneurial spirit and skills can only be fully harnessed when the communities are welcoming and inclusive" (Guo-Brennan & Guo-Brennan, 2018, p. 31). The requisite commitment to inclusion of refugees has failed in many communities on both a macro and micro level. For example, the past decade alone has seen harmful, anti-refugee events like Brexit, the EU-Turkey Deal, and the US "Muslim Ban." These macro-level policies both inform and are anchored in micro-level anti-refugee rhetorics and attitudes, with both Guo-Brennan and Guo-Brennan (2018) and Hello Neighbor (2022), a Pittsburgh-based organization that works alongside resettled refugees, finding that refugee participants experienced discrimination and did not feel welcomed in their new local contexts.

These experiences of discrimination are often compounded when the focus is shifted to newcomer youth. Only 34 percent of eligible refugee youth are enrolled in secondary schools, and these youth are half as likely to complete lower-secondary school as their non-refugee peers (USA for UNHCR, 2023). These challenges relate directly to anti-refugee policies and sentiments, with Mendenhall et al. (2017) reporting that 70 percent of refugee-background students encountered "discrimination and xenophobia as a barrier to education" (p. 13). Resettled refugee students are also on the frontlines of language education, which often emphasizes writing in English over other languages and modalities of communication. Indeed, as Lazar et al. (2022) lament, "literacy pedagogy in many schools is not centered on students' experiences, knowledge, traditions, or heritage" (p. 2). In fact, in school settings, the measure of success for newcomers is often integration to dominant US white, middle-class standards, creating a deficit paradigm around students' existing cultural and linguistic knowledge. This dynamic puts immense pressure on both educators and students, especially those at risk of aging out of the secondary school system before graduating.

Within this context, we see out-of-school programs that work alongside resettled refugee youth as crucial supports to center the perspectives of newcomer youth and expand access to and engagement with civic futures. As Outley and Skuza (2019) explained, there needs to be "space for youth to negotiate, resist, and respond to their sociopolitical marginalization by using their voices, telling their stories, and writing about their experiences" (p. 1). Throughout the rest of this essay, we detail our work with the Alliance for Refugee Youth Support and Education (ARYSE) working with newcomer youth on multimodal (simultaneously engaging more than one of the five modes: linguistic, visual, aural, gestural, and spatial) projects, including a collaboratively authored book and individually crafted zines. We argue that out-of-school contexts like ours have unique opportunities to democratize knowledge production, leading to more robust civics education for *all* students when resettled refugee youth voices are heard, and to blurring the barrier around citizenship as a requisite for civic engagement. We see these multimodal projects not necessarily as solutions but as *tools* for collaboratively building solutions *with* and *led by* newcomer students. By centering refugee youth voices and taking a vested interest in the stories they want to tell, we can create sites of change where students can build new civic futures.

Framework: Counterstories

In this essay, we use the framework of counterstory (Martinez, 2020) to actively disrupt what MacDonald (2018) called the "discriminatory, binary constructions" of refugees, such as victim or villain, that limit their civic engagement through vastly unequal power dynamics. This means that even those who are seemingly "pro-" refugees can fall into neoliberal paradigms in which refugees are infantilized as pure victims, creating a dynamic that positions the learner "as a problem and the sponsor as a solution" (MacDonald, 2018, p. 39). Counterstories resist these assumptions and provide perspective on how we can expand civic education and engagement to be relevant to refugee youth.

Counterstories are a framework that, according to Martinez (2020), allow "minoritized people to intervene in research methods that would form 'master narratives' based on ignorance and assumptions about minoritized people" (p. 21). These counterstories are all the more urgent given McDonald's (2013) observation that "despite the implications refugee experience might have for understanding literacy in global contexts, the perspectives of refugees have been given only cursory attention" (p. 95). For educators who seek to veer away from deficit discourses, we need to support refugee youth in telling their own stories on their own terms. Reinforcing youth agency is crucial in any storytelling endeavor; while Montero and Al Zouhouri (2022) asserted that "refugee children and youth are empowered when they become the authors and arbiters of their stories, when they control what they want to share, how to share, and to whom to share their stories" (p. 89), the power dynamics and deficit views above stand to get in the way of this authentic expression of creativity and criticality. Multimodal counterstories are one way of centering youths' agency in order to build more active and just civic futures.

Context

The projects that we discuss within this essay were created within youth programs at ARYSE, an equity- and student-centered organization that supports forcibly displaced youth living in Allegheny County, Pennsylvania, through advocacy and educational, art, and leadership programs that affirm and celebrate youths' identities, goals, and visions for their futures. ARYSE works with middle and high school youth within out-of-school-time spaces and began in 2013 from the volunteer efforts of undergraduate students at the University of Pittsburgh. As the organization evolved, particularly after the 2016 US elections that brought anti-immigrant rhetoric to an unprecedented public scale, ARYSE began orienting itself toward showing stronger and more consistent solidarity with immigrant and refugee youth, developing more programs, and learning how to play a more active role in dismantling structural barriers that forcibly displaced communities face. Currently, ARYSE has four different summer and year-round programs. Students that participate represent over fifteen different countries of origin, speak over thirty different languages, and attend nine different school districts in twenty-one distinct schools. Both of us have worked with ARYSE in different capacities (Megan as a long-time academic partner and Meg as a program manager). The Zine and Book Projects came out of two ARYSE programs: PRYSE Academy and the Afghan Youth Program.

PRYSE Academy is the oldest and largest program at ARYSE. It is a five-week summer program that enrolls approximately 100 students from grades 6–12 annually. The focus of PRYSE Academy includes developing English language skills, building community, and generating creative expression through art workshops. Students engage in English language-learning activities facilitated by counselors in the morning and arts-based workshops facilitated by local teaching artists in the afternoon. In the summer of 2022, Megan led a creative workshop on zine-making with twenty-five students as part of an IRB-approved study (IRB 22-073-EXT). Zines are small, handmade booklets with art and writing in them that come from a lineage of rich counter-cultural practice, including political pamphlets, riot grrrl media, and more. The 2022 zine workshop met for ninety minutes a day, four days a week, for all five weeks of PRYSE Academy. Of the twenty-five students enrolled, sixteen completed individual zines and three participated in the formal study. After the success of the 2022 workshop, Megan led the zine workshop again in 2023 with a new group of about twenty-five students, all of whom finished zines. In both workshops, students were given creative prompts as well as free making time and later curated from these creations the content they wanted to put in their final zine.

The Afghan Youth Program was developed in 2021 through funding from the PA Department of Education's Refugee School Impact Grant in response to many youth from Afghanistan resettling in Pittsburgh. The goals of this program were to foster peer support and connect students to local resources during an incredibly challenging transitional time. Throughout the three-year life of this intentionally temporary program, Meg worked as the program coordinator alongside a total of sixty-five high school students, with an average of nineteen students attending each monthly meeting throughout the school year. The Book Project happened in the second year of the Afghan Youth Program (2022–2023), stemming from the interest and familiarity that students, many of whom had also attended PRYSE Academy, had in zine making. Due to the larger group context and the less frequent meeting schedule, we opted to make a book together. Students expressed a desire to engage more broadly with the Pittsburgh community and the communities they were connected to (families, friends, teachers). The initial prompt for the book was: What do you want others to know about you? What do you want them to know about Afghanistan? To get ideas flowing in the beginning, we had conversations with students about what culture is and the cultural diversities within the group. We also emphasized that there isn't one essentialized experience of being Afghan or part of any community and encouraged students to create whatever felt true for them.

Themes

In collaboratively analyzing students' creations in these two programs and in discussing students' work with them, we (the authors) found four interconnected themes that focus on the importance of 1) expanding civic perspectives, 2) crafting counterstories, 3) leveraging multimodal tools, and 4) fostering counterpublics. In particular, by expanding civic perspectives to include refugee youth, we out-of-school practitioners could center youths' agency and create spaces in which they could create their own counterstories against the victim/villain binary. Furthermore, by leveraging multimodal tools, the students with whom we worked could also prefigure a different and better future by fostering the growth of counterpublics.

Expanding Civic Perspectives

Refugee youth have transnational perspectives that are necessary for expanding our understanding of civic engagement. For these youth, the US context is often not the only nor the strongest frame of reference. Especially among the youth from Afghanistan, symbols and visuals they created in the zines and book showcased how they engage with civic identities in both America and Afghanistan. For example, one Afghan participant in Megan's zine workshop and study in 2022 drew the Afghan flag in her zine and wrote below it, "I love my flag / I am from Afghanistan" (see Figure 1). During Meg's book project, that same student (who wished not to be named) and two others, Jami and Hawa (all names selected by students to represent themselves throughout) collaborated on an image (see Figure 2) that would become the cover of the book, highlighting a mix of Afghan and American cultural references. Later in the book, Jami created a page with the Afghan and US flags (see Figure 3). When prompted about the page, she explained, "I told [a volunteer], you make flag American and I make flag Afghan." These creative decisions by students demonstrate their global citizenship and the ways in which they straddle—or indeed, mesh—multiple cultures and experiences into their civic perspectives.

Figure 1. One student's Afghan flag zine page.

Figure 2. Cover of the Afghan youth program book by Jami, Hawa, and another student.

Figure 3. Jami's flag page in the Afghan youth program book.

Crafting Counterstories

While we found that our students' identities across cultural and geographic contexts were central in many of their creations, their creative expression was not limited only to topics about the countries in which they have lived or with which they identified. Although we certainly agree that refugee youth are politicized subjects, we argue that practitioners should expressly *not* demand or expect that these students' work be deliberately political. For example, we need to acknowledge that students are allowed to like things just because of their aesthetic and remove the pressure that everything they make must be an overt political statement. In fact, we see an important aspect of their counterstories as pushing back against this presupposition and instead creating a space in which youth can represent themselves and their interests authentically.

Both the zine workshop and the book project were designed intentionally to be open ended, such that whatever students chose to create was seen as important. When Megan talked to two Afghan students in the 2022 zine workshop and study, they both explained that their creative decisions were based on their own personal preferences in ways that couldn't be parsed analytically. Rahil, for example, shared in Dari, "انیا زا هک دمآ مهنذ مرادن یصاخ لیلد مدوخ .مکن هدافتسا"—"There was no specific reason. I just wanted to use those pictures, and it was coming to my mind and I used them." The book project also yielded similar themes with students carefully composing aesthetic spreads around travel (see Figure 4) and fashion (see Figure 5), among other topics.

When Meg prompted these students for more information about the creation of their pages, Liza (Figure 4) responded, "I like all the pictures and this is it," echoing the aesthetic themes of Rahil's comments to Megan. For the spread in Figure 5, Emal told Meg, "I like Nike. These are summer clothes. These are winter clothes." These choices, based on internal aesthetics or preferences, are counterstories in the sense that they push back against the pressure for resettled refugee youth to be constantly political and politicized, as well as against the neoliberal savior complexes that can lead to extractive and transactive approaches to storytelling.

Providing space for youth to show up authentically and express what matters to them—or just what they like—can help them find more opportunities to connect within their new communities, leading to more robust civic futures for both them and their neighbors.

Figure 4. Liza's travel page from the Afghan youth program book.

Figure 5. Emal's Nike page in the Afghan youth program book.

Leveraging Multimodal Tools

There are very real pressures on newcomer youth to learn English and linguistically assimilate upon resettlement in the US. With few exceptions, access to citizenship is quite literally dependent on fluency in English speaking, reading, and writing (USCIS, 2023). In educational spaces, high school students are also expected to navigate academic forms of English. While the pressures and urgency to learn English may be accurate, MacDonald (2018) importantly identifies that "they also reflect the larger, unquestioning discourse that treats English as a language of opportunity" (p. 56). Instead, within out-of-school-time learning environments, we can and must get creative. In an effort to expand understandings of civic education and engagement, we must acknowledge the inadequacy of relying solely on English as a tool. Multimodal avenues for expression are important in order to include resettled refugees in civic dialogues equitably.

In the zine and book projects, students used multiple modes of expression: writing in several languages, completing sentence frames, drawing, and collaging (see Figure 6 for an example of many of these modalities). By approaching the zine and book projects multimodally, we were able to better center youths' authentic perspectives, both in the projects themselves *and* in striving together to prefigure (Spade, 2016) a new and better future reality for and with students. Listening to refugee youths' multimodal counterstories about their lives is an important first step in changing micro attitudes and macro-level policies that impact young refugee learners. Practitioners can fall into traps of making assumptions of what youths' stories are or will be, but we have found through these projects that youth always surprise us—and that's a wonderful thing! For example, many youth in the zine workshops featured a number of expensive status symbols in their collages, including an entire zine on cars (Figure 7), a travel-themed zine (Figure 8), and an "I Love" collage (Figure 9) with fancy watches and cars. These aspirational expressions certainly demonstrate youths' dreaming around their own futures, which are valid and important in and of themselves.

The affordances of multimodality further work to broaden the diversity of voices that communities, educators, and policy makers can access. Often when voices of refugees *are* considered by policy makers, it is the voices of those who are most linguistically and socially accessible—those who are more comfortable and confident communicating in English—that make us consider whose voices are being left out. Multimodal tools are especially rich for collaboratively prefiguring a different civic future in which English literacy is not necessarily so crucial to citizenship and educational pathways in the US or to whose voices are considered in policy decisions.

Figure 6. Rahil's "If I Could Change the World" fill-in-the-blank poem zine spread.

Figure 7. Emal's car zine cover.

Figure 8. Excerpt from Madina's travel zine.

Figure 9. One student's "I Love" collage zine spread.

Fostering Counterpublics

Multimodal tools like zines and books can facilitate and elevate refugee youth expression and perspectives, allowing opportunities to craft counterpublics. Fattal (2018) defined counterpublics as a particular kind of public that "stand in conscientious opposition to the dominant ideology and strategically subvert that ideology's construction in public discourse" (p. 1). In this sense, non-citizen refugee youth and those who are centering their voices can be considered a counterpublic against neoliberal assimilationist discourses.

One powerful example of youth prefiguratively crafting their own counterpublics is evident in one of Liza's pages from the Afghan youth program book (Figure 10). The spread itself demonstrates the attention to aesthetics described above but also to political realities of hijabi women in the US. When asked about this page, Liza explained, "This is for hijab girl, and I want people to know about hijab girl and Muslim girl." Liza is implying her audience here—both Muslim girls *and* people who need to know about Muslim girls. The counterpublics she is prefiguring here are ones of alliance between Muslims and non-Muslims, between hijabis and those who choose not to cover their heads, and between girls and those of other genders. This cross-sectional building of accompliceship is crucial to how we see refugee youth prefiguring more inclusive civic futures—for themselves and for others.

Figure 10. Liza's "Hijab Girl" page in the Afghan youth program book.

Moving Forward: Reimagining Civic Realities

Understanding citizenship through the US legal system provides a narrow view of how people develop affinities to a place and, in turn, an orientation toward civic engagement. Legal statuses can impact every aspect of participation in society: the ability to travel, work, vote, receive government services, etc. An expanded understanding of civic engagement must operate beyond these logics if we are to fully embrace refugee youth. In particular, while schools have many distinct pressures around assessment and standards, orientations such as cultural sustaining literacy pedagogy that seek to sustain the cultural and linguistic expertise of students have already been used in classrooms (Cantrell et al., 2022). Through multimodal projects such as the zines and collaborative books, educators can also work with students to understand and critique power dynamics that inform their and their peers' lives. We encourage teacher-scholars to build upon these examples as a springboard for planning, implementing, and assessing the impact of such multimodal literacy projects, making sure the process is youth and community led.

Furthermore, while it's important to elevate youth perspectives, the responsibility of creating better civic realities shouldn't fall on individuals sharing their stories. Rather, those in power must work to identify and disrupt systemic barriers that inhibit refugee communities' civic participation. This necessitates intentional collaboration with refugee youth and open-mindedness to utilizing a variety of tools and modes of knowledge production. Truly listening to youth perspectives also requires us to relinquish the power we hold as adults and through other positionalities and to approach storytelling in a less extractive way. Such reorientations pose the question as to what possibilities exist in out-of-school spaces to engage youth in political education that provides context for their multiple social and cultural identities and evolving perspectives? Ultimately, it is the knowledge of refugee youth that will provide important insight as to how we might build these new societal systems that not only support forcibly displaced youth but seek to eradicate future displacement.

Works Cited

Cantrell, S. C., Walker-Dalhouse, D., & Lazar, A. M. (2022). Enacting culturally sustaining literacy practices: Toward more socially just teaching. In S. C. Cantrell, D. Walker-Dalhouse, & A. M. Lazar (Eds.), *Culturally sustaining literacy pedagogies: Honoring students' heritages, literacies, and languages* (pp. 159–170). Teachers College Press.

Fattal, A. L. (2018). Counterpublic. In H. Callan (Ed.), *The international encyclopedia of anthropology* (pp. 1–2). John Wiley & Sons. https://escholarship.org/uc/item/73t260cm

Guo-Brennan, M., & Guo-Brennan, L. (2019). Civic capacity and engagement in building welcoming and inclusive communities for newcomers: Praxis, recommendations, and policy implications. *Journal of Community Engagement and Scholarship*, *11*(2), 31–42.

Hello Neighbor Network. (2022). *How do refugees and migrants come to understand race and racism in the United States?* www.neighbornetwork.io/research

KidCentral TN. (2018). *The importance of civic education*.www.kidcentraltn.com/education/community-after-school-care/the-importance-of-civic-education-.html

Lazar, A. M., Walker-Dalhouse, D., & Cantrell, S. C. (2022). Introduction: Culturally sustaining literacy pedagogy: From relevance to permanence. In S. C. Cantrell, D. Walker-Dalhouse, & A. M. Lazar (Eds.), *Culturally sustaining literacy pedagogies: Honoring students' heritages, literacies, and languages* (pp. 1–15). Teachers College Press.

MacDonald, M. T. (2018). Governing sponsorship in a literacy support program for resettled refugee students. *Reflections, 18*(1), 39–70.

Martinez, A. Y. (2020). *Counterstory: The rhetoric and writing of critical race theory.* National Council of Teachers of English.

McDonald, M. (2013). Keywords: Refugee literacy. *Community Literacy Journal, 7*(2), 95–99.

Mendenhall, M., Russell, S. G., & Buckner, E. (2017). *Urban refugee education: Strengthening policies and practices for access, quality and inclusion.* Teachers College, Columbia University. www.edu-links.org/sites/default/files/media/file/Urban-Refugees-Full-Report.pdf

Montero, M. K., & Al Zouhouri, A. (2022). Fear not the trauma story: A trauma-informed perspective to supporting war-affected refugees in schools and classrooms. In L. J. Pentón Herrera (Ed.), *English and students with limited or interrupted formal education: Global perspectives on teacher preparation and classroom practices* (pp. 83–100). Springer.

Outley, C., & Skuza, J. A. (2019). Special issue: Perspectives on immigrant, refugee, and border youth. *Journal of Youth Development: Bridging Research and Practice, 14*(2), 1–9.

Spade, D. (2016, December 21). *Part 1: Prison abolition & prefiguring the world you want to live in* [Video]. YouTube. www.youtube.com/watch?v=aQ9iGoZ4s3k

United Nations High Commissioner for Refugees. (2024). *Figures at a glance.* www.unhcr.org/figures-at-a-glance.html

US Citizenship and Immigration Services. (2023, August 25). *The naturalization interview and test.* www.uscis.gov/citizenship/learn-about-citizenship/the-naturalization-interview-and-test

USA for UNHCR. (2023). *Refugee statistics.* www.unrefugees.org/refugee-facts/statistics/

De- and Re-Constructing Journalism: Storytelling and Social Action

EMILY PLUMMER CATENA

In this age of instant access and updates—when cell phones and social media make on-the-scene "reporting" by all citizens possible—journalism is no longer about being the first to "break" a story (Kovach & Rosenstiel, 2014). Youth are taking to the digital realms that have become synonymous with adolescence to engage in new forms of journalism, ones that critically examine inequities and engage in activism against them (e.g., McDaniel, 2024). Given the rise of "citizen" and "social media" journalism (Bruns & Highfield, 2016; Chorley & Mottershead, 2016), the genre has become a liminal space characterized by constructions that are interpersonal, collaborative, and ever-shifting (Papacharissi, 2015). Such "connected civics" (Ito et al., 2015) is more possible through digital activism, but not all student engagement is equally received in public arenas (e.g., Blades, 2018).

Youth are utilizing the shifting genre of journalism to engage civically, entering political news and commentary across scales, acting as journalists and expanding understandings of civic engagement. Students do so through international social media campaigns like #BLM, #climatestrike, and #NeverAgain (e.g., McDaniel, 2023) but also local in-person protests or critical writing programs, like the journalism camp I facilitated with youth in Philadelphia.

I planned, moderated, and researched an eight-day journalism summer writing camp for adolescents that took place over a two-week span in August 2018. Fifteen middle and high school students from in and around Philadelphia attended. The students had multiple opportunities to publish their journalistic work, including a culminating radio broadcast with a local community media center and a newspaper publication created during and mailed out after the camp.

Students also interacted with a different journalistic mentor each day of the camp; each presented the genre in line with their own practices and understanding, including journalism as activism, and through ethnography, narrative, podcast, and even dramatic monologue. For example, one of the journalistic mentors was a local public media organization employee who shared about his years-long efforts to reframe negative stereotypes around a local urban high school attended by predominantly Black, poor, urban youth by writing a news article about a pregnant teenager as she started and ultimately graduated from the school (McCorry, 2017).

An emphasis on journalism as social action through creativity and "the personal" cohered across and emerged from these various journalistic forms (Plummer Catena, 2020). Much like this journalistic mentor (and others), I attempted to interrogate issues and understandings of power surrounding youth writing, civic engagement, and journalistic positioning through a focus on adolescent voices.

In our journalism summer writing camp, journalism was a grounding means of looking at and working in a writing genre as fluid—but doing so with particular attention to positioning. How does the genre of journalism already position youth, especially when youth are attempting to use journalistic writing to affect change? What factors influence that positioning? What are our understandings of journalism? What are different ways that the genre can be approached in media, modes, and more? What does it mean to be a student journalist? The genre of journalism was a means for us to examine our individual choices and movements as writers with critical eyes toward how journalism—particularly in the media—positions youth writers and activists.

These discussions of how youth utilize writing, particularly digital, for social justice aims across audiences and spaces highlights "the increasingly murky line between journalism and activism" (Neason & Dalton, 2018, para. 2). But it also emphasizes the unequal potential of journalism to foster change in this age of social media and this ongoing civic season of "fake news." Urban students of color, their words, their causes, and even their identities are not met with the same enthusiasm and applause as those of their white suburban peers, as surfaced in the local newspaper headline "The world is listening to Parkland teens. Some Philly kids wonder: Why not us?" (Graham, 2018)."

Students' choices as writers and changemakers are rooted in what they perceive as likely, possible, and/or necessary—when writing with or in certain genres and conventions, to or for particular audiences, and both in and out of school. How and why writing is taken up and identities and experiences are represented is inextricably linked to systems of power (Stornaiuolo, Smith, & Phillips, 2017). Fostering spaces and conceptualizing genres in fluid ways that facilitate critical attunement to identities and power are much needed in these shifting times.

In this essay, I will unpack elements of our summer camp curriculum through which we critically deconstructed youth representations in journalistic media, specifically how we analyzed ways headlines differently position youth activists (Appendix A). I will then discuss how we reconstructed journalistic practices and publications, emphasizing the role of one camp journalist mentor who invited students to "workshop" their news articles into dramatic monologues, exemplifying how literacy educators can engage student writers in speculative civic literacy learning (Mirra & Garcia, 2020, 2022) by approaching journalism as personal and creative.

Our camp space, the journalism genre, and our individual and collective civic engagements converged to create new writing practices and forms of knowledge—"transformations" (Gutiérrez, 2008) that are imperative "in yet another civic season of 'great need'" (Mirra & Garcia, 2023, para. 1).

Critical Literacies: Redesign Cycle

Collaborative engagement in the "redesign cycle" (Janks, 2010) was a means of working toward these types of transformation: knowledge production and sharing and civic engagement across writing processes, relationships, and spaces. Janks (2010) calls for teachers and students to work together in moving through this cycle, as the students and I did during the journalism camp. The "redesign cycle" involves iterative movement between "Design/Construct/Make a Text," "Deconstruct/Unmake," and "Reconstruct/Redesign/Remake" (p. 183), as the orientations are interdependent. Students continuously engaged in reconstructions of journalism while they grappled with the genre as readers and writers both positioned by journalistic coverage and repositioning journalism through their expanded understandings of what it can look like and do.

Deconstructions

When we participated in a deconstruction activity on the final day of the camp, students had already written their news articles and shared pieces of their writing on the culminating radio broadcast, whether the news articles or other reconstructed forms.

The activity involved critically examining headlines about student activism covered by a wide range of journalistic media outlets, from local ones like *The Inquirer* to national ones like *CNN*, *The New York Times*, and *The Washington Post*, for the impact of journalists' diction and the positioning of youth as change agents. The students and I collaboratively unpacked representations, positionings, and uptakes of youth across aspects of identities and lived experiences, like geographic location (e.g., urban versus suburban), race, socioeconomics, and more.

Students were given ten headlines I had chosen and then presented with strategically missing words, which they worked in pairs or small groups to "correctly" fill in; students were also given the subhead text that appeared just under the headline, which was usually one to two sentences. After students completed all ten headlines, I revealed the original headlines. We drew on discrepancies between words students imagined would fill in the blanks and the words the headlines actually used—e.g., why did a journalist choose that word instead of another? What impact might a different verb have had on readers?

I designed the headline omission activity to fit our focus on critically examining the journalism genre and how it positions youth as change agents. Given the temporal (2018) and topical relevance of the Parkland students' activist efforts around gun control, I emphasized articles on Parkland in relation to other student groups. Literacy educators can consider issues of student activism relevant to and in their contexts, curating journalistic headlines that allow them to address those issues in their classrooms or spaces. (See Appendix A for a list of the ten headlines I selected.) Figure 1, on the following page, is a particularly powerful headline example.

This headline originally appeared on *Time.com* as "'They Are Lifting Us Up.' How Parkland Students Are Using Their Moment to Help Minority Anti-Violence Groups." The article explores the Peace Warriors, a Chicago-based student group of predominantly Black youth that has similarly been engaging in activism for nearly a decade about gun violence without capturing the nation's attention and overwhelming positive uptake in ways the Parkland students so quickly did.

Many students had strong reactions to this headline. Brielle,[1] an Asian American rising high school senior, perceived this headline as dichotomizing the Parkland youth from youth of

1. Student names here and throughout are pseudonyms.

Figure 1. Example headline from activism headline omission activity.

'They Are Lifting Us Up." How Parkland Students Are ______ Their ______ to ______ Minority Anti-Violence ______

The Peace Warriors, a group of predominantly black high school students from Chicago, have been fighting gun violence for 10 years without garnering much attention from the outside world. The students from Parkland, Fla. brought the issue to national prominence in a matter of days.

color, exalting the efforts of the former and downplaying those of the latter. However, she resisted this pulling apart of youth activists in her response to the headline, offering both that it "was very passive aggressive to say that they [Parkland students] get more attention" but also at the same time that it was passive aggressive to imply the Parkland students' activism amounted to nothing more than "their 15 seconds of fame" (Brielle, personal communication, August 16, 2018). While Brielle did use the collective "we" when expanding on how the headline positions youth of color—"We're not as important. We're more resilient but not as important" (personal communication, August 16, 2018)—her words push back on this unequal positioning by highlighting how it places both groups in problematic relationships to one another and is detrimental to both.

In deconstructing the headline, Brielle reconstructed how we discussed it—she surfaced the racial disparities evident without erasing that it simultaneously did harm to all student activists. Brielle more strongly identified with how the headline positioned youth of color, reconstructing it around the resilience of minority students rather than the authors' implied unequal placement of them as in need of white students' help. But Brielle resisted the journalist's positioning of both white, suburban students as well as urban youth of color. Her words and the stance behind them demonstrate the importance of resisting dichotomization and solely deconstruction and instead working toward reconstructed and transformed writing approaches and practices for civically oriented ends.

Reconstructions

The students reconstructed the genre with adults/mentors in the space and with one another, ultimately centering journalism on stories they wanted to tell about social change issues, aligning journalism with speculative civic literacy engagement (Mirra & Garcia, 2020, 2022). Camp students' reconstructions of journalism cohered around the power of incorporating the personal. In particular, "the personal" included three expanded understandings of what journalism can involve and/or look like in practice: journalism as creative, journalism as narrative, and journalism as activism.

Each of these three expanded understandings of journalism will be discussed in turn; however, all are intertwined and overlapping. To represent these interconnections, I will focus on how journalism emerged as creative, narrative, and activist during and as a result of interactions and composing with one journalist mentor, Maurice.

Maurice was the only mentor who structured his time as a "workshop," making it both the most targeted and the most widely impactful. Maurice's workshop centered on dramatic monologues and how they connect to journalistic writing. Nearly every student commented on Maurice in reflective discussions and interviews as having broadened how they understood and subsequently engaged in journalism, making it more personally relevant and more interesting and useful to others. Aspects of writing they had previously separated from journalism—i.e., creativity and personal voice—were brought to the fore, as was perspective-taking in considering who tells a story, how, and why.

Maurice was a podcast producer and connectivity manager for a local educational nonprofit that works with urban schools to engage students in playwriting where theater programs do not exist. I had intentionally reached out to Maurice because of the potential I saw in his podcast to break down this often-perceived binary between journalism and creativity. The podcast was a newer project of the nonprofit centered on students' writing related to social issue topics rooted in real, local experiences. An episode of Maurice's podcast had been filmed at a local public school where I was separately doing field work, so I had previously watched firsthand how a student's piece of writing about gun violence was transformed into a dramatic monologue that was then read live on the podcast by a professional actor. Following the reading was a discussion between students and experts on gun violence, all facilitated and broadcast through the podcast. This was the general format of all podcast episodes. I imagined Maurice could work with camp students on shifting their news articles into dramatic monologues, thereby expanding their understandings of journalism.

While Maurice remained certain throughout our camp collaboration that a dramatic monologue was not a form of journalism, he articulated seeing the two as sharing important elements. Those connections emerged during his conversations and activities with the students and included writing about issues significant to individuals and their communities, offering multiple perspectives on a story, and fostering empathy. Activities included examining the medium of podcast, or "writing for the ear," as Maurice termed it; considering journalism's relation to activism; and thinking through relationships and perspectives when writing about something that impacts real people. Maurice had students read and talk about a *Los Angeles Times* article on podcasting and journalism as a shifting genre (Saidi, 2018). After unpacking the article, Maurice invited students to rework their news pieces into dramatic monologues.

At the core of Maurice's work with the students was a sense of students' agency—an agency that involved drawing on multiple genres and forms both selectively and simultaneously in the pursuit of their own civic literacies goals. Maurice emphasized how students could take up elements of dramatic monologues with the aim of writing journalistic news articles about social justice issues, positioning journalism as deeply personal. Maurice was direct in discussing with students how their personal voices and writing practices were powerful forces, particularly in relation to journalism as a liminal genre, as when he said the following:

> Journalism is always changing. You all, if you continue to go on this path, are going to make decisions about what journalism looks like and how people receive it that are going to affect me and the way I consume it 20 years from now. (Personal communication, August 14, 2018)

As "traditional" notions of journalism continue to mix with social media and citizen journalism as well as youth activism, what the genre is or can be becomes increasingly open. Centering youth agency and civic engagement, Maurice called on students to recognize their power to shape journalism and to be cognizant of their own writing practices and purposes as they raise awareness about issues.

Journalism as Creative

Among the students—and in society writ large—there remained an initial tendency to associate journalism with fact telling and, further, to dichotomize facts from creativity, personal voice, and a variety of writing forms. However, students spoke about their reconstructed understandings of and approaches to journalism as coming to incorporate creativity. I use "reconstructed" intentionally here because these new conceptualizations—of the genres and of themselves as writers—were actively arrived at through de- and re-construction activities with mentors and peers and students' own reflections and engagements.

Brielle drew a direct connection between journalism, creativity, and the personal when reflecting on why she most enjoyed writing the monologue with Maurice as compared to other forms of writing explored during the camp. Brielle researched and wrote on her selected topic of immigration issues in her home city of Philadelphia, specifically if it were going to become a sanctuary city. She shifted this work across multiple different genres and mediums: news article (see Figure 2), dramatic monologue (see Figure 3), and radio broadcast.

Brielle explained her preference for the monologue during an end-of-camp interview:

> I think writing the monologue . . . made me think about it more. It was something different. And now I'm like, okay, I want to do this more . . . creative writing-wise . . . In my case, when I wrote the monologue, I feel like I connected with my topic because it was more of a personal account of what might have happened in the personal aspect. (Personal communication, August 16, 2018)

Brielle chose her topic because of its personal proximity to her family, describing many of its members as undocumented immigrants. However, she felt the "traditional" news article format distanced her from that personal connection while the monologue gave her "creative license" to explore it. In the monologue, Brielle wrote from the perspective of an undocumented immigrant who was pursued by Immigrant and Customs Enforcement agents and arrested in front of his mother. How immigration laws are unfolding in a major city is inarguably a topic of journalistic relevance. What the dramatic monologue workshop called into question was what makes for an especially impactful news piece about that issue. Exploring the topic through the creative monologue form surfaced how important personal perspectives and experiences can be to news stories and to civic engagement more broadly.

Figure 2. Brielle's news article.

Philly: Is it Becoming a Sanctuary City?

I

Listen, can you hear the sounds around you? Can you hear the loudness of the city? But the real question is, can you hear the tick of time, the heavy breaths, the shaking eyes, and the whispers of the heart? Many undocumented immigrants view Philly as a city for a beginning, something new, somewhere safe to start a home: a city where dreams are nurtured. But is it really?

Philly has always been battling between being a sanctuary city or not, but what does "sanctuary" mean? Sanctuary means that the city limits its cooperation with the national government's effort to enforce immigration law. This creates a place of safety for immigrants that are undocumented or without legal status.

Although Philly is a city made of many immigrants, we still have this ongoing battle to protect the people and treat each other like humans. The city has had incidents in which Immigration and Customs Enforcement (ICE) has arrested people without warrant, and people have not spoken out or reached out to police to ask for help out of fear. Although the time seems grim for undocumented immigrants, there are community organizations like Juntos that are helping immigrants. Olivia Vásquez, a former community organizer for Juntos, says to all immigrants, "We have always been deported. Yes, the chances increase under the Trump administration, but that does not mean we stop. I want them to remember two things, and one is that you are not alone and to not be afraid. We have to stay together and continue to fight."

On July 28, 2018, Mayor Kenney did not renew the contract that allows federal ICE agents to access a key law-enforcement database known as PARS and use that information against undocumented but otherwise law-abiding immigrants in Philadelphia.

"I cannot in good conscience allow the agreement to continue," he said.

Philly will also be offering municipal IDs to anyone who does not have one. A municipal ID, or a city ID, allows a person

to have access to everyday citizen needs. In Philly it pertains to getting groceries from food pantries, treatment for drug addiction, entry to City Hall, entry to municipal buildings, and possibly more. The cards will be issued to anyone 13 and above to provide some form of identification when asked. They will cost probably around $10-$15 judging from Chicago's price.

However, there is a big controversy. With the municipal IDs being provided in the most ideal situations, the people who would most likely apply for them are the undocumented. If they were stopped by ICE and asked to take out their IDs that might create a problem; considering that most Philadelphians would have a PA state ID, having a city ID would hint that the person is possibly undocumented, possibly making it easier for ICE to identify them. On the other hand, many people argue that Philadelphia is on its way to becoming a sanctuary city and that this is a first step to help people.

Meeting interesting people with interesting background

Figure 3. Brielle's dramatic monologue.

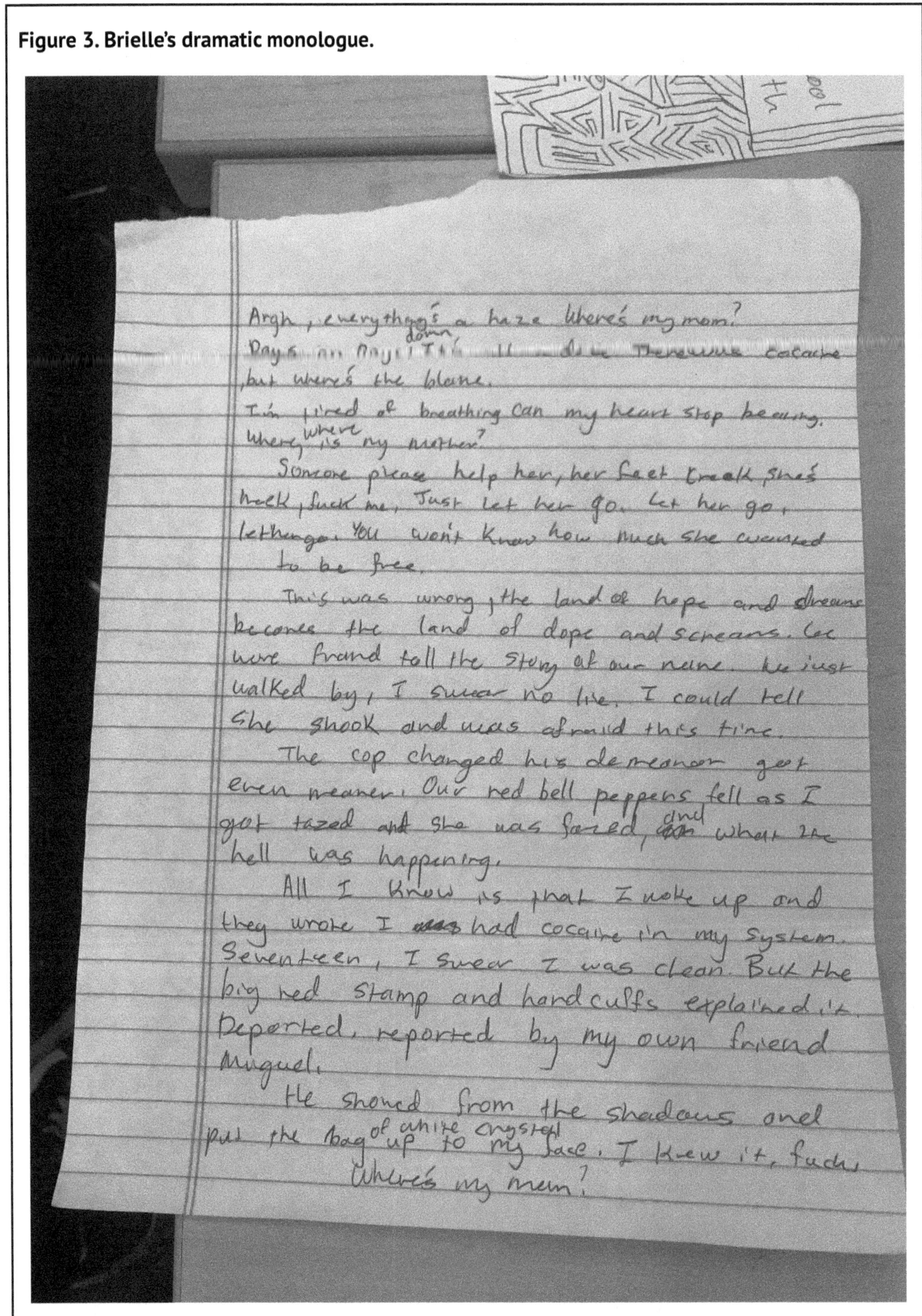

Argh, everything's a haze where's my mom?
Days on days [illegible] down [illegible] There was cocaine
, but where's the blame.
I'm tired of breathing can my heart stop beating.
Where, where is my mother?
Someone please help her, her feet break, she's
weak, fuck me, Just let her go. Let her go,
let her go. You won't know how much she wanted
to be free.
This was wrong, the land of hope and dreams
becomes the land of dope and screams. We
were [illegible] tell the story of our name. He just
walked by, I swear no lie. I could tell
she shook and was afraid this time.
The cop changed his demeanor got
even meaner. Our red bell peppers fell as I
got tazed and she was fazed, and what the
hell was happening.
All I know is that I woke up and
they wrote I had cocaine in my system.
Seventeen, I swear I was clean. But the
big red stamp and handcuffs explained it.
Deported, reported by my own friend
Miguel.
He showed from the shadows and
put the bag of white crystal up to my face. I knew it, fuck.
Where's my mom?

Brielle equated creativity with the personal and described journalism as more meaningful to herself and others when allowed to approach it in her "own ways." Just as Maurice was very clear in articulating that a dramatic monologue is not necessarily a form of journalism, Brielle did not say all structures of journalism should be erased or all news articles should be written from a first-person perspective. They instead highlighted how they can choose to draw on elements of multiple genres and forms simultaneously when writing journalistically and engaging civically. And, further, they articulated that doing so makes for more complicated and, therefore, more powerful pieces of "news." By delving with Maurice into dramatic monologues alongside and intertwined with news articles, students began to speak into being the shifts in journalism that Maurice emboldened them to move forward with during his workshop.

Journalism as Narrative

Another way students reconstructed journalism and worked toward greater understandings of themselves as writers and civically engaged changemakers was through perspective-taking in their writing. Students discussed and then acted on journalism as a means to tell personal stories—first-person accounts of real-life experiences with issues in their communities, schools, and lives. News articles can incorporate aspects of storytelling inherent to fiction and dramatic monologue—first-person perspectives, in-depth description, and opportunities to see self and others differently. Broadening understanding of the genre likewise broadened its impact for both writer and audience—students felt they could write as journalists "in so many different ways" once the role was framed as storytelling, whether in relation to their own narratives, others' narratives, or societal narratives.

Maurice positioned both news articles and dramatic monologues as grappling with complex personal and social issues through stories. He described the first-person narrative inherent to dramatic monologue as a "way into" multifaceted social issues that journalists can tackle with news articles. Maurice offered an extended example about a journalistic piece on the George Foreman Grill and how it had become the "go-to-stove for people experiencing homelessness" (Personal communication, August 14, 2018). When the journalist writing this story approached Foreman about his grill's significance in homeless populations, Foreman was unaware but then shared his own experiences with food instability as a child. Through his George Foreman Grill example, Maurice showed how a news article can be narrative and be factual and, as a result, be more impactful for readers because the combination opens up challenging issues in new, person-centered ways.

Presenting journalism as including and made more powerful by personal stories is a reconstruction—literally—of the inverted pyramid's call to begin with only the most important "facts" (Purdue University, 2020) and broadly of how students understood their preferences for fiction and creative writing in relation to journalism as social action.

Journalism as Activism

Maurice acknowledged that positioning journalism in an activist stance around issues of personal importance "is a shift in thinking," using the podcast medium as an example through the aforementioned article on journalists' podcasts as changing the genre. He shared a quote from the podcast article

(Saidi, 2018), situating it between activism and fact telling:

> **"Although traditional reporting emphasizes the facts,"** and I've bolded that because I think that's very important about journalism, "and lets readers draw their own conclusions, podcasters are not shy about trying to change people's minds. We have," and this is a quote from someone, I think they worked at NPR [National Public Radio], "some pretty old school journalists, and they may bristle at the idea of journalism being activist, but I don't. We are out there to make the world a better place, to make it more just." (Maurice, personal communication, August 14, 2018)

Amid the article quotes, Maurice highlighted that a fact-telling orientation to journalism—although "old school"—is particularly constitutive of and important to the genre. But he did so with equal attention to how those facts can be framed by the personal, in this instance a journalist's activist agenda.

Journalism as activism became the culmination of telling revealing stories and drawing on elements of creative writing like dynamism, perspective, and emotion. Maurice summed up these interrelations as "journalism can be activist. There can be a voice and call for change inside of the presentation of an issue in a journalistic way" (Personal communication, August 14, 2018).

Students broadened reconstructions and expanded understandings even further, opening up who and what counts as a journalist and as a form of activism. Tina, in an end-of-camp interview, stated the following:

> Anyone can be a journalist. Like it may seem difficult, but well . . . as any other skills, you have to learn, but it's like writing or issues that's going on in the world and standing for a change. And that's, like, a way of becoming a journalist, standing up. (Personal communication, August 16, 2018)

Tina did not directly reference the workshop with Maurice. However, she similarly recognized the duality of needing to understand and draw on key structures within journalism while simultaneously taking a clear stance on an issue of personal importance. Connecting journalism to activism made journalism more inclusive for Tina, as she offered the most challenging part as needing to "learn." In addition to learning more about the core tenets of "traditional" journalism, a writer also necessarily learns about others, self, and the complexity of social issues in question while engaging in journalism as activism. Here again "the personal is the political," as journalism comes to include genre conventions as well as a writer's aims and beliefs in the service of a broader social message and purpose.

Tina focused on how journalism as activism expands who can participate. Jasmine further opened up what counts as participation in journalism and in activism. When I asked Jasmine at the camp's end if she considered herself an activist, she first described physical activities she participated in that demonstrated her activism, i.e., rallies and marches. However, as she went on, she clarified that "activism can go way farther than, like, just participating in these sorts of events . . . I also write about things online, whether it's an actual . . . serious paragraph or just . . . a random Tumblr post made to tell people" (Jasmine, personal communication, August

16, 2018). Writing, whether "serious," factual, fictional, and/or creative, is a way of engaging in activism. Journalism, as reconstructed by Jasmine, Tina, Brielle, Maurice, the other campers, and me, is a shifting, more inclusive and action-oriented form of writing than first conceptualized by many in our space.

Journalism as Civic Engagement

By providing students opportunities to draw on their personal experiences and civic dreams—by not dichotomizing the personal and the "academic," factual, and/or journalistic—students can come to produce knowledge in agentive ways that motivate them as writers. Students can engage civically while building awareness about their writing choices and practices. They can consider questions such as why they want to write about a particular topic, how it will be received, and where they might publish it. In news articles and dramatic monologues from our journalism summer writing camp through to #NeverAgain tweets, we see students emphasizing their beliefs and passions and pushing back against the conventions of a writing genre (journalism) and the representations and reactions of the media. All of this helps students, educators, and researchers to see writing—their own and others—in ways that can create an impact.

Intertwining the personal, creative, and activistic in writing pushes for more expansive approaches to and understandings of genres, including journalism but also others and whether digital, print, or hybrid. Journalism is, however, a critical space for students to circulate their stories and to see how others' stories are circulating—both forms of civic engagement. This approach to engaging in journalism as writers and with journalism as media consumers is something that can and should occur in secondary literacy classrooms and other literacy learning contexts and is especially important in these contentious times for in- and out-of-school literacy learning and civic engagement.

Appendix A

Headline omission activity during journalism summer writing camp.

1. Like Parkland students, Philly teens _______ for their _______ on gun violence

Maureen Boland worried when she started seeing the nasty comments piling up under the column that I wrote about her Philadelphia students as the National School Walkout approached.

2. Parkland's David Hogg _______ students to _______ activists, even if they don't go to _______

One of the most prominent students leading the fight for stricter gun laws got meetings on Capitol Hill with top lawmakers, airtime on prime-time cable news and a key speaking spot at one of the largest marches in recent years.

3. Parkland Students Bring _______ to Town _______

To keep the momentum going on their #NeverAgain protest movement, student activists from Marjory Stoneman Douglas High School in Parkland, Fla., have been pushing members of Congress to hold town hall meetings.

4. Harry Potter _______ the Parkland _______

After the 2016 election, I was bewildered by many things. One of them was how 41% of millennials voted for Trump when they had been raised on Harry Potter.

5. 'They Are Lifting Us Up." How Parkland Stu-

dents Are ______ Their _______ to _______ Minority Anti-Violence _______

The Peace Warriors, a group of predominantly black high school students from Chicago, have been fighting gun violence for 10 years without garnering much attention from the outside world. The students from Parkland, Fla. brought the issue to national prominence in a matter of days.

6. How the Parkland Students _______ So Good at ______ _______

The secretary of education, Betsy DeVos, had only just announced that she would visit Marjory Stoneman Douglas High School when the students began to react.

7. For Parkland Students, a _______ Journey From '_______' to a _______ March

WASHINGTON — Little has returned to normal for the students of Marjory Stoneman Douglas High School since Feb. 14, when a gunman killed 14 of their classmates and three staff members.

8. The world is ______ to Parkland teens. Some Philly kids ______ : _________ ______ us?

Milan Sullivan is horrified that 17 people died in a mass shooting at a Parkland, Fla., high school. And she does not disagree with the teenage survivors who have stood up since the massacre, demanding action on gun violence.

9. Parkland students _____ clear backpacks: 'We ______ _____ _____'

PARKLAND, Fla. — Students at Marjory Stoneman Douglas High School are not happy about the clear backpacks they've been issued as a safety measure, decrying them as a temporary fix to a larger issue and bemoaning their sudden loss of privacy.

10. Trying to ____ post-Parkland ____, students again ____ gun violence in Philly

For the second time in as many months, high school students around the country walked out of school to protest gun violence and call for more gun control.

Works Cited

Blades, L. A. (2018, February 23). *Black teens have been fighting for gun reform for years.* Teen Vogue. www.teenvogue.com/story/black-teens-have-been-fighting-for-gun-reform-for-years

Bruns, A, & Highfield, T. (2012). Blogs, Twitter, and breaking news: The produsage of citizen journalism. In R. A. Lind (Ed.), *Produsing theory in a digital world: The intersection of audiences and production in contemporary theory* (pp. 15–32). Peter Lang.

Chorley, M. J., & Mottershead, G. (2016). Are you talking to me? An analysis of journalism conversation on social media. *Journalism Practice, 10*(7), 856–867.

Gutiérrez, K. D. (2008). Developing a sociocritical literacy in the Third Space. *Reading Research Quarterly, 43*(2), 148–164.

Ito, M., Soep, E., Kligler-Vilenchik, N., Shresthova, S., Gamber-Thompson, L., & Zimmerman, A. (2015). Learning connected civics: Narratives, practices, infrastructures. *Curriculum Inquiry, 45*(1), 10–29.

Janks, H. (2010). *Literacy and power.* Routledge.

Kovach, B., & Rosenstiel, T. (2014). *The elements of journalism: What newspeople should know and the public should expect* (3rd ed.). Three Rivers Press.

McCorry, K. (2017, August 30). *Don't call it the Badlands: The story of Savannah Zayas.* WHYY. https://whyy.org/articles/dont-call-it-the-badlands-the-story-of-savannah-zayas/

McDaniel, D. S. (2023). Supporting justice-oriented English instruction through teens' digital activist literacies. *English Journal,*

113(1), 49–57.

McDaniel, D. (2024). Tatum's social media activism as multiliteracies: Connecting, advocating, and resisting social injustices. *Journal of Language and Literacy Education, 20(*1), 1–26.

Mirra, N., & Garcia, A. (2020). "I hesitate but I do have hope": Youth speculative civic literacies for troubled times. *Harvard Educational Review, 90*(2), 295–321.

Mirra, N., & Garcia, A. (2022). Guns, schools, and democracy: Adolescents imagining social futures through speculative civic literacies. *American Educational Research Journal, 59*(2), 345–380.

Mirra, N., & Garcia, A. (2023, October 17). *Call for proposals—special issue of Research in the Teaching of English.* National Council of Teachers of English. https://ncte.org/blog/2023/10/call-for-proposals-special-issue-of-research-in-the-teaching-of-english/

Neason, A., & Dalton, M. (2018, February 21). In Parkland, journalism students take on role of reporter and survivor. *Columbia Journalism Review.* www.cjr.org/analysis/parkland-school-shooting.php

Papacharissi, Z. (2015). Toward new journalism(s): Affective news, hybridity, and liminal spaces. *Journalism Studies, 16*(1), 27–40.

Plummer Catena, E. C. (2020). Journalism and activism anew: Participatory movements with adolescents writing for change [Doctoral dissertation, University of Pennsylvania]. Proquest Dissertations & Theses.

Purdue Online Writing Lab. (2020). *The inverted pyramid structure.* https://owl.purdue.edu/owl/subject_specific_writing/journalism_and_journalistic_writing/the_inverted_pyramid.html

Saidi, J. (2018, August 2). How podcasts are being used by journalists and how they are changing journalism. *Los Angeles Times.* www.latimes.com/entertainment/movies/la-ca-et-podcast-journalism-20180802-story.html

Stornaiuolo, A., Smith, A., & Phillips, N. C. (2017). Developing a transliteracies framework for a connected world. *Journal of Literacy Research, 49*(1), 68–91.

Tales of Resistance: Rebuilding Social Realities in Civic Imagination Workshops

FABIO C. CAMPOS

The reader might find counterarguments, but, in several aspects, the United States and Brazil mirror each other. Notwithstanding the military and economic abyss that separate both nations, the US and Brazil are behemoths in size and population, have a past marked by colonization, slavery, independence and internal conflict, and face similar political challenges in current times. The capitol buildings of both nations have been stormed by right-wing insurrectionists—on January 6, 2021, in Washington, DC, and January 8, 2023, in Brasília—and free press is under attack by citizens who act under the banner of free speech. Perhaps the most interesting similarity between these giants-in-the-mirror is how much civic education is, on one hand, defunded by the state and, on the other, weaponized as a means to establish political dominance and to ban any trace of civics that might mean developing critical thought and fighting for social justice. From the book bans in the US to the "civic military" schools in Brazil—where students learn to comply and are taught by reserve military officers—school-based civic education is falling short of accounting for both countries' marginalized youth.

In the absence of national standards—and considering a significant disparity in the availability of learning opportunities (Kahne & Middaugh, 2009)—civic education programs still adopt instructionist pedagogies centered on factual knowledge and government-related issues (e.g., voting, branches of government, etc.). On top of these limitations, the research and practice around civic education focus on program evaluation or the quantification of civic knowledge as a proxy for learning or intervention success. Beyond concluding that intervention B has superior results to A, civic learning needs to delve into which mechanisms, principles, and decisions make an intervention effective and why.

Luckily, other suns insist on rising. A nascent body of scholarship—often called "new civics"—emphasizes the importance of additional skills, literacies, and dispositions in order for youth to engage with complex social issues and envision potential solutions (Mihailidis & Gerodimos, 2018). Such fluencies include civic self-efficacy (Hipólito-Delgado & Zion, 2017), participatory literacies (Mihailidis, 2018), sociocritical literacies (Gutiérrez & Jurow, 2016), locative literacies (Headrick Taylor, 2017), and civic imagination (Jenkins et al., 2020). Also on this side of the spectrum are speculative and utopian pedagogies (Garcia & Mirra, 2023), two of such approaches that invite students to elaborate diverse and even multiversal scenarios as alternatives to current situations of inequality.

Designing civic interventions that ally speculative thought and well-rooted structural critique, however, is not a given. The field of education is still devoid of robust interventions that blend these two elements in a way that does not tokenize social challenges—perhaps by creating a mere aestheticization of the dystopian (Nooney & Brain, 2019)—nor engage in a form of critique that hampers mobilization and hope.

This essay narrates in depth the findings from a series of civic imagination workshops conducted in two cities: Santa Ana in the US and Rio de Janeiro in Brazil. The study sought to answer how educators might design mechanisms and processes in a learning environment that are imaginative enough to go beyond the constraints of reality while sufficiently grounded to one's lived experience. To address this pursuit, this study adopted a Design-based Research Approach (DBRA) (Hoadley & Campos, 2022) in which a civic imagination workshop was designed and refined in four consecutive iterations. For this task, adolescents of marginalized communities were recruited in a *barrio* of the city of Santa Ana and at Rocinha, a *favela* in the heart of Rio de Janeiro. The workshops employed a myriad of tools from card games to community mapping and from roleplaying games to exercises with generative artificial intelligence. All such tools and tasks were designed to reflect the work of Brazilian educator Paulo Freire (1970), who wrote extensively about the dialectics between criticality and imagination and who professed that it is through dialogue that marginalized students elaborate, tell stories, and learn about their historicized selves.

Background

Imagining means mentally developing scenarios and representations not perceived by the physical senses (Gotlieb et al., 2016). A notable advocate for integrating imagination into the core of education was Maxine Greene, who posited that looking at things "as if they could be otherwise" (Greene, 1993, p. 225) should not be devoid of solid social critique. Greene's notion of wide *awakeness*—or the critical awareness of one's lived experiences—remains fundamental to a critical pedagogy of possibility and social change. Similarly, Freire (1970) posited that learning should not be organized around teaching scripts but instead based on supporting students in moving away from a culture of silence—or a lethargic acceptance of one's limit-situations (or situations of oppression)—into a culture of informed participation.

Speculative Pedagogies

Speculative pedagogies are an expansive set of ideas that transcend conventional boundaries and focus on visionary, future-oriented approaches to teaching and learning. Such pedagogies provide educators and learners with tools and environments to devise alternatives of collective thriving beyond existing horizons guiding educational policy, research, and practice (Garcia & Mirra, 2023).

As proposed by Garcia and Mirra (2023), speculative pedagogies take a multiversal approach, encouraging deep interrogation, innovation, and collective action toward other realities that "can and do exist" (p. 17). Such approaches to teaching and learning include an expansive set of futuristic and visionary methods of teaching that start with dreaming in the present about liberatory alternatives to capitalism, gender inequality, patriarchy, and other related forms of oppression. Similarly, Jenkins and colleagues (2020) suggest a pedagogical approach based on civic imagination, "the capacity to imagine alternatives to current social, political and economic conditions (. . .) even if those alternatives tap the fantastic" (Jenkins et al., 2020, p. 5). Their approach, highly contingent on popular culture, contends that understanding that change is possible is necessary for civic engagement and participation. This definition implies that individuals cannot contribute to changing current societal conditions without imagining what a new society (or aspect of it) might look like.

Civic Storytelling

Storytelling conveys information, emotions, or concepts through narratives that may incorporate characters, events, and plots. Storytelling is crucial in civic learning because it can connect people emotionally and intellectually with complex societal challenges. By intertwining personal narratives, larger societal forces, and popular culture, civic storytelling prompts individuals to establish a personal connection with civic concerns (Jenkins et al., 2020; Mirra & Garcia, 2023). Civic storytelling has been described as a group of approaches to provide young people with tools to express their lived experiences, voice social issues, and advocate for change. Greene and colleagues (2018), for example, argue that telling stories contributes to fostering a sense of community and empowerment and to emphasizing critical consciousness, community organizing, and social justice. Telling civic stories about situations of oppression has also been described as a form of activism (Greene et al., 2018), connecting personal narratives to broader sociopolitical contexts. Youth who engage in civic storytelling—by building fictional narratives or sharing their own stories—can reclaim, reshape, or reaffirm their identities as civic actors.

Setting Up the Workshops

This study employed design-based research (DBR), an approach focusing on real-world testing of multiple design iterations to understand learning phenomena. DBR involves successive cycles of data collection, contextual consideration, intervention adjustment, and methodological review (Hoadley & Campos, 2022). Through four consecutive implementations of civic design workshops over a year (see Figure 1), adolescents from Santa Ana and Rio engaged in imaginative activities related to self-identified *limit-situations* (Freire, 1970), with each workshop informing the findings of the next one. Adolescents (thirteen to sixteen years old) in both cities were recruited through partner community organizations; gender and age balance were kept whenever possible. At Santa Ana, all thirteen participants (three in iteration 1 and ten in iteration 2) were of Latine background with roots in various Central American countries such as Mexico, Honduras, and Guatemala. In Rio, of a total of seventeen participants (eight in iteration 3 and nine in iteration 4), fourteen were Black or Brown with roots either in Rio or in cities in the northeast of Brazil.

All workshop sessions were recorded and transcribed using Zoom and Brazilian Portuguese-specific services. Interview data underwent topical coding, where similar excerpts were grouped into topics without a predetermined scheme. Workshop data underwent exploratory topical and process coding approaches to identify main topics, standpoints, tensions, and decisions, thus generating themes for further analysis.

The Workshops

The length and specific procedures of each iteration varied and changed throughout the implementation of the workshops based on intensive data collection and analysis, which

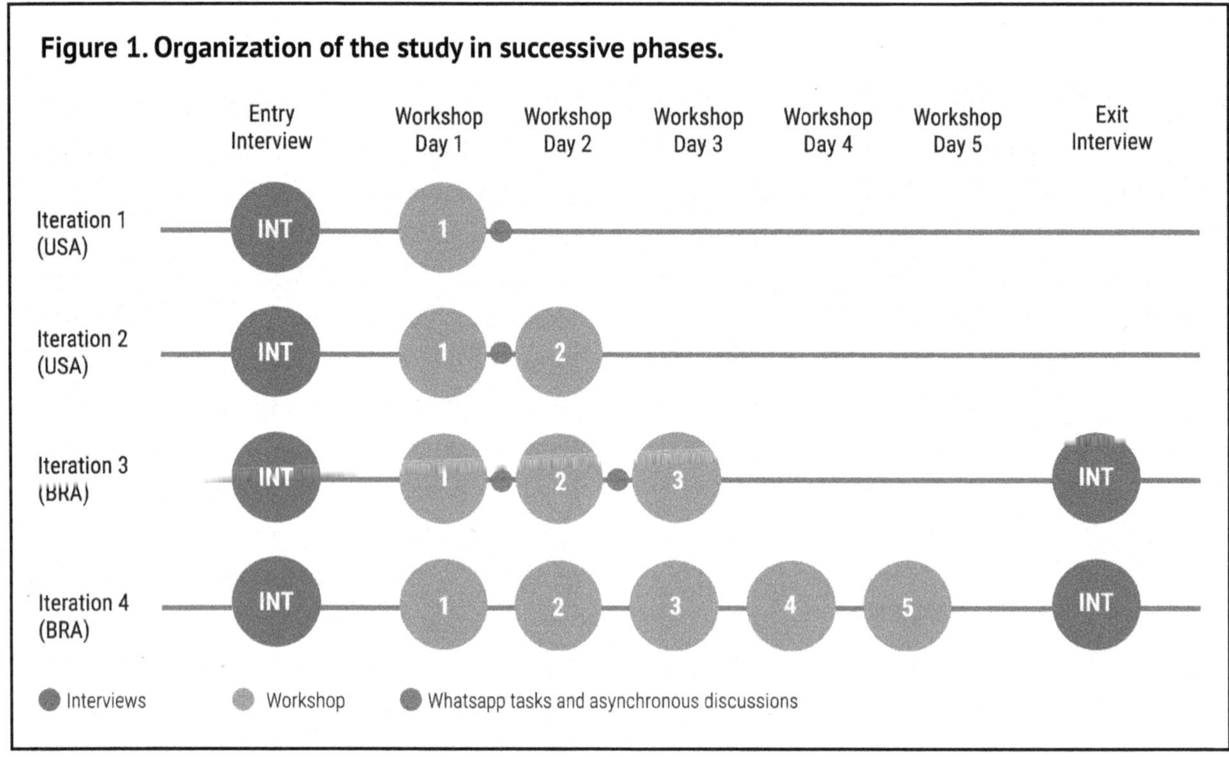

Figure 1. Organization of the study in successive phases.

characterizes the DBR approach. Below, some of the procedures utilized in iteration 4 (Rocinha, Brazil, which built on prior phases) are outlined. Iteration 4 spanned five days, each lasting 2.5 hours, with daily plans focusing on leveling participants' knowledge, fostering wild imagination, or grounding adolescents in solid critiques of lived experiences.

1. **Thematic Card Games:** Adolescents engaged in a card game addressing local challenges and potential solutions, fostering knowledge sharing and deep discussions. In all versions of the workshop, card decks and rule sets were deployed at the beginning of the activities to promote conversations, reveal opinions and standpoints among participants, and elicit new themes that were dear to the group. This procedure is based on Paulo Freire's concept of *generative themes* (1970), topics collected from the student population that are powerful enough to promote dialogue and anchor learning.
2. **Wicked Problems:** Complex societal issues were tackled using visual representations like causal loop diagrams and concept maps, facilitating analysis and understanding of topics.
3. **Mapping and Counter-Mapping:** Participants mapped localities and challenges, then dream mapped to reimagine physical spaces, fostering critical and imaginative fluencies.
4. **Seeing What You Think:** Generative AI platforms (e.g., Midjourney) were used to materialize participants' dreams and wishes. Through simple text prompts, adolescents explored possibilities, sparking reflective conversations and revisions based on lived experiences.

Santa Ana (California, USA)

Santa Ana is a crossroads of intense cultural diversity and a strong Latine identity. The city has a youthful population, with a median age of around 31 years, and faces severe socioeconomic challenges such as gang violence and homelessness.

Iterations at Santa Ana started with adolescents playing a game with a deck of cards (Figure 2). Throughout the four iterations, new cards were added and eliminated and, most important, rules for how to play them were co-developed between researcher and participants. As expected, themes reflecting major topics of social justice emerged at each site. For example, at Santa Ana, conversations generated during the card game phase revolved around the homeless population of the city and its alleged connections with the increase in gang violence.

The card game was readily followed by the deeper dive activity, in which participants were divided into two groups to 1) talk about a social problem, 2) build a diagram of connections representing a "wicked problem," 3) watch videos about said social problem to dive deeper into its complexities, 4) return to the diagram to represent further insights, and finally 5) present their diagrams to the group, followed by a discussion. For stage 3 of the activity, the group watched YouTube videos portraying in-depth stories of homeless people in California, the reasons behind their current situations, and their struggle for better living conditions. Consider the dialogue below:

> **Fabio**: What else do you know about homelessness?
>
> **Carmen:** All those people are unhygienic. They smell a lot.
>
> **Evo:** They do drugs. Pot. Use plastic water bottles that people leave on the road.

The answers above reveal how participants' accounts are usually based on deficit views or

Figure 2. Initial version of the card game activity, with cards made by participants.

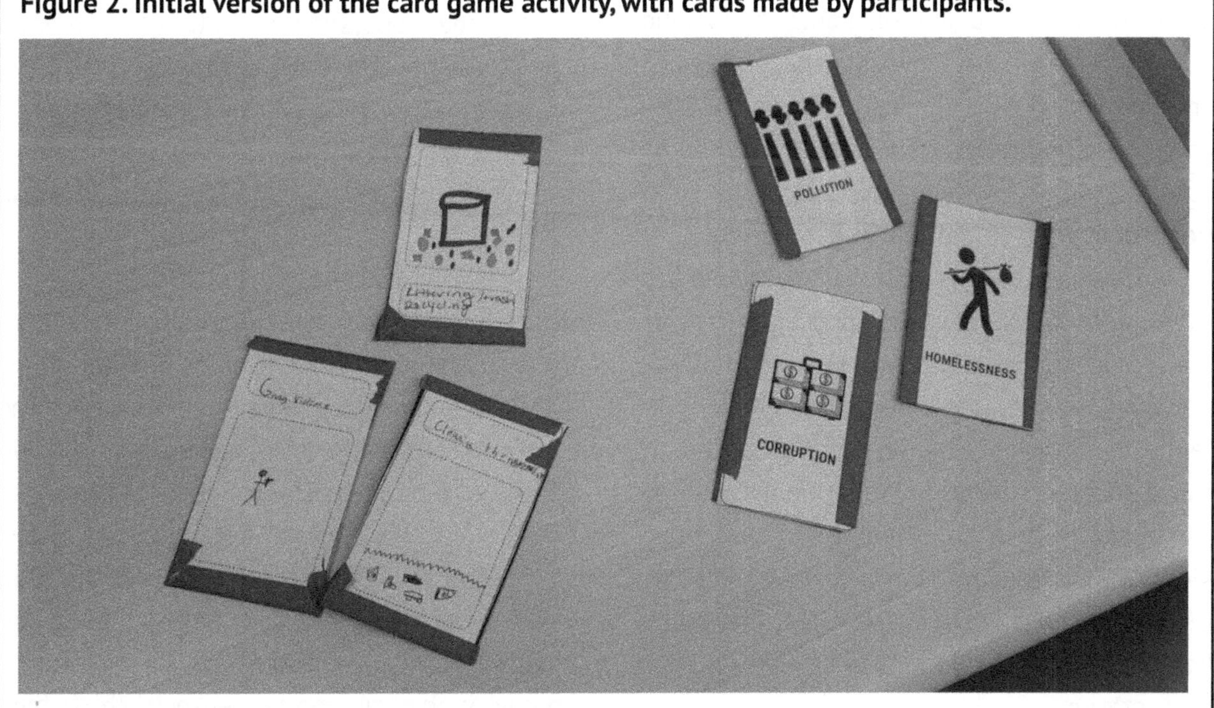

derogatory assumptions about homeless populations, as evidenced by words such as "unhygienic," "problems," and "drugs." Conversely, after the deeper dive and especially after watching real-life homeless men and women speaking to the camera, participants' words became not more structured but, most important, more empathetic toward the subject. Consider the two examples below:

> [The] reasons why they're homeless is because they lose their jobs [. . .] because of bankruptcy of companies. They have bad hygiene, so no one wants to help them.

The redesign activity brought together pieces of knowledge built by participants in the two days of the workshop. In this segment, adolescents were asked to give form to the ideas they had verbalized so far that would mitigate the limit-situations lived by the homeless. Additionally, the exercise prompt suggested that they gather ideas from all previous activities—from the card game to wicked problem diagrams—by looking into all artifacts that now furnished the walls around them. The prompt also clarified that they could use their imagination freely but would be asked to explain why and how a particular solution would work on the challenges discussed.

After completing a gallery walk around the room and taking several notes, participants started designing what they understood as initiatives with the potential to reduce the challenge of homelessness. Artifacts produced by the participants ranged from a highly detailed campus with housing, hospital, and other services to a network of free showers around town. Beyond artifacts, gains in civic learning could be seen in the observations that followed each presentation:

> For that idea, some homeless people actually get claustrophobic after being out on the streets for so long. So we'd have to think about that—many windows if they are going to be in enclosed spaces. (Claire, Santa Ana, Day 2).

The intervention above highlights how civic storytelling and design were instrumental for considering trade-offs and potential risks of one specific design. It also foregrounded Claire's own research about the lived experiences of homeless people during the deeper dive activity, when she searched for stories on the web.

By the end of the second day, adolescents started to tell stories—real and imagined—about the homeless populations surrounding their homes. These stories are evidence of how their once deficit views (unhygienic and drug users) evolved into more empathetic ones:

> They don't get enough resources. People don't ask for their consent on doing things or moving their stuff. [. . .] if they need food, shelter or if they have mental health problems . . . or those who have children: who can take care of [them]? They don't want them to be unsafe in the streets.

Rocinha (Rio, Brazil)

Rio de Janeiro, Brazil, harbors significant inequality, with about 10 percent of its population residing in *favelas* (i.e., slums, in Portuguese). The most iconic favela, Rocinha, houses over 100,000 people who often lack basic services like sanitation and security. Rocinha has also been historically plagued by armed violence and the drug trade. Government initiatives have aimed to improve infrastructure, but some critique the focus on improving physical aspects over social challenges.

In iterations 3 and 4, held at a public library in the heart of the favela, notions of citizenship were rooted in the *favelado*[1] identity and the idea that Rocinha is a "City within the City of Rio." In Brazil, favelas are highly segregated spaces—physically, socially, and politically—that suffer from exclusion and prejudice from residents of the *asphalt society*.[2] During the card game, one participant explained some of the factors that create an "infrasociety" at Rocinha:

> There's no social justice here. You look at us, and you look at a guy from Copacabana. The difference is big. If you look in the newspapers, there's no good thing about Rocinha. We have a lot of good things happening here [...]. People judge us by things that happened here.

In her response, the participant compares herself with a resident of Copacabana, an upper-middle-class neighborhood in Rio. The mention of "what happened here" refers to the gang wars that often happen at Rocinha. This us-and-them psyche was manifested by most of the participants and revealed an identity formed not only by affirmation but mainly by exclusion.

Among the activities held at Rocinha, the fourth version of the card game (the game evolved through participants' direct input from iterations 1 through 4) included a series of imagination prompts that, used in conjunction with wicked problem diagrams and maps of the favela, gave rise to highly charged, deeply rooted, and personal civic stories (see Figure 3). From societal issues identified by themselves, adolescents created characters and fictional narratives that reflected personal situations of oppression. Consider the summary of the stories for each group below, voiced by adolescents themselves:

> **Group 1:** We talked about gender inequality and created a multiverse story. In this other universe, everything is upside down: LGBTQIA+ people are considered the standard people of society, and straight people are treated as abnormal people. Rodrigo is a straight man and thus abnormal in this reality. Rodrigo likes girls and is the most popular person in school, but in this universe, being a popular person is considered negative, and nerds are seen as positive. One day, Rodrigo looks into his bathroom mirror and sees that there's another world behind it, where LGBTQ+ people are frowned upon. Rodrigo needs to decide what to do with his findings. But opening that door caused ripples in both worlds.

> **Group 2:** Our theme is racism and violence. Our history happens in the present but with a connection to the past, because racism has been around for a long time. Marcela is a trans, Black, and *nordestina*[3] woman who migrated to Rio and went to live in Rocinha. Marcela decides to move into a pension, where she is offered free housing in exchange for work as a maid. The owner of the pension, Alberto, is a 38-year-old white man who initially treats Marcela with kindness but soon starts showing signs of racism, prej-

1. A derogatory word in Portuguese for a Black woman.
2. Middle and upper classes or simply those who do not live in favelas, which are often located on hills.

3. "Nordestino" refers to people from the northeast of Brazil, a region known for poverty and drought. The recent history of Brazil saw frequent migration waves from the Northeast to cities such as Rio and São Paulo. Such migrants make up the bulk of Rocinha's population.

> udice, and xenophobia against her: "For a Black woman, you're actually pretty, *neguinha.*[4]" Marcela suspects that a dark spirit moves Alberto's actions. One day, sad and exhausted, she sees a little bug trying to escape from the window. When she approaches the bug, Marcela notices it's a tiny fairy. Could she do something to change that story?

Both stories are examples of how elements of identity and historicity were manifested during iteration 4. For example, group 1 manifested how adolescents experience gender differences in the school environment and how sometimes a single "world" may house multiple normal and abnormal, mirrored realities. Similarly, group 2's narrative reflects participants' own historicity as the first generation born in Rio from migrant parents and shows the prejudice of white men toward other *nordestino* migrants.

The stories created by participants were a structural element that supported the whole workshop experience. After each activity, stories were changed and new narrative elements added. First, after a short introduction to generative AI prompt engineering, participants generated images that represented their stories (see Figure 4). This move allowed adolescents to go further in the narrative by discussing additional elements such as race, gender, environment, and even magical companions.

Groups were then asked to build a diagram of connections and to think about how such elements impacted the two stories they had been creating so far. New evidence came in various forms from personal stories to experiences lived by friends and from major news to YouTube videos. The facilitation team also contributed information about the two chosen topics (e.g., a *New York Times* reporter in Rio sent voice messages to

4. A derogatory word in Portuguese for a Black woman.

Figure 3. Card decks containing imagination prompts to facilitate civic storytelling.

Figure 4. AI-generated images representing aspects of two stories.

the group recounting her coverage of gender inequality in Rocinha during the pandemic). Consider how one participant added to the diagram her experience as a Black girl in a cosmetics store:

> My mother and I went to O Boticário.[5] It's big and there's security. My mother is Black and the security man started following us . . .

Similarly, the excerpt that follows was taken from a larger dialogue held when groups presented their diagrams.

After being questioned by other participants about why her group drew an arrow toward "Religion and Culture" in a poster about the causes of gender-based hate crimes inside Rocinha, an adolescent responded: "People say that God said he doesn't like LGBT people, people who like other genders."

The excerpts above reveal how participants were able to go beyond rote descriptions of common situations and shallow solutionism (i.e., mechanist and simplistic forms of thinking about a problem, such as "if this, then that") and engage their own personal narratives to understand larger societal phenomena.

Discussion

Civic education comes in many flavors in the United States and Brazil. Although such approaches do have enough particularities to set them apart, they all carry the torch of preparing learners for engaging with representative democracy and the civic space. This, per se, represents a pressing educational challenge: how might schools contribute to informing and

5. A major Brazilian cosmetics brand.

preparing citizens for democratic life without proper funding and conceptual clarity, as well as highly irregular offerings, a curriculum that privileges factual knowledge, and a focus on grinding for standardized tests (Garcia & Mirra, 2023)? Moreover, how might educators and policy makers open space for pedagogies that privilege complacency over action?

The answer might rest upon going beyond the standard ELA curriculum and practices. ELA—as well as its Brazilian analogue—affords the creation of unique learning environments where students can develop critical thinking skills through consuming and creating stories. It is precisely this type of flexible, protean learning environment that may be fruitful for significant term civic imagination experiences. In the absence of structured civic education curricula in several parts of the US and Brazil, ELA is often the single chance to develop long-term projects that blend criticality and imagination and discuss in depth how power, resources, and opportunities are so poorly distributed in communities and nations. And even more importantly, for adolescents from low-income backgrounds, such as the ones from Santa Ana and Favela da Rocinha, ELA might be the only space in the curriculum in which their own stories can be further elaborated, reflected upon and, hopefully, recreated.

Some principles, however, need to guide this endeavor. First, not all stories are created equal nor will any form of storytelling lead to critical civic imagination. In this study, adolescents used their own *historicity* and *identity* as vehicles for learning about social issues before jumping into creating fantastic alternative scenarios. In this process, the facilitator guided adolescents into recognizing and discussing deficit views, avoiding shallow explanations to social phenomena and, most importantly, steering the learning process away from mere—yet beautiful—idealizations of what is foreign or dystopian (Nooney & Brain, 2019).

Second, ELA interventions designed to promote social justice learning must take into account not only curricular and educational aspects but also broader political, ethical, and sociocultural dimensions (Gutierrez et al., 2016) and reach beyond normative, factual knowledge. Instead, they ought to underscore the importance of unconventional, non-factual knowledge that can be a catalyst for challenging existing power structures, systems of inequality, and conventional wisdom. Encouraging students to tell and create their own stories—much as Paulo Freire did since the mid-1950s—might just be the first step.

Works Cited

Freire, P. (2000). *Pedagogy of the oppressed* (M. B. Ramos, Trans.). Continuum. (Original work published 1970)

Garcia, A., & Mirra, N. (2023). Other suns: Designing for racial equity through speculative education. *Journal of the Learning Sciences, 32*(1), 1–20.

Gotlieb, R., Jahner, E., Immordino-Yang, M. H., & Kaufman, S. B. (2016). How social-emotional imagination facilitates deep learning and creativity in the classroom. In R. A. Beghetto & J. C. Kaufman (Eds.), *Nurturing creativity in the classroom* (2nd ed., pp. 308–336). Cambridge University Press.

Greene, M. (1993). Imagination, community and the school. *Review of Education, Pedagogy, and Cultural Studies, 15*(3–4), 223–231.

Greene, S., Burke, K. J., & McKenna, M. K. (2018). A review of research connecting digital storytelling, photovoice, and civic engagement. *Review of Educational Research, 88*(6), 844–878.

Gutiérrez, K. D., & Jurow, A. S. (2016). Social design experiments: Toward equity by design. *Journal of the Learning Sciences, 25*(4), 565–598.

Headrick Taylor, K. (2017). Learning along lines: Locative literacies for reading and writing the city. *Journal of the Learning Sciences, 26*(4), 533–574.

Hipolito-Delgado, C. P., & Zion, S. (2017). Igniting the fire within marginalized youth: The role of critical civic inquiry in fostering ethnic identity and civic self-efficacy. *Urban Education, 52*(6), 699–717.

Hoadley, C., & Campos, F. C. (2022). Design-based research: What it is and why it matters to studying online learning. *Educational Psychologist, 57*(3), 207–220.

Ito, M., Soep, E., Kligler-Vilenchik, N., Shresthova, S., Gamber-Thompson, L., & Zimmerman, A. (2015). Learning connected civics: Narratives, practices, infrastructures. *Curriculum Inquiry, 45*(1), 10–29.

Jenkins, H., Peters-Lazaro, G., & Shresthova, S. (Eds.). (2020). *Popular culture and the civic imagination: Case studies of creative social change*. New York University Press.

Kahne, J., & Middaugh, E. (2009). Democracy for some: The civic opportunity gap in high school. In J. Youniss & P. Levine (Eds.), *Engaging young people in civic life* (pp. 29–58). Vanderbilt University Press.

Mihailidis, P. (2018). Civic media literacies: Re-imagining engagement for civic intentionality. *Learning, Media and Technology, 43*(2), 152–164.

Mirra, N., & Garcia, A. (2023). *Civics for the world to come: Committing to democracy in every classroom*. W. W. Norton & Company.

Nooney, L., & Brain, T. (2019). A "speculative pasts" pedagogy: where speculative design meets historical thinking. *Digital Creativity, 30*(4), 218–234.

Coalitional Civic Literacies: Tracing Urban Migrant Girls' Democratic Sense-Making in Two Virtual Inquiry Communities

ANKHI G. THAKURTA

On July 21, 2021, a group of Indonesian American girls based in a large Northeastern city join me (an Indian American scholar-practitioner) on Zoom. After we warmly greet each other, I invite the youth to discuss any civic issues that are impacting their communities. As we are convening amid the COVID-19 pandemic, they begin organically reflecting on how this crisis is impacting people in and beyond their communities. One youth, for instance, expresses concern about uneven levels of masking she has observed in her city. She notes that this practice is central to keeping "everyone safe," especially those with preexisting health conditions. Another girl, tracking the spread of COVID-19 in her family nation of Indonesia, highlights its effects on other vulnerable populations (e.g., the elderly). As these girls sense-make about the effects of the pandemic, they strive to understand its full scope by imaginatively assuming the perspectives of those with experiences different from their own.

A few days later, I'm on Zoom again with another group of youth: predominantly Bihari internal migrant girls who are based in an Indian megacity. I invite them, as I did the Indonesian American girls, to reflect on civic issues they are noticing. They, too, begin discussing the effects of COVID-19 on multiple populations. One girl observes how schools are closed even though other parts of society are opening. She wonders: "If importance are given to all the departments, why . . . not given to the schools?" Another youth notes how deepening economic precarities in her neighborhood are contributing to rising rates of child marriage. Like their US-based peers, the girls on this call are demonstrating their curiosity and care for multiple groups (e.g., students, neighborhood girls being positioned for marriage) whose experiences entangle with, but also diverge from, their own.

These two vignettes foreground how urban migrant girls from India and the US—two of the world's largest and most inequitable democracies—engaged in civic learning in two virtual out-of-school inquiry communities. Though separated by geographic and cultural divides, these young people faced comparable forms of civic marginalization in their home nations (e.g., economic instabilities, vulnerabilities to COVID-19, heteropatriarchy). As culturally minoritized transborder youth, they also navigated sociocultural exclusions amid deepening hegemonic nationalisms in both nations (Garcia & De Rook, 2021). These included US white supremacist movements and Indian pivots toward Hindu nationalism.

While the girls negotiated multiple marginalities, they were not *themselves* marginal figures. Across the inquiry communities, they mobilized their experiential knowledges and multiple literacies for civic learning. This essay highlights one dimension of their meaning making by exploring their *coalitional civic literacies*—that is, literate practices through which they explored how those beyond their communities negotiated civic injustices. It emphasizes how they did so by transacting with civic texts (e.g., poetry, maps), rendering civic experiences beyond their own. Girls' coalitional civic literacies in conversation with these texts revealed their capacities for envisioning linkages across diverse struggles and orientations to working alongside others for more just civic futures.

In what follows, I discuss the theoretical underpinnings of *coalitional civic literacies*. After describing my study, I trace how youth in the two inquiry groups mobilized their coalitional civic literacies in conversation with two texts—the poem "Identity Card" in the US and a map depicting urban racial segregation in India. I conclude with the pedagogical implications of these findings.

Coalitional Civic Literacies

My understanding of youths' *coalitional civic literacies* draws on Campano et al.'s (2013) discussion of *coalitional literacies*—a term arising from their work in a research-practice partnership in which university researchers based in a large Northeastern city conduct educational research alongside local Black, Latine, and Asian communities. As a doctoral student, I was a member of this partnership; as I describe later, a portion of the project I discuss here arises from my work in this community.

As partnership members primarily research issues of educational equity and access, their work entails centering multiple perspectives and learning across identificational and experiential boundaries. Campano et al. (2013) describe these cross-border forms of knowledge building and communication as coalitional literacies or

> . . . critical social practices whereby community members enact language and literacy across cultural boundaries in order to learn from others, be reflective with respect to social location, foster empathy, cultivate affective bonds, and promote inclusion in the service of progressive change. (p. 315)

This concept helps frame my discussion of how urban migrant girls in my study cultivated their coalitional civic literacies by learning about sociopolitical issues impacting communities beyond their own. Unlike the researchers in Campano et al.'s (2013) project, they did not directly engage with those communities; rather, they learned from their engagements with textual representations of them in diverse texts. I thus build on Campano et al.'s (2013) concept to consider how literacy curricula can invite youth to cultivate their coalitional civic literacies—a precursor to imagining more just conditions for themselves and others.

Transnational Girlhoods

I also anchor this work in transnational girlhood perspectives (Vanner, 2019). Drawing on transnational feminism (Anzaldúa, 1999; Mohanty, 2013), this highlights globally marginalized girls as sociopolitical actors whose lives are constrained by intermeshing oppressions (e.g., heteropatriarchy, colonialism) (Vanner, 2019).

Central to this perspective is the concept of intersectionality—deriving from Black feminism, this underscores how girls exist at the nexuses of "systems of domination whose effects doubly or triply constrain individuals at the intersection of multiple subordinated identity categories" (Vanner, 2019, p. 118).

A transnational girlhoods lens highlights, too, marginalized girls' agentic capacities as actors and meaning makers. Discussing US girls of color (GoC) literacies, for example, Player and González Ybarra (2022) echo transnational girlhoods perspectives by observing how Black, Asian, Latine, Indigenous, and other marginalized girls generate literacies about the world that are "rooted in their cultural, linguistic, raced, and gendered experiences" (p. 1665).

Relatedly, other transnational girlhoods-aligned scholars emphasize how marginalized girls draw on their experiential knowledges and multiliterate repertoires to pursue social change. Taft (2011), for example, notes the following about the political lives of girls in the Americas:

> . . . from the young Zapatistas with the braids and bandanas who climbed the fence at the WTO protests in Cancun to throw flowers at the police to the U.S. high school students designing curriculums to educate their peers about child labor and sweatshops, teenage girls in the Americas are participating in a variety of struggles for social justice. (p.3; cited in Vanner, 2019, p. 112)

Drawing on transnational girlhoods, I underscore how urban migrant girls' intersectional identities (e.g., ethnicity, class, race, religion, gender) positioned them to face uniquely situated civic oppressions in their nations. Simultaneously, I use the lens to foreground the knowledges they mobilized for literacy-infused civic learning—conceptions of the world that underscored their critical sociopolitical capacities.

Study Overview

This essay draws on a comparative case study (Bartlett & Varvus, 2017) that examined the civic identities, learning, and literacies of Indonesian American girls and Indian Bihari internal migrant girls. These youth (aged between fourteen and seventeen years old) were based in two cities with deep migration histories. Our collaboration arose from our existing relationships. In the US, I was a doctoral researcher on the partnership described by Campano et al. (2013). Through my involvement, I cultivated close relationships with Indonesian American girls who were on the frontlines of conducting educational research. Observing their passionate social engagement, I was inspired to form an out-of-school community in which they could further nurture their vibrant civic perspectives. After I recruited six youths, they welcomed two additional girls from their wider networks to join my study.

My work with the Indian girls began a little more distantly. Since 2020, I had worked remotely as an educational volunteer with a non-governmental organization (NGO) that served them and other marginalized youth in their city. In my role, I provided girls with virtual asynchronous activities (e.g., written reflections) through which they contemplated local civic issues (e.g., urban poverty, gender disparities). As I poured over youths' assignments, I was struck by their fierce and critical social imaginations. I thus solicited permission from the NGO to develop a virtual literacy inquiry space in which they could, like their US counterparts, explore their democratic perspectives. With the help of the organization, I recruited five girls into the India side of my study.

Curricula for Civic Coalition Building

In this project, I employed practitioner inquiry (Cochran Smith & Lytle, 2009)—that is, a method in which educators theorize issues of practice (Cochran-Smith & Lytle, 2009). As practitioner research is often conducted alongside those most impacted by the issues under study (Campano et al., 2022), it is a democratic approach to knowledge production positioning youth, families, and other community stakeholders ". . . as creators of knowledge with agency to inform and change the work in the classroom and . . . research" (Wissman, 2011, p. 413). Finally, practitioner inquiry is committed to social justice and "breaking inequitable patterns" in the education system (Campano et al., 2013, p. 104).

My use of practitioner research reflected my larger aim of supporting my youth partners' civic learning. I thus constructed two separate virtual out-of-school inquiry communities that were anchored by literacy curricula that I designed and which invited youth to cultivate their civic perspectives (Thakurta, 2023, 2024). While the curricula for each community was distinct and connected to youths' contextual realities, they similarly emphasized three focal areas:

- How girls' intersectional identities connect to their civic roles;
- How girls' democratic priorities were shaped by their community connections in and beyond urban and national borders; and
- How they understood and shaped those communities through literacy.

Youth explored these areas through diverse literate activities (e.g., discussions; text-based engagements; composing).

Curricula on both sides of the study emphasized coalitional civic learning. I promoted this by centering diverse literary and nonfiction texts that highlighted narratives from social groups to which the youth themselves claimed membership (e.g., girls; migrants; cultural and racial minorities). For instance, in the US community, we read texts centering Asian American experiences (e.g., the graphic memoir *The Best We Could Do* by Vietnamese American author Thi Bui). Likewise, on the India side, we engaged with narratives of internal migration (e.g., *Somaru Misses Home* by Shivani Taneja, which is a picture book depicting an internal migrant youth's educational journey). Such texts enabled youth to deepen their understandings of issues impacting communities overlapping with their own. Additionally, to highlight a plurality of civic perspectives, we also engaged with texts centering the perspectives of those from other social groups (I discuss examples below). Curricular resources like these helped youth explore the democratic issues mattering to themselves and others, thereby bolstering their coalitional civic literacies. To further explore these practices, I next discuss examples from each inquiry community.

US: A Coalitional Reading of "Identity Card"

My first example stems from sessions in the US inquiry community during late May–early June 2021—a timeframe when the Israel-Palestine conflict intensified. The girls, who were observing Free Palestine protests in their city and on social media, wanted to deepen their understandings of it. As one youth noted, "I definitely need to educate myself more on the issue because I really don't know much about it." To respond to youths' inquiries, I introduced the situation through a focus on the poetry of

Mahmoud Darwish—one of Palestine's most beloved poets. After facilitating a discussion regarding a *Vox* article and video that mapped the broader contours of the conflict, we explored how Darwish used his poetry to centralize Palestinian yearnings for liberation. Though he suffered injustices like exile and incarceration for his art, we discussed how he held close the transformative potential of poetry by stating that "every beautiful poem is an act of resistance" (Darwish, quoted in Saber, 2024).

To explore Darwish's work, we read "Identity Card" (1964), one of his most celebrated compositions. The piece centers the voice of an ordinary Palestinian speaking directly to "an Israeli government official" (Behar, 2011, p. 196). Though speaking from a position of structurally enforced submission, the poet-author subverts this power dynamic by commandingly directing the official, "Write down!/I am an Arab" (Darwish, 1964). The rest of the composition similarly centers themes of dignity, self-determination, and resistance.

After reading the poem, the girls expressed their coalitional orientations toward it. Emma (names are pseudonyms), for example, traced parallels between the experiences of displaced Palestinians and US-based immigrants. Responding to a moment when the poet highlighted his oppressed "status," she noted,

> I feel like a lot of immigrants, especially *my family*, could relate to that as like—Um. Status is something that—I—I don't wanna speak on every immigrant, but a lot of immigrants are, like, worried about . . . and in this situation [the poet is] talking about like his class and stuff . . . I feel like that can be interpreted in many ways where everyone can connect to it.

For Emma, this moment illuminated some of the potentially similar ways Palestinians and immigrants negotiated structural oppressions. This was a coalitional move, since it represented her effort to understand and connect experiences of oppression across cultural boundaries (Campano et al., 2013).

Besides tracing continuities between the Palestinian struggle and barriers facing their own communities, the girls also used "Identity Card" to imaginatively assume the perspective of the Palestinian speaker. Noticing the oppressive conditions of coloniality rendered in the poem, a youth named Ruby observed,

> I feel like [Palestinians] are being discriminated against, and the government wants to take everything away from them.

Youth also coalitionally read the ending of the composition. Darwish's text concludes on a warning note: while the speaker positions himself as peaceful, he signals his willingness to fight oppression if he is provoked. A youth named Monica was drawn to this part of the poem, noting,

> I liked the last few lines . . . I think that it shows kind of passive aggressiveness but also trying to be a better person, and not like, letting your past or the people who have wronged you . . . but also trying to be strong and fighting for yourself.

In her reading, Monica used second person (e.g., "your") to clarify the perspective of the poet for the rest of the group. She invited those of us on the call to understand how the speaker strove for goodness within conditions of injustice but also refused to submit to them (e.g., "fighting for yourself"). This coalitional move, which compelled the rest of us to consider the interpretive and experiential horizons of the speaker, deepened our feelings of empathy for Palestinians and a sense of solidarity with their cause.

India: Reading Urban Inequities across Borders

The second examples I'll share stem from sessions in the India-side inquiry community when we explored the spatial dimensions of sociopolitical injustice. Most girls resided in urban slums where systemic oppressions shaped their material environments (e.g., inadequate housing, unsanitary living conditions). Thus, they were especially interested in how civic inequities were perpetuated through space.

I responded to their interests by facilitating an inquiry into mapmaking—that is, the practice of producing (multi)literate representations of space. We first discussed how maps were not objective representations of the world but rather were positioned texts that could reify power asymmetries. For example, we talked about how mainstream maps (e.g., the Mercator Projection) have historically solidified Eurocentric understandings of world geographies. Concurrently, we considered how maps could perform liberatory functions like critically foregrounding (and thus problematizing) the spatialization of injustice. During two February 2022 sessions, for example, we read a map rendering the segregation of Black American communities in my city—one of the most racially segregated contexts in the US. To introduce this text to India-based youth, I briefly discussed categories of racial difference in the US that were highlighted on the map key. Youth then asked clarifying questions. During one session, for example, a girl named Indira said: "Di [sister], I want to know who are Latino and Hispanic." This led to a longer discussion about US-based racial categories.

As we then discussed the map further, the girls were curious about whether the spatial segregation of African Americans were rooted in US history. In response, I briefly explained the transnational history of slavery as well as the social, legal, and political underpinnings of anti-Blackness in the US. These contextual framings prompted youth to contemplate the spatial distribution of African American communities in my city through a critical lens. In one session, for example, a girl named Zara asked: "Why are they treated like this, the Black people?" Similarly, in the next session, Indira wondered:

> **Indira:** Di, why they have made a different place or a different area for the Black people to live, because in the map, by looking at the map, I can see that Black community lives together or in a particular area? It's because of them only, because of the discrimination they live in that area, because everyone is like that only, they don't feel safe?
>
> **AGT:** That is—
>
> **Indira:** Yes.
>
> **AGT:** No, no. Go ahead. Finish your question.
>
> **Indira:** Or the countrymen has decided that this area should be for them, and they would live there?

In this exchange, Indira used the map to trace connections between space, power, and racial injustice. Her inquiries sparked a longer discussion about the sociopolitical underpinnings of racial segregation in the city and how these especially impacted the Black community. Indira's questions provided evidence of her coalitional civic literacies—that is, her attempts to better understand how civic inequalities confronting Black Americans in the US left visible markings on distributions of urban space. Also, by grappling in our group with the injustices confronting this community, she demonstrated a coalitional orientation to analyzing inequalities that transcended the boundaries of her city and nation.

Youth also used their coalitional readings of this US-based map to draw connections to their own contexts. Two girls, Maheen and Nazia, made the following observations:

> **Maheen:** In [our city]—there is some communities, caste-wise live . . . one group, then another . . . Muslim group, then Hindu group, different, different places, different caste live. I just see that.
>
> **AGT:** Excellent, excellent observation. . . . If you were to make a map, maybe, it might be interesting to make a map of even—the city that's based on caste, and what caste lives in what part of [our city] can tell us something about social inequality in the city, right? Or maybe even other parts of India.
>
> **Maheen:** I've seen in my locality, also.
>
> **AGT:** What have you seen?
>
> **Maheen:** I've just like caste system, live—in other, other places.
>
> **AGT:** And would you say you yourself are part of that system?
>
> **Maheen and Nazia (both):** Yes.
>
> **Nazia:** It's just the caste system. Rich, poor, middle-class families, they're all just located in different, different areas.

Here, Maheen and Nazia drew on a US-based text to foreground local forms of spatialized, caste-based stratification. Such theorizing was coalitional in the sense that it represented youths' efforts to "learn from others" and to highlight the convergences between manifestations of urban injustice in and beyond their city (Campano et al., 2013 p. 315). Such meaning making could, in turn, theoretically inform their imaginings of future collaborations alongside marginalized communities far beyond their own neighborhoods.

Educating toward Civic Coalitional Imaginaries

This essay explored how India and US-based urban migrant girls cultivated coalitional civic literacies through text-based engagements that inspired them to explore the experiences of marginalized communities beyond their own. Their meaning making in their two inquiry groups began shaping their civic coalitional imaginaries—that is, their capacities to empathetically explore the challenges faced by others and, by extension, to begin envisioning how to build a more just world for themselves *and* those distant individuals.

Though focusing on two groups of marginalized girls, this essay has implications for ELA/literacy educators serving youth across various settings. Amid deepening forms of geopolitical fragmentation worldwide, it is imperative for educators to centralize the perspectives of those dwelling beyond the localities, states, and even nations in their instruction. Doing so can orient youths' coalitional literacy and imagination building toward the complexities of our deeply unequal yet fundamentally shared world. In this essay, I provided a model of how text-based pedagogies can support this educational priority. For example, responding to current events and youths' interests in the two inquiry groups, I centered Mahmoud Darwish's artistry and a rendering of urban racial segregation. Educators might similarly draw inspiration from geopolitical events and student interests to select texts and other learning materials that render perspectives from communities beyond the students' own. These can include geographically distant communities or groups with whom their learners do not share social identities (e.g., the Indonesian American girls engaging with Palestinian poetry). As such selections can invite students to step beyond their own experiences, they might productively shape their coalitional civic literacies and imagining.

My second recommendation is for educators to foster students' coalitional civic imaginaries through diverse learning invitations. I highlighted here how the girls in my project did so through readings and shared discussions. Following the needs (and, indeed, leads) of their own students, they should design instruction inviting youth to center their "plurality of literacies" (Sánchez & Ensor, 2020, p. 276)—be these linguistic, aural, spatial, gestural, visual, or multimodal—to grapple with the civic realities impacting them and others (New London Group, 1996). This could be accomplished through activities like shared readings, discussions, and opportunities for youth to themselves construct "multiple authentic texts" (Sánchez & Ensor, 2020, p. 276).

Finally, educators must highlight the resources that youth themselves bring to the work of coalitional civic imagining. In this project, girls consistently summoned their abundant civic knowledges and multiple literacies as low-income urban transborder youth to explore the experiences of others. Educating toward coalitional civic imaginaries thus entails constructing opportunities for youth to consider how their own civic identities situate their public life and how these equip them to strive toward coalitional justice. I offer such suggestions as guidelines for teachers across borders who seek to undertake the messy, rewarding, and profoundly urgent work of cultivating more a more just civic future for all.

Works Cited

Anzaldúa, G. (1999). *Borderlands/La frontera.* Aunt Lute Books.

Behar, A. (2011). Mahmoud Darwish: Poetry's state of siege. *Journal of Levantine Studies, 1*(1), 189–199.

Campano, G., Ghiso, M. P., & Sánchez, L. (2013). "Nobody knows the…amount of a person": Elementary students critiquing dehumanization through organic critical literacies. *Research in the Teaching of English, 48*(1), 98–125. www.jstor.org/stable/24398648

Campano, G., Ghiso, M. P., & Thakurta, A. (2022). Community-based partnerships: Advancing epistemic rights through improvement research. In D. Peurach, J. L. Russell, L. Cohen-Vogel, & W. Penuel (Eds.), *The foundational handbook on improvement research in education* (pp. 189–210). Rowman & Littlefield.

Campano, G., Ghiso, M. P., Yee, M., & Pantoja, A. (2013). Toward community research and coalitional literacy practices for educational justice. *Language Arts, 90*(5), 314–326. www.jstor.org/stable/24574990

Cochran-Smith, M., & Lytle, S. L. (2009). *Inquiry as stance: Practitioner research for the next generation.* Teachers College Press.

Darwish, M. (1964). *Identity card.* https://tinyurl.com/2shyvrmj

Garcia, A., & de Roock, R. S. (2021). Civic dimensions of critical digital literacies: Towards an abolitionist lens. *Pedagogies: An International Journal, 16*(2), 187–201. https://doi.org/10.1080/1554480X.2021.1914058

Mohanty, C. T. (2013). Women workers and capitalist scripts: Ideologies of domination, common interests, and the politics of solidarity. In M. J. Alexander & C. T. Mohanty (Eds.), *Feminist genealogies, colonial legacies, democratic futures* (pp. 3–29). Routledge.

New London Group. (1996). A pedagogy of multiliteracies: Designing social futures. *Harvard educational review, 66*(1), 60–92. https://doi.org/10.17763/haer.66.1.17370n67v22j160u

Player, G. D., & González Ybarra, M. (2022). Re-imagining literacy and language education for girls of color. *Urban Education, 57*(10), 1663–1672. https://doi.org/10.1177/00420859211003924

Saber, I. (2024, March 13). *"The war will end": Remembering Mahmoud Darwish, Palestine's poetic voice.* Al Jazeera. https://tinyurl.com/kcw6fs6f

Sánchez, L., & Ensor, T. (2020). "We want to live": Teaching globally through cosmopolitan belonging. *Research in the Teaching of English, 54*(3), 254–280. https://doi.org/10.58680/rte202030521

Taft, J. (2011). *Rebel girls: Youth activism and social change across the Americas.* New York University Press.

Thakurta, A. G. (2023). Solidarity-as-project: Charting democratic co-inquiries in an Asian American girl and woman-centric English education community. *English Education, 55*(4), 257–278. https://doi.org/10.58680/ee202332697

Thakurta, A. G. (2024). Reading and (re)writing democracy: Asian American girls claim civic space through literary inquiry. *English Teaching: Practice & Critique, 23*(3), 352–367. https://doi.org/10.1108/ETPC-09-2023-0124

Vanner, C. (2019). Toward a definition of transnational girlhood. *Girlhood Studies, 12*(2), 115–132.

Wissman, K. K. (2011). "Rise up!": Literacies, lived experiences, and identities within an in-school "other space." *Research in the Teaching of English, 45*(4), 405–438. https://doi.org/10.58680/rte201115255

Place-Based, Community-Engaged Learning in Challenging Contexts

SHANNA PEEPLES

Is anger a good reason to start a project? Anger felt better than despair as I faced the wave of restriction and censorship sweeping Texas schools in recent years. Legislators deemed anything "woke" subject to bans, with one representative creating a list of 850 books to challenge. Texas now leads the nation in book bans with some schools locking up entire libraries out of fear. This chilling effect across content areas produces a siege mentality among faculty.

As a university professor, I wondered how to counter this trend: *What if we could create our own texts?* With like-minded colleagues, I discussed the possibility of connecting with local leaders to develop "living textbooks" built on questions about where we live, who has lived here before, and what the land may remember that we have forgotten. This led us to the concept of *place-consciousness*. Place-consciousness in education means grounding learning in the local environment, culture, and experiences of a particular place. It involves developing awareness of how places shape us and how we shape them, connecting curriculum to students' immediate surroundings, exploring local history and ecology, and empowering students to actively engage with and care for their communities (Greenwood, 2013). This approach allows us to think deeply about our area and collaboratively build a *pedagogy of place* that uses our immediate environment and its people as a starting point to teach concepts across the curriculum (Azano, 2011). It emphasizes hands-on, real-world learning experiences, helping students to develop stronger ties to their community, it enhances appreciation for the natural world, and it creates a heightened commitment to serving as active, contributing members of their cities, towns, and villages.

This process counters current restrictions and equips young people with skills they'll need to participate in a complex, digital, and interconnected world. Grounding learning in contexts of place and space fosters deeper involvement and prepares learners to become active, responsible citizens in an increasingly global society. One example of how a specific place can illuminate broader historical and cultural narratives is the US highway Route 66.

Route 66, nicknamed the "Mother Road" by author John Steinbeck, is a historic 2,400-mile highway stretching from Chicago to Los Angeles. It played a central role in twentieth-century American history, particularly during the Great

Depression of the 1930s when it served as an escape route for impoverished farmers, known as "Okies," fleeing the Dust Bowl.

Growing up in Texas, which sits in the middle of Route 66 as it bends toward the Southwest states of New Mexico and Arizona, I was aware of its nostalgic appeal but needed more understanding of its deeper historical significance. My education largely overlooked the diverse communities along its path. For instance, more than half of Route 66 runs through 25 tribal nations (Beal, 2018), and its construction came at the cost of forced displacement of Indigenous peoples like the Comanche and Kiowa.

Similarly, I knew little about the Hispanic Los Barrios neighborhood in my hometown of Amarillo or the hidden history of segregated railroad workers known as *traqueros* (track workers). It wasn't until graduate school that I learned of my city's connection to the Green Book, a guide that helped Black motorists navigate safely through segregated America (Taylor, 2020).

This limited perspective exemplifies what Nigerian author Chimamanda Ngozi Adichie calls "the danger of a single story" (2009). When applied to civics education, this concept highlights the importance of embracing multiple perspectives and voices to understand our area's complex, multifaceted reality.

Much of the standard curriculum presents a singular, dominant narrative of a place's history, values, and institutions. The viewpoint often prioritizes the experiences and perspectives of those in power while marginalizing or erasing the stories of minority groups, oppressed communities, and dissenting voices. By presenting a single story of civic life, traditional texts risk perpetuating stereotypes, reinforcing power imbalances, and limiting students' understanding of their society's complexity.

Benefits of Place-Based Learning in a Fragmented and Distracted Time

As teachers, we've all felt the struggle of competing with smartphones, social media, and a world that seems daily to grow more complex. Localized learning approaches offer a fresh solution while addressing many obstacles unique to our digital age. Connecting academic content to our students' immediate surroundings unlocks a powerful source of engagement and motivation (Peeples, 2018; Sobel, 2004). This enhanced engagement often translates into improved performance across subjects, including reading, writing, math, science, and social studies (Lieberman & Hoody, 1998). As our students tackle real-world issues in their communities, they develop stronger critical thinking and problem-solving skills (Smith, 2002) while also learning to critically evaluate information sources—an essential skill in our information-saturated environment (Mihailidis, 2018; Mirra & Garcia, 2023).

According to Semken and Freeman (2008), place-conscious education seamlessly weaves together various subjects, creating rich, cross-curricular experiences that enhance teaching effectiveness and efficiency. Beyond academic benefits, this approach nurtures civic responsibility and deepens students' connections to their surroundings (Gruenewald & Smith, 2008). In our digital age, we cannot overstate the value of such localized engagement; it promotes face-to-face interactions and builds social connections, offering a powerful antidote to the growing trend of isolation that Putnam (2000) identified. Place-based learning, especially when it involves outdoor experiences, can help alleviate what Richard Louv (2008) calls "nature-deficit disorder." Engaging with nature through place-based activities can positively affect students' mental health and well-being

(Chawla, 2015), providing a much-needed balance to screen time and digital distractions.

This way of project-based learning, emphasizing multisensory experiences and varied forms of expression, can be particularly well-suited to neurodiverse learners. It organically accommodates a wide range of learning styles and abilities. For instance, while some students might shine when conducting oral history interviews, others could discover their forte in crafting visual maps of historical sites. Students on the autism spectrum often contribute uniquely detailed observations about architectural changes, unveiling insights that might otherwise go unnoticed.

In our politically polarized climate, place-based learning offers a unique opportunity to bridge divides by grounding discussions in shared experiences. By encouraging young people to engage with distinct place-conscious perspectives, you can help them develop greater cultural awareness and competence (Gruenewald, 2003). This method can foster a strong sense of area identity and belonging (Greenwood, 2013) while also preparing students to engage thoughtfully with global issues.

Global Competencies Embedded in Place-Based Learning

- **Digital Citizenship:** Students learn to navigate digital spaces responsibly and engage in constructive online dialogue by creating and sharing community stories online.
- **Data Literacy:** Collecting and analyzing local data equips students with crucial skills in statistical interpretation and evidence-based decision making.
- **Cross-Cultural Competence:** Students cultivate the cultural awareness and empathy essential for effective cross-cultural collaboration by exploring diverse local narratives.
- **Environmental Stewardship:** Local ecosystem studies instill a sense of planetary responsibility, preparing students to address future sustainability challenges.
- **Adaptive Problem Solving:** Navigating area partnerships cultivates flexible thinking for addressing evolving complex situations.

Preparing for Future Civic Engagement

Place-conscious learning equips young people with critical skills for future civic participation and global competence, as highlighted by the OECD's Program for International Student Assessment (PISA) (Schleicher, 2020). These kinds of projects develop core proficiencies that align closely with global competence, defined as the capacity to examine local and global issues, understand different perspectives, interact respectfully with others, and take action toward sustainability and collective well-being.

PISA results show that teachers can significantly foster these competencies, particularly for disadvantaged young people. Schools offering curricula that value global openness, provide inclusive learning environments, and prepare teachers for global competence instruction can help bridge gaps in intercultural learning opportunities.

By developing these competencies through place-conscious learning, we prepare all learners, regardless of their backgrounds, for effective participation in an interconnected global society. Teachers are then able to address immediate needs for a multifaceted and contextualized education and build a foundation for future civic engagement connecting the local to the global.

Countering the Single Story

The 2892 Miles to Go program exemplifies how Adichie's concept can be combined with place consciousness to create interdisciplinary civics learning that amplifies divergent voices. The project, initiated by writer and award winning educator Ashley Lamb-Sinclair, was inspired by a profound experience at a 2020 Healing Ceremony in Louisville, Kentucky. During the ceremony, held amid protests following Breonna Taylor's killing, city leaders revealed Louisville's hidden history as a former auction block for enslaved individuals.

> I never knew that every step I took in my own community stepped upon and over an opportunity to remember the humanity of the people who walked before us. And those steps also represented so many who lead work for change in the present. It was that moment when I realized that as long as these steps are taken without truly knowing the history of our land and the true stories of the people who lived and continue to live here, we will never escape the shame of our past, heal our present, or walk into a just future. (Lamb-Sinclair, 2021)

As a 2020 National Geographic Education Explorer tasked with developing the concept of "real-time learning," Lamb-Sinclair saw an opportunity to create a transformative educational experience. Motivated by the growing demand from educators and young activists for more equitable learning approaches, she founded 2892 Miles to Go—an initiative that connects current social justice activism, place-based narratives, and the real-time experiences of educators and youth.

The program's name symbolizes the 2,892 miles spanning the contiguous United States, with each mile representing countless untold stories that could reveal truths about race and equity in communities nationwide. The project, shaped by different voices and leaders including educators and youth from across the US, emphasizes the responsibility we all share in learning from those who came before us and contributing to the knowledge of those who will come after.

As a university professor and researcher, I sought to contribute to this transformative work by combining my research agenda of diversity, equity, inclusion, and belonging (DEIB) with my experiences as a writing teacher. By recommissioning the writing project site I direct, I found a creative way to engage people from the area in the research process and to amplify their voices through accessible storytelling tools.

For me, the process of creating this living textbook began with asking questions and seeking out regional leaders who could provide valuable insights and perspectives. Connecting with nonprofits, professional networks, and conference speakers is an effective way to locate partners who can lead this work. Involving people from the area with direct experiences or ties to the places you want to study is essential for creating authentic and meaningful content. When it comes to resources for sharing the stories, I ask myself three central questions:

- What do I have?
- Who do I know who can help me?
- What can I do with this information?

The mistake is trying to do it alone. The foundation for success is collaboration with partners who can connect you with people already working in the area you're interested in. Joining with technically savvy friends and colleagues helped me find solutions to the issues of how to capture interviews with people. A Diné documentarian, Ramona Emerson, helped us to understand how easily we could use basic film techniques like pans to show the places mentioned, and mid-range and close-ups in the interviews to create visual variety. You can edit that footage using free tools already installed on most brands of laptops.

By using the power of free interactive storytelling platforms like StoryMaps from ESRI (https://learn.arcgis.com/en/paths/teacher-resources/), smartphone video capabilities, and free online audio-sharing services, we created a place-conscious multimedia learning site that we shared on a university's National Writing Project page, freely accessible to anyone. This approach can help educators who might be hesitant to do this work inside their classrooms or with school resources. As described in the "2892 Miles to Go StoryMap Learning Guide" (2022), these textbooks are "voiced by many and rooted in collective wisdom," providing young people with the opportunity to learn history and culture directly from those who have lived it.

While the creation of the StoryMap was the main publication, ensuring its accessibility was equally important. Our partnership with a university's National Writing Project site proved instrumental in making our StoryMap freely accessible to everyone. By housing the project within this platform, we ensured students could access the content outside of school, regardless of their personal technology resources. This strategy broadened the reach of our place-based learning initiative and provided a model for how educational institutions can leverage existing resources to support locally engaged projects. The free, open-access nature of the StoryMap aligned with our goal of creating living textbooks that were truly accessible to all learners, further democratizing the educational experience.

Throughout the project, we navigated various obstacles and ethical considerations with meetings that fostered open communication, collaborative problem solving, and prioritizing the needs and histories of the communities we sought to highlight. By engaging members with multiple perspectives as active partners in the research process, we ensured that our work remained respectful, inclusive, and accountable to those whose stories we aimed to amplify.

Getting Started

Community-based learning connects young people with their communities, fostering civic engagement and active citizenship. This approach grounds education in regional realities, including history, environment, culture, and economy. To begin, invite students to observe and listen to their surroundings. These next steps and suggested questions can help you to explore your locale:

- Oral histories and interviews: Students interview area people about their experiences.
- Question: What was this place like when you were my age?
- Soundscapes: Create audio recordings of neighborhood sounds.
- Question: What do the sounds around us reveal about our neighborhood's relationships?
- Found objects: Collect nearby artifacts for discussion and writing prompts.
- Question: What can these objects teach us about our neighborhood's members and their history?

- Visual representations: Encourage sketches or drawings of significant neighborhood places.
- Question: How do these places make us feel, and why are they special?
- Digital storytelling: Use tools like Google Earth or ESRI's StoryMaps to create virtual tours.
- Question: How can we use technology to uncover and share our area's hidden stories?
- Community participation: Attend area events and festivals.
- Question: What do these events tell us about our area's values, and how can we contribute?

Educators facilitate reflection and action, allowing learners to wrestle with localized issues and develop confidence and agency. Engage parents and people from the area to tap into proximate sources of knowledge and strengthen school-community ties.

To make sure you can complete this project without inviting scrutiny, I offer this advice based on our Route 66 project:

- Identify supportive organizations, especially nonprofits already working with folks in the neighborhoods you'd like to explore.
- Collaborate on interdisciplinary, standards-aligned projects.
- Provide opportunities for place-conscious action through service-learning.

Place-conscious learning with critical consciousness acknowledges how history, politics, and power shape places (Gruenewald, 2003). Engaging with these realities, we help young people become informed, empathetic citizens ready to work toward a just and sustainable future.

Table 1. Ten strategies for navigating challenging contexts in place-based learning.

Strategy	**Description**
1. Frame as Local History	Present projects as explorations of area history and cultural heritage
2. Prioritize Primary Sources	Focus on primary sources, archival materials, and oral histories
3. Align with Curriculum Standards	Connect projects explicitly to state or national curriculum standards in ELA, civics, history, and geography
4. Engage Diverse Stakeholders	Involve a wide range of community members from the beginning of the project
5. Emphasize Student Agency	Frame projects as student-led inquiries into regional history and culture
6. Develop Clear Communication	Prepare positive messaging about the project's educational goals and benefits. Emphasize its unique ability to capture people and places
7. Create Supportive Networks	Form or join networks of educators engaged in similar work
8. Document Process and Outcomes	Thoroughly document the project process and student learning outcomes
9. Incorporate Multiple Perspectives	Include a range of perspectives on historical events or area issues You can create an acknowledgment of them as mentors and technical experts
10. Focus on Skill Development	Emphasize development of twenty-first century skills like digital literacy and critical thinking

Table 2. Empowering educators and communities through place-based learning.

Historical Connections	Cultural Connections	Economic Connections	Ecological Connections
Example inquiry question from our project How did Route 66 affect and shape the history of the Diné culture and communities it passed through?	*Example inquiry question from our project* How did Route 66 impact the cultural identity and community dynamics of the Los Barrios neighborhood?	*Example inquiry question from our project* How did Route 66 affect Black-owned businesses before, during, and after its construction and use?	*Example inquiry question from our project* What can we learn from our region's Indigenous communities about surviving climate change?
Questions you can apply to your community What decisive events or moments in history have shaped the development and identity of this place? How have different groups of people experienced and influenced the history of this community? What can we learn from the stories and experiences of the people who have lived and worked in this place throughout its history?	*Questions you can apply to your community* What diverse cultures and traditions exist in this community, and how have they shaped its identity and heritage? How do art, music, food, and other cultural expressions reflect this place's unique character and influences? How can we celebrate and learn from the cultural contributions of different groups within this community?	*Questions you can apply to your community* What industries or economic activities have been important to this community, and how have they shaped its development? How have changes in the broader economy (e.g., globalization, technological shifts) impacted this community? What economic challenges and opportunities does this community face today, and how are they connected to its history and location?	*Questions you can apply to your community* What natural features or ecosystems are important to this community, and how have they influenced its development and identity? How have human activities impacted the environment in this place, both positively and negatively? What challenges and opportunities does this community face regarding environmental sustainability and resilience, and how are these connected to larger regional or global issues?

Mapping the connections: Possibilities for your community

Framing your project as an exploration of the area's history and cultural heritage allows you to resist internal and external political pressures and position it as a celebration of regional identity. For example, in our Route 66 project, we emphasized the road's role in shaping nearby economies and cultures rather than explicitly framing it as a social justice initiative. This method allows for exploring complex issues while grounding the work in shared experiences of place.

The 2892 Miles to Go StoryMap was created by Shanna Peeples, Ramona Emerson, Melodie Graves, and Ruth DeAnda through a National Geographic Education grant project led by Ashley Lamb-Sinclair. The resource is hosted by the Route 66 Writing Project at West Texas A&M University.

Clear communication about your project's goals and methods is imperative. Consider developing an FAQ document that shows how your project enhances student learning and benefits the region. Creating or joining supportive networks of educators in organizations like the National Writing Project can provide valuable resources and moral support. These networks can offer strategies for addressing difficulties and sharing success stories. Documenting your project's process and outcomes through student reflections, diversified feedback, and concrete learning outcomes creates a record of its educational benefit. Such documentation can be a powerful resource if you must defend your work to administrators or others from the area. By incorporating multiple perspectives on historical events or area issues, you demonstrate a commitment to balanced inquiry. This plan of action can help counter accusations of bias or indoctrination. In our Route 66 project, we included voices from various ethnic, economic, and age groups to create a multifaceted narrative of the road's impact.

The key is to root your work deeply in your context, involve your community authentically, and always keep the focus on student learning and growth.

Localized learning projects serve a dual purpose: they deepen students' understanding of their present-day communities while simultaneously cultivating the skills necessary for active, informed citizenship in the future. These experiences, rich in opportunities for digital literacy, data analysis, cross-cultural communication, and adaptive problem solving, equip our youth with the tools they'll need to navigate and address the complex civic challenges that lie ahead.

Educators, researchers, and community organizations inspired by this vision can start in many ways. See Tables 1 and 2 for some strategies. The 2892 Route 66 StoryMap offers a compelling example of how educators can implement place-based, place-conscious in practice. We offer examples of promoting civic participation, social justice, and creative problem solving, even in the face of political attacks and censorship. By centering marginalized voices, collaborating with diverse partners, and leveraging accessible multimedia tools, it is possible to co-create living textbooks that inspire learners and communities to become active co-creators of knowledge and agents of change.

Works Cited

2892 Miles to Go. (2022). *2892 miles to go: Storymap learning guide for educators & youth.* https://storymaps.arcgis.com/collections/a3be16e5495344679e1baac600bad1aa?item=2

Adichie, C. N. (2009, July). *The danger of a single story* [Video]. TED. www.ted.com/talks/chimamanda_ngozi_adichie_the_danger_of_a_single_story

Azano, A. (2011). The possibility of place: One teacher's use of place-based instruction for English students in a rural high school. *Journal of Research in Rural Education, 26*(10), 1–12.

Bear, C. (2018, August 20). *From false advertising to cultural exchange: Native Americans, New Mexico, and Route 66.* National Trust for Historic Preservation. https://savingplaces.org/stories/from-false-advertising-to-cultural-exchange-native-americans-new-mexico-and-route-66

Chawla, L. (2015). Benefits of nature contact for children. *Journal of Planning Literature, 30*(4), 433–452.

Greenwood, D. (2013). A critical theory of place-conscious education. In R. B. Stevenson, M. Brody, J. Dillon, & A. Wals (Eds.), *International handbook of research on environmental education* (pp. 93–100). Routledge.

Gruenewald, D. A. (2003). The best of both worlds: A critical pedagogy of place. *Educational Researcher, 32*(4), 3–12.

Kerski, J. J. (2022). Online, engaged instruction in geography and GIS using IoT feeds, web mapping services, and field tools within a spatial thinking framework. *The Geography Teacher, 19*(3), 93–101. https://doi.org/10.1080/19338341.2022.2070520

Lamb-Sinclair, A. (2021, April 14). *2,892 miles to go—A geographic walk for justice.* National Geographic Education Blog. https://blog.education.nationalgeographic.org/2021/04/14/2892-miles-to-go-a-geographic-walk-for-justice/

Louv, R. (2008). *Last child in the woods: Saving our children from nature-deficit disorder.* Algonquin Books.

Mihailidis, P. (2018). Civic media literacies: Re-imagining engagement for civic intentionality. *Learning, Media and Technology, 43*(2), 152–164.

Mirra, N., & Garcia, A. (2023). *Civics for the world to come: Committing to democracy in every classroom.* W. W. Norton & Company.

Peeples, S. (2018). *Think like Socrates: Using questions to invite wonder & empathy into the classroom, grades 4–12.* Corwin.

Putnam, R. D. (2000). *Bowling alone: The collapse and revival of American community.* Simon & Schuster.

Schleicher, A. (2020, October 22). *Are students ready to thrive in an interconnected world? The first PISA assessment of global competence provides some answers.* OECD Education and Skills Today. https://oecdedutoday.com/students-ready-thrive-interconnected-world-first-pisa-assessment-global-competence/

Taylor, C. (2020). *Overground railroad: The Green Book and the roots of Black travel in America.* Abrams Press.

Theobald, P., & Curtiss, J. (2000). Communities as curricula. *Forum for Applied Research and Public Policy, 15*(1), 106–111.

Enacting Speculative Futures with Youth at Fan Conventions

KARIS JONES, M'MAH CISSE, ANAIS SANTIAGO & KIMONYE MAYS

When you enter the Javits Center for New York Comic Con (NYCC), you are greeted by a large banner that reads, "Welcome Home Heroes." Pushing your way through the crowd wearing brightly colored badges, your head is on a swivel as you take in the many posters and TV screens blasting promotions for new shows and books. As you weave between wizards and Spider-Men, you see people of all ages, ranging from babies in strollers to young girls dressed as Batman to grown men in full body suits. Piling onto a packed escalator, you peer past the checkered hats and purple wigs to see what waits below. The escalator deposits you on the show floor, a huge room filled with booths selling comics, plushies, art, pins, merch, clothing, and anything fandom-related you can imagine. Squishing through the fans, vendors, and cosplayers, you might run into a character you know and ask a cosplayer if you can snap a picture. Are you worn out from the show floor? You can head over to a panel of comic artists or a premiere of a new show. You might drop by Artists Alley to search for hand-drawn portraits of your favorite character or swing by Cosplay Central to patch up your costume. Even if you are there all day, it feels like there is always more to see.

Practicing Civic Futures at Fandom Conventions

What does attending a convention like New York Comic Con have to do with practicing civic futures? In fandom spaces like the one described above, youth have many opportunities to make decisions, from what they wear and where they go to who they interact with and what they buy. These decisions can be critically informed by their personal experiences and issues that matter to them. Together, youth's collective decisions can shape what the future can look like. For instance, youth can choose to consume and talk about diverse media that align with their own modern values instead of media that reproduce stereotypes or inequalities from the past. Choosing to invest in different kinds of media shapes the future, because mass support for new paradigms in media promotes the establishment of new cultural norms and shifts what the media industry attends to or prioritizes.

In this essay we take up the concept of *speculative civic literacies*. Usually when civics is mentioned, we may think about politics, voting, or civil rights movements—concepts that relate to formal government structures. The concept of speculative civic literacies helps us to think about changing public life more broadly, such as ways that our everyday actions shape the future. We share this definition from Mirra and Garcia (2022):

> Our framework of speculative civic literacies ... encourages boundary-pushing and youth-centered creative thinking about how to fully re-story (Thomas & Stornaiuolo, 2016) public life by putting lived and participatory approaches to democratic learning into conversation with the agentic resistance and public dreaming of futurist literary world-building. (p. 351)

For instance, this might refer to ways youth shift public conversations through intentional social media usage or day-to-day purchasing choices.

This concept is closely connected with fandom media spaces, public communities that often deeply involve youth. Fandoms are compelling for youth because these communities are building on media that already interest them and often provide public space for them to make their own contributions to the conversation via analysis, speculation, or artistic creations such as fanfiction or fan art. You might be interested to learn that the framework of speculative civic literacies is actually grounded in concepts from fandom media spaces! Specifically, this framework takes up the idea of *restorying* (Thomas & Stornaiuolo, 2016), which refers to fan rewritings of popular media texts that remix storylines in more socially just ways, such as centering marginalized characters or changing the ending of stories to make them more satisfying. As fans identify issues and take steps in their own communities to address them through artwork, social media campaigns, or even petitions, they can work toward addressing longstanding issues in the media industry. Grassroots fan movements addressing problematic or normative characters and storylines, while asking for new or more diverse storylines, can affect the industry in a bottom-up way, because viewership matters so much. In taking up this concept of speculative civic literacies, we are interested in how youth learn to navigate and resist toxic practices in participatory fandom discourses as well as exclusionary trends in the media industry. Youth can change their individual media consumption and engagement practices to shift larger structures of social inequalities toward imagining more just futures.

In this essay, we consider implications for civic engagement through youth place-based participation at in-person fan events, whether these be official conventions or local events organized by nonprofits, libraries, or universities. Specifically, we will share speculative civic literacies practices to consider before, during, and after place-based conventions.

Our Context

This project stems from the course Meaningful Media, a month-long series of virtual seminars taking place through a performing arts nonprofit serving urban youth. The seminar series focused on developing critical media skills in youth-selected contexts, culminating in field trips to local anime and comic conventions. The class participated in a field trip to both a local college's anime convention (5,000 attendees) and to New York City Comic Con (200,000 attendees). All youth participants in the course, ten in total, were BIPOC high school students hired as instructors for first through eighth grade youth in music, sports, or academics. During a staff meeting, youth received a description of the class and were invited to opt into the course based on their interest in media. The primary instructor was a white female university instructor and researcher (Karis) implementing weekly activities and coordinating the convention trips, while M'mah, Anais, and Kam were both youth participants and co-researchers. Meet the authors in Figure 1 and Table 1 (Karis, front center; M'mah, left; Anais, left; Kam, right).

Figure 1. Meet the authors.

Table 1. Youth authorship team.

Name (Racial Identity, Pronouns)	Grade	Meaningful Media Presentation Topic	Anime Cosplay	Comic Con Cosplay
M'mah (African American, she/they)	10	*Erased* and fan controversy over the ending	Saiki K from *The Disastrous Life of Saiki K*	Haru from *Beastars*
Anais (Latine, she/they/he)	11	*Batman: Under the Red Hood* and Jason Todd's characterization	Jason Todd from *Batman* (DC)	Jason Todd from *Batman* (DC)
Kam (Black, they/she)	11	*Berserk* and animation quality	Starfire/ Princess Koriand'r from *Teen Titans*	Zir from *Invader Zim*

Figure 2. Youth seminar prompt.
Select a media artifact and some connected fan discourse that is important to you in some way. (Bonus points if it's something you might cosplay and/or something relating to [local anime convention].) This could be a social media post, a video, an article, part of an anime episode, a song, posters, etc. Be prepared to give some background on the media artifact including who made it and why as well as how the audience engaged with it. Bring any critical questions that you have and be prepared to guide the group in a reflection.

Over the course of the class, youth were tasked with making a presentation about a fandom they loved in order to spark a class discussion (see Figure 2).

During these presentations, participants asked critical questions about current issues in the media industry such as lack of diversity and stereotypes as well as fan toxicity and gatekeeping in preparation for attending a fan convention together (see Table 2).

Before the convention, the youth prepared ideas for critical "life skills" that they might practice at the convention for addressing such issues (see Figure 3). Attending conventions such as NYCC surfaced critical thinking about media corporations' priorities as well.

Data for this case include transcripts from seminar discussions and artifacts with a focus on GoPro video recordings and pictures collected by M'mah, Anais, and Kam from the two local anime and comic conventions. Our authorship team met to analyze photos and video recordings taken by youth at the two conventions they attended. We also analyzed youth reflections about the convention collected both during the day of the convention as well as at post-convention meetings.

Figure 3. Digital bingo board co-generated with youth.

Meaningful Media Life Skills Bingo!

Someone changing their mind	Acceptance of media from various cultures	Connecting emotionally with a character
Making an ethical evaluation of characters' chocies	Identifying a harmful ideology (racism, sexism, etc.)	Speaking back to someone being rude for no reason
Giving reasons grounded in evidence for a fan opinion	Persistance leading to positive effects	Resisting a toxic fan opinion

Practicing Speculative Civic Literacies before, during, and after Fan Conventions

Across the next three sections, the authors of this piece suggest topics for youth and educators to consider with respect to *speculative civic literacies* at fan conventions. Similar to classroom structures in which youth consider how they might engage with a text before, during, and after reading, Table 2 (see next page) suggests speculative youth practices to consider before, during, and after a convention. These topics were developed by the youth authors in conversation with their instructor based on reflecting on what the class learned through participation at fan conventions. Such conversations can help support intentional and targeted engagement by youth as well as help educators to think expansively about the value of live participation in these media spaces.

Table 2. Meaningful Media class topics.

Session #	Topics	Media Texts
1	What makes media meaningful? Introduction to fan conventions Instructor-led Meaningful Media seminar	"Waiting in the Wings," song from *Tangled: The Series*
2	Youth-led Meaningful Media seminars and class generation of "Life Skills"	Goku from *Dragon Ball Z* Scene from *Batman: Under the Red Hood* Scene from *Violet Evergarden* anime Scene from *Erased* anime Scene from *Berserk* anime
3	Youth-led Meaningful Media seminars and class generation of "Life Skills"	Scene from *I Want to Eat Your Pancreas* anime From Software Games fan tweets TikTok clip of Joe Budden commenting on BTS
4	Field trip to anime convention	Anime panels, cosplays, video games, concerts, merchandise
5	Anime convention debrief Sharing moments we enjoyed and discussing artifacts from convention	Youth cosplaying photographs and video clips
6	Preparation for Comic Con Closet cosplay advice Discussion about centering joy as well as unpacking, dismantling, and resisting toxicity	Cosplay pictures
7	Field trip to Comic Con	Comic Con panels, cosplays, screenings, comics, merchandise, art

Before the Convention

Choice of Convention

The choice of convention matters as we think about what type of impact youth can have in a media ecosystem. At larger conventions, youth may attend packed sessions with popular celebrities, artists, or media producers but have less of an opportunity to interact with them personally. Large conventions may afford them the opportunity to watch special new releases of shows, which youth can then evaluate to decide whether to engage with further or to promote on social media. At smaller conventions organized by local nonprofits, libraries, or universities, youth may have less access to new releases or famous guests, but there may also be fewer barriers to interacting with these guests.

We found that youth in this course were less familiar with celebrity guests featured at NYCC, whereas at the local convention they had the opportunity to see artists they knew from Instagram or TikTok. We speculated that the professionals organizing the large conference had more connections with established

Table 3. Speculative practices for supporting youth civic futures.

	Speculative Practice
Before	• attending to youth potential for networking and impact when choosing a convention • supporting intentional choice of character for cosplaying, writing youth identities into less inclusive mainstream franchises, or promoting less popular characters • putting together material cosplays with attention to environmental sustainability
During	• celebrating diverse identities by restorying popular media and dismantling toxicity through in-person interactions with other fans • making shareable creations such as photos or video essays that address issues of justice in media spaces • financially investing in newer and more diverse media
After	• intentionally forming connections with creators, businesses, and other fans on social media, including younger and more diverse media influencers • participating in post-convention surveys in intentional ways to shape the convention for subsequent years • creating your own local convention aligned to speculative goals

guests from the media industry while the college students organizing the local conference were more likely to find up-and-coming guests who were popular online with fans and familiar to youth. This afforded different opportunities at each convention. For instance, several youth from our program were excited to attend a concert at the local convention by the indie performer Madds Buckley, an artist on social media who performs original songs inspired by anime. Though we attended panels of comic book artists at NYCC, youth did not recognize these artists by name. However, these larger conventions allowed youth to see inequalities playing out in the industry, as they noticed panels of popular franchises at NYCC were composed of primarily white men.

Youth noticed that different sized conventions had different audiences and goals. For instance, the larger conventions expected participants to pay to participate in activities such as one-to-one meetings with celebrity guests, whereas the local convention allowed attendees to meet guests directly. The youth expressed feeling overwhelmed at the larger convention, whereas at the local convention, they were more likely to seek out artists they knew or run into friends from school (possibly because this convention was more affordable and accessible to youth). Overstimulation also affected their bandwidth to network or to form connections with others at the large convention.

Cosplay and Costuming Choices

When youth are deciding what character to cosplay, they often want to choose a character who aligns with some aspect of their identity. For instance, Kam, an extroverted and bubbly person, chose to cosplay Starfire from *Teen Titans*, an excited and energetic character. As youth choose characters that they relate with, they might decide to write themselves into the fandom (Thomas & Stornaiuolo, 2016) by bending aspects of the characters' gender and race. Many of the anime characters that youth in our class chose to cosplay are racially ambiguous or white presenting, but that did not stop our diverse class from choosing those characters, successfully cosplaying them, and being recognized as that character. This kind of identity bending through cosplay can call attention to ways that media franchises leave out certain identities.

Once youth decide on a character to cosplay, they can make choices that affect the future through their costuming choices. Instead of purchasing new materials and contributing to problems of fast fashion and consumerism, cosplayers often consider ways to reuse or recycle when putting together a cosplay. Youth might also consider environmental impacts as they make intentional choices about what they want to wear to conventions. During one of the Meaningful Media class sessions, youth reflected on ways to repurpose or borrow costume elements instead of buying a store-bought one. We discussed how to make a "closet cosplay," or a cosplay out of materials you already have in your home. For instance, M'mah chose to cosplay an anime character Saiki K because she already had everything she needed from his uniform in the show (white shirt, cardigan, pants), and she added his distinctive pink hair and glasses. Anais decided to make a Jason Todd costume out of clothing she already owned, such as a red COVID-19 mask and a gray hoodie to represent a superhero suit. She ordered a t-shirt with a red bat symbol that she could also wear again.

Additionally, the youth noted ways that cosplayers made choices to bend the gender and race of the characters. For instance, youth took photos with a punk *Kingdom Hearts* cosplayer who racebent the character Roxas with the Oblivion Keyblade (this series has very few Black characters). M'mah also noted that Black cosplayers often chose to wear curly wigs instead of straight-haired wigs regardless of the character's original design. These costuming choices write the cosplayers' identities into franchises that may originally exclude them.

During the Convention

In-Person Visibility

Youth can leverage their cosplays to intentionally connect with others. At conventions, it is easy to tell what fandoms or franchises people love based on their highly visible costume choices, and our class was able to identify other fans they might not know personally but wanted to chat with. They also made connections with others cosplaying the same character; M'mah, for example, met many other cosplayers dressing as Saiki K, even taking some pictures together. Youth noted it was much easier to have a positive interaction at a convention than on the street or at school. In person, we saw many instances of people's cosplaying choices being validated and celebrated, in contrast to online spaces where trolls can heckle cosplayers if they feel their identity and appearance does not perfectly match the character. After attending a panel where a cosplayer talked about biases against her in the industry because of her body type, our class committed to celebrating cosplayers of all races, genders, and body types.

Youth were also able to consider ways their actions impact people in the media industry. There are prevalent problems in online fandom spaces with parasocial relationships (when fans have one-sided imagined relationships with actors or artists whom they don't know personally). Fans can make Q&As with actors and artists awkward by asking intense, charged, or inappropriate questions about the panelists or fandom content. Educators can help youth practice interacting with creatives in positive and productive ways. As the youth in our class often felt shy about talking with artists, cosplayers, or panelists, we worked together to forge social connections they wanted to make. For instance, Karis sometimes talked to cosplayers on behalf of the youth or offered to take pictures when they needed a photographer. She also arranged for youth to attend panels with famous writers and then meet them at their booths on the show floor or in Artists' Alley later in the day.

Finally, identities of participants in the mainstream media industry were more visible at in-person conventions. Youth could attend panels and reflect on whose voice was included as authors, actors, animators, producers, etc., and who was left out. Youth noticed a clear difference between the diversity of fans walking around the convention and the popular characters that were available to cosplay. These kinds of interactions made the stakes of access, inclusion, and representation all the more tangible.

Critical Content Creation and Engagement

There were several ways that youth engaged in building speculative futures through composition. The most prevalent method was through taking photos of or with other cosplayers whose costumes we admired. For instance, Kam was excited to celebrate Black reimaginings of characters, taking pictures with cosplayers racebending mainstream characters like Scarlet Witch from the MCU and Raven from *Teen Titans* (see Figure 4). She also created live video essays of her own accord. While the class walked from place to place, Kam used a video camera to narrate what was going on around her and to share critical takes on media she liked, combining a livestreaming-like commentary with critical tools and practices discussed in the Meaningful Media seminars. In one of her videos, she analyzed why she liked the 2018 version of *Teenage Mutant Ninja Turtles*, explaining how she felt like this version of the characters felt the most like Black teenagers to her. Her classmates listened in while she made these compositions and engaged with her opinions.

In addition to celebrating content the class already liked, it was easy to encounter types of media and franchises that were new to us. For instance, Kam admired a Black cosplayer with an amazing punk costume and prop key and took a picture with him, and this cosplayer was so cool that the authorship team later looked up the character, learning more about the *Kingdom Hearts* video game franchise. Youth were excited about the possibility for people at conventions to learn to accept and celebrate all types of media, such as anime, which everyone in the class liked but which can be deemed "nerdy" by mainstream media standards. These sorts of positive interactions can be in contrast with online media interactions, which youth discussed as toxic, as people attack newcomers for not knowing everything about a franchise or not agreeing with their opinions. Reflecting on the positive experiences we had at the convention, our class talked about how to help fandoms both in-person and online become more positive spaces to express interests and likes.

Intentional Purchasing Choices

An important speculative practice at fan conventions was making decisions about what to purchase. Conventions have opportunities to buy texts such as manga, comics, or books as well as art or merchandise inspired by these

Figure 4. Kam's photo with Scarlet Witch and Raven.

source texts. Considering what to buy was an important decision youth made at the convention, as fan purchases are a valued outcome for conventions organizers, who pay close attention to what fans want when deciding who or what to feature. Thus, youth purchasing decisions at scale can contribute to shifts in industry decision making. The instructors decided that purchasing decisions were such an important part of attending conventions that we designated programmatic funding toward 1) buying tokens that youth could use to select small anime-themed trinkets from various machines as well as 2) providing Visa gift cards for youth to practice making purchasing decisions at the convention. Since the youth were earning a salary as employees of the nonprofit, they also brought their own money to spend.

Across the conventions, we were interested in ways that youth chose to financially invest in newer and more diverse media, as well as ways they prioritized fan-made products over more official texts and merchandise. For instance, though Anais loves DC Comics and browsed many comic book options at NYCC, she ultimately decided not to purchase older issues of comics. Indeed, while browsing these classic comics, Anais and Kam discussed how this older artwork did not feature female characters in empowering ways or in healthy relationships. Subsequently, when they saw pin-up artwork on the show floor sexualizing Harley Quinn, they did not want to purchase that art. They instead decided to purchase character-driven artwork of Harley Quinn and Poison Ivy from Artists' Alley, inspired by more recent iterations of the franchise that "ship" Harley and Poison Ivy together instead of the more toxic relationship of Harley and the Joker.

After the Convention

Sustained Networking

Throughout their trip, youth were constantly engaged by individuals who made demands for sustained attention. Panels streamed newly released episodes and invited them to follow the show when it was released. Authors gave away new comic issues and books for youth to sample. As they traveled the show floor and Artists' Alley, they were bombarded with giveaways and advertisements as well as names and contact information. Companies tried to solicit ways to stay in touch, such as booths that promised prizes in exchange for email addresses. Others asked for them to connect on social media, such as a cosplayer who carried a sign with their Instagram handle.

As we rode the subway back from the convention, youth sorted through the many materials they had gathered over the course of the day and decided what to keep and what to discard. They scrolled through social media and decided who to tag or follow. These decisions shaped the community and their media ecosystems in lasting ways. They could decide to empower younger and more diverse influencers by giving them a follow or to support a show they wanted to see succeed by shouting it out or following its social media page. There were also opportunities to learn about online communities to join, such as Discords dedicated to a particular fandom. Such choices had the potential to shape their future interactions with fans and fandoms.

Participating in Survey

Most conventions share surveys after their events. Participating in such surveys helps to shape the convention for next year, as conventions aim to make their events attractive for wide fan audiences and are incentivized to make changes based on feedback. Youth can share both positive feedback about what they liked as well as critical observations about issues they saw at the convention. Youth can intentionally suggest guests that the convention organizers should invite, such as younger or more diverse artists. As these surveys can often get lost or go to spam, educators can remind youth to take the surveys when they go out. If educators are buying tickets on behalf of youth, they may have to be intentional about forwarding on such surveys to the class. We suggest that discussing youth opinions together collectively before answering the surveys can allow youth to build power in numbers by making similar suggestions across their responses.

Creating Your Own Convention

Finally, the teens were interested in creating their own local version of a fan convention for the elementary and middle school youth they worked with, with the goal of helping the younger youth move beyond passive consumption of texts/media and instead supporting their growth into enthusiastic and impactful fans of franchises that they enjoyed. We brainstormed aspects of the convention that teens found engaging, such as having the opportunity to dress up as characters, browsing new books and texts, and collecting freebies relating to media they enjoyed. Based on their experiences, the teens planned a "Literacy Celebration" for the children they worked with. They developed five customized stations including character-related face painting, a comic-book makerspace, a poem-related craft, and a *Jeopardy!* game relating to reading trivia. The teens also coordinated with the local library to create a customized culturally responsive booklist for children in the program, and teens and librarians worked together to help children choose new books and graphic novels to take home with them. Each station provided a sticker as a giveaway and children were encouraged to "collect them all."

Conclusions

Fan conventions may primarily be seen as entertainment, not necessarily contexts for learning or places for civic participation. We hope that through this essay, our readers have gained a new perspective on speculative practices that youth can develop by engaging with fandoms at conventions. In-person conventions are valuable contexts for learning because they make fandom participants and the media industry visible in ways that can be harder to see when consuming content alone and/or online. This visibility opens up space for critical reflection and speculative changes to participation. Additionally, we see opportunities for intentional decision making that may be harder to see at the individual level but that can be impactful at scale.

Almost a decade ago, Booth (2015) argued that critical educational involvement with fandoms was necessary to resist "an encroaching turn to neoliberal education and corporate-focused fandom" (1.1). He urged educators to engage with fandoms alongside youth in ways that encouraged critical dialogue and commitment to activism in light of corporate encouragement of passive consumption. The turn he predicted has arrived, as these issues have not dissipated in the modern day but instead have intensified.

With respect to education, youth's fandom interests are sometimes framed as addictive, distracting to educational goals, or even dangerous. It is true that fandoms can perpetuate societal issues, both through fan-to-fan interactions and the media industry itself. However, this does not mean that educators should avoid or compete for attention against these interests. Instead, educators can be valuable allies as youth learn to navigate these complex spaces. In this essay, readers can see ways that educators and educational organizations can support youth with access to the backstage of media production as well as facilitate breaking into conversations that intentionally or unintentionally exclude them. We invite youth and educators to reflect on these speculative practices and to continue to develop them. If we engage critically with popular media and culture together, we can build powerful coalitions to demand that our entertainment reflect our values and priorities instead of passively allowing the industry to shape us.

Grant Funding: *Meaningful Media programming was made possible by a grant from the New Jersey Council for the Humanities, state partners of the National Endowment for the Humanities. Any views, findings, conclusions, or recommendations expressed in this publication do not necessarily represent those of the National Endowment for the Humanities or the New Jersey Council for the Humanities.*

Works Cited

Booth, P. J. (2015). Fandom: The classroom of the future. *Transformative Works and Cultures, 19.* https://doi.org/10.3983/twc.2015.0650

Mirra, N., & Garcia, A. (2022). Guns, schools, and democracy: Adolescents imagining social futures through speculative civic literacies. *American Educational Research Journal, 59*(2), 345–380. https://doi.org/10.3102/00028312221074400

Thomas, E. E., & Stornaiuolo, A. (2016). Restorying the self: Bending toward textual justice. *Harvard Educational Review, 86*(3), 313–338. https://doi.org/10.17763/1943-5045-86.3.313

Transnational Fan Activism: Digital Literacies and Global Civic Futures

GRACE MYHYUN KIM

Emerging forms of youth activism on social media have been dismissed as weak ties that do not lead to collective action or effect social change (Gladwell, 2010), yet events over the past decade suggest otherwise. For example, in 2020, a Dallas Police Department software application designed for people to report "illegal" protest activities crashed within 24 hours after being flooded by Korean popular music (K-pop) videos posted by international K-pop fans. This "fancamming" continued as K-pop fans flooded hashtags such as #whitelivesmatter and #whiteoutwednesday with K-pop content in an effort to dismantle ostensible countercalls to the Black Lives Matter (BLM) movement. In addition to advocacy for Black lives and racial justice, K-pop fans have reached out to global peers to raise awareness and support for other current issues. For example, Armenian K-pop fans have stood in front of cameras holding signboards written in Korean to raise global awareness among global K-pop fans of the conflict between Armenia and Azerbaijan (JeonAe, 2020; Lee & Kao, 2021). These digital engagements underscore the growing role of social media in civic literacy, transnational activism, and global empathy among today's youth. Moreover, these examples illustrate young people's creative digital literacy practices not only to imagine the world they want but also to engage in current issues and organize with other youth around the world.

With the rise of new media, new avenues and forms of political expression have also emerged. Indeed, young people have been pursuing knowledge and participation in political and social issues "by any media necessary" (Jenkins et al., 2016). Studies show civic learning can emerge when youth explore their civic identities with local peers (e.g., Mirra & Garcia, 2020) as they express their views and experiences about issues within a local or national context (Garcia et al., 2020; Lee, 2018; Mihailidis, 2020). Students may also be engaged in online communities in which they learn about and connect with others around civic issues that are not immediately local to them. For example, youth in the United States participated in digitally mediated, grassroots activism concerning the Arab Spring and "Kony 2012" movements (Jenkins et al., 2016).

Importantly, these examples highlight myriad ways youth may be engaged in out-of-school civic learning and literacy practices. However, studies tend also to focus on US youth and organizations. Extending the research on digital civic literacy, this essay focuses on how youth in and beyond the United States, in the transnational sphere (Bean & Dunkerly-Bean, 2020), practice civic futures. In this essay, I discuss examples of young people whose civic imagination is transnational in its exploration of and concern for peoples, communities, and issues that may be outside of their immediate locales. I argue that their creative digital literacy practices convey a future-oriented vision of civic learning and engagement that could be supported within English language arts education to cultivate youth as actors of global social change.

After a brief overview of civic literacy within out-of-school digital environments, I review transnational fan activism as a potential site of civic literacy. I then discuss examples of how some youth who identify as K-pop fans connect with other fans and issues outside of their local contexts through transnational fan activism within digital out-of-school learning environments. Following these examples, I conclude with ways these examples might inform the perspectives and practices of teacher education and English language arts, along with questions for educators to consider for literacy teaching and learning.

Civic Literacies in a Digital Age

Recent studies have shown the limitations of existing school curriculum for effectively engaging students' interests for civic learning and a need to attend to out-of-school environments for developing youth civic voice (Lee et al., 2021; Shapiro & Brown, 2018). Researchers of new forms of youth civic learning have emphasized *civic imagination* (Jenkins et al., 2016) and *civic literacies* (Mirra & Garcia, 2020) that youth practice to imagine alternatives to current issues and institutions. For example, some use video blogging (vlogging), memes, and social media to express their views on current events and political issues (Jenkins et al., 2016; Mihailidis, 2020). Much of this research on the intersection of digital literacy and youth civic identity draws on the concepts of *participatory culture* (Jenkins et al., 2009), peer-based social networks often facilitated by digital media, and *participatory politics* (Cohen et al., 2012), everyday individual and group practices that aim to discuss and influence public issues.

Studies also indicate a key role of popular culture texts in participatory cultures for mobilizing youth engagement in real-world issues. For example, fan activism studies suggest popular stories can be an entry point for youth interest and involvement in social change, although researchers of participatory cultures and politics have acknowledged two limitations. First, "new youth activism" studies are often US based; the activities and concerns within this research are often located within US politics and of White American youth (Jenkins, 2016). For example, research on youth civic engagement within the online community Nerdfighters acknowledged limited inclusivity, as it comprised of mostly white American teenagers (Jenkins et al., 2016). Second, within the scarce research on transnational social activism, exclusivity is an issue due to necessary insider knowledge of the popular literature around which the fan activism is based, such as *The Hunger Games* series. A "White savior" narrative has also surfaced in studies featuring US-based efforts and leadership, as in research on youth engagement in the "Kony 2012" movement, which has revealed a focus on stories about US youths' activist efforts, funds directed at growing US youth capacity, and an absence of Ugandan voices (Jenkins et al., 2016).

This essay broadens the extant research on civic learning and digitally mediated youth activism by focusing on how some transnational fan communities practice civic futures through their digital literacy practices. One fandom that has a massive international following is Korean popular culture, an expansive industry of cultural products that has been transnationally exported, circulated, and bolstered with the use of digital technologies (Jin, 2016; Jin & Yoon, 2017; Kim, 2019). In this essay, I discuss examples of K-pop fans engaged in transnational fan activism, including examples of a specific fandom: ARMY (Adorable Representative Master-of-Ceremony for Youth). ARMY is a participatory culture brought together by their devotion to BTS (Bangtan Songyeondan), a K-pop group that has become an international phenomenon. ARMY is a noteworthy contemporary case of how some young people practice global civic futures through their digital literacy practices for a few key reasons. First, research on literacy practices facilitated by new technologies, or, multiliteracies for "designing social futures" (Cazden et al., 1996), shows some youth pursue transnational affiliations for their identity development (e.g., Kim, 2016a). On-screen texts that combine writing with other modes of representation (e.g., images and animations) can support a wider range of literacy practices for youth to access and maintain transnational networks and identities than written communication only (e.g., Cingel et al., 2019). Second, the civic discourse and engagements within the online community emanate from a shared interest in media texts produced in South Korea; therefore, participation does not rely on the cultural preferences and knowledge or taste politics (Bourdieu, 1984) of existing fan activism studies that tend to center on Western literary texts and popular culture, including American musical artists and celebrities. The case of global K-pop fans is notable given the need for research on citizenship education that is not based on singular national values, heroes, and concerns (Banks, 2017) and for more research on online platforms for engaging students from different backgrounds in developing civic voice (Garcia et al., 2021).

Transnational Fan Activism

In addition to the fancamming of the Dallas Police Department application, K-pop fans have engaged in other instances of transnational organizing for political action. Leading up the US 2020 presidential election, K-pop fans distorted the expected attendance for a Trump rally to be held in Oklahoma. They reserved tickets for the rally, although they did not plan to attend it. The inflated attendance expectation and lower turnout than anticipated led Democratic Representative Alexandria Ocasio-Cortez to tweet that the Trump campaign had been "rocked" by teens. Her tweet about the fake ticket reservations for the rally underscored the potential role of K-pop fans in civic and social justice issues: "Kpop allies, we see and appreciate your contributions in the fight for justice too" (Hollingsworth, 2020). Again, whether viewed as a youthful prank or a significant organizing tactic, the "call to action in K-pop circles revealed a growing realization that fans' efficient social-media tactics for fund-raising or making a song go viral can also be used for political activism" (Coscarelli, 2020).

Although many fandoms can be intense with zealous fans, or *stans*, the relationship between BTS and its ARMY is uniquely based in a continual reciprocity happening largely on social media (Lee, 2019). A contributing factor that could explain ARMY organizing around social changes issues is fans' take-up of BTS's ethos. For example, BTS has launched a "love myself" campaign focused on promoting self-esteem and well-being, offered encouraging messages to audiences about the importance of mental health, and served officially as cultural ambassadors of South Korea. These actions of BTS could be seen as calls for charity to oneself and care for others—BTS as engaged in mutual support with fans through concerns for their development. The reciprocal spurring on to support BLM between fans and BTS is evident, for instance, in their fundraising for the BLM movement in 2020. After the group and its company, Big Hit Entertainment, donated $1 million to BLM on June 4, 2020, fans raised an additional $1 million for BLM within 24 hours through a hashtag campaign, #MatchAMillion (Coscarelli, 2020). Importantly, through this sequence of events, not only the K-pop artists but also their fans gained attention as actors in social change (Lee et al., 2021).

The expression of support for BLM and the donation made by BTS to BLM were not made in isolation and illustrate the potential power of transnational fan activism for practicing global civic futures. The Black ARMY Lives Matter Movement had tweeted calls for BTS support of BLM because the K-pop group had not issued any public statements in the days following the killing of George Floyd on May 25, 2020. Criticisms about BTS's initial silence were also met with some non-Black ARMY members' derailing of these criticisms through calls for group cohesion. These critiques of BTS and fan reactions generated crucial cross-racial dialogue, including discussions about anti-Blackness among ARMY, statements of Black pride, and expressions of allyship from non-Black ARMY (Evans, 2022; Park et al., 2021).

This dialogue about race and racism among and within ARMY illustrates how online fan communities espouse a collective identity through a shared affinity, yet issues of equity and conflict can also arise across group members' identities, experiences, and perspectives. In a study of a queer fan community dedicated to queer media representation, for example, Navar-Gill and Stanfill (2018) found marginalization of Black members within the fandom's advocacy for social justice. Online communities formed on social media are fraught with inequalities that permeate offline community formation and discourse; however, ARMY exchanges suggest a transnational fandom community can still become a generative site of civic dialogue and learning.

One In An Army (OIAA): A Transnational Fan Collective for Social Change

One particular ARMY fan collective is explicit about its goals for improving the world. This online community is defined by two main commitments: BTS and global causes for social change. One In An Army (OIAA)'s Twitter (now X) is a transnational, participatory culture brought together by a loyalty to BTS and "using our collective power for global good" (One In An Army, oneinanarmy.org). This fan collective garners support from fans to give micro-donations to nonprofit organizations around the world. Founded in 2018, OIAA takes a multiple-issues approach to real-world problems rather than focusing on a single cause. Example issues on @OIAA include food insecurity, climate change, and sex trafficking.

The global following of @OIAA is striking. Many following accounts suggest location-based groups (e.g., "@MyanmarARMY"). For example, replies and retweets index accounts in countries such as Kenya, Iran, Malaysia, Colombia, Ghana, Australia, India, Nicaragua, the United States, and Egypt; some posts include self-reported locations, such as the United Arab Emirates, Indonesia, Tunisia, and Bangladesh. User profiles also sometimes indicate imagined locations—a digital literacy practice that some fans engage in as they envision and learn about lives in different contexts, as well as share their imaginative views of the world based on their readings of Korean media texts (Kim & Omerbašić, 2017). For example, a few of the locations on @OIAA included "The end of the rainbow," "The hearts of BTS," and "The Internet & NYC."

In October 2020, @OIAA had over 172,000 followers. OIAA is not led by US youth; according to its website, it is "a fan collective comprised of volunteers around the globe." In 2020, a team of twenty volunteers from ten different countries managed OIAA. Importantly, OIAA does not accept money; any fundraising efforts within @OIAA go directly to identified organizations. Unlike some social and political activism that gets expressed on social media platforms without responses from or dialogue with those most directly affected by the topic or issue, transnational feedback on the community's activism occurs within @OIAA, which allows for "cross-cultural readings" informed by "'on the ground' engagements with people and their communities" (Tierney, 2020, p. 48). For example, discussion threads related to combatting deforestation in Indonesia include a video of Indonesians responding to @OIAA supporters of this cause.

On @OIAA, by identifying as either an individual in ARMY or a subgroup within the umbrella of ARMY (e.g., LGBT ARMY, BLACK ARMY, NIGERIAN ARMY), K-pop fans in countries outside of Korea engage in transcultural digital literacy practices (Kim, 2016a) through their reading of K-pop media (specifically, all things BTS) and by signaling their membership within this global social community. In addition, an ethic of cross-cultural respect and responsiveness that resists "the conceit of universalism" gets demonstrated within the "critical and creative expression of one's identity" (Tierney, 2020, p. 43) that surfaces within the @OIAA discourse. Many posts include the use of symbol systems that index one's own or appreciate others' cultural identifications, such as national flags attached to following accounts and likes that show support of those cultural affiliations across national borders.

Some who identify as ARMY on @OIAA may also encounter new learning about issues of social and political change through their engagement within this global community. ARMY's shared central interest is an affinity for BTS, not a religious or political affiliation that could otherwise result in a social media echo chamber of discourse, geographically or ideologically. Some studies even suggest that a shared affinity for Korean popular culture has brought together people from countries and cultures that have histories of conflict, such as fans of Korean dramas in Japan (Oh & Lee, 2014), and fans in Israel and Palestine (Otmazgin & Lyan, 2013). ARMY may be "the most inclusive and diverse fandom of the world today," and it may also be disproportionately comprised of minoritized peoples (Lee & Kao, 2021, p. 167; Saeji, 2020). Whatever the reasons may be for the international fandom and its diverse composition, ARMY has been able to sustain transnational community building amid—and sometimes around—social and political issues.

Global Meaning Making

Global interconnectedness has been laid bare through the COVID-19 pandemic and ongoing crises such as climate justice, forced migration, and food insecurity. These issues are not only local or national concerns but are global problems that will require the next generation to connect and coordinate across cultural and geographic borders. Teaching and learning can support the digital literacy practices that youth are already engaged in for *global meaning making* (Tierney, 2018) as *global readers*: "The shift to global reading entails support for readers and writers to navigate cross-cultural concerns—that is supporting meaning makers moving beyond their own cultural bubbles and self-interests to weighing information from multiple informants and multiple sources" (Tierney, 2020, p. 42). Social media has, for quite some time now, been the most common source of news for thirteen- to eighteen-year-olds (Robb, 2017). New uses of digital media have also stimulated new practices (Ito et al., 2013), including dynamic ways youth connect around shared interests, learn about and express views on political and social issues, and creatively participate in large-scale movements (Garcia et al., 2021).

The online activism and organizing of some K-pop fans, such as ARMY, illustrate how youth connect online in joyful exchanges around media texts and across national borders in ways that may include civic learning. Their transnational social media activism documents their reading and writing "across spaces, people and times and beyond oneself" (Tierney, 2020, p. 42). Global citizenship has been a popular term in educational research and practice, including teacher education, yet moving this discourse to students' civic participation in global contexts continues to be a challenge (Estellés & Fischman, 2021). As students participate in a global society through their digital lives, K-pop fans are demonstrating how transnational digital literacy practices can cultivate empathy and action for the concerns of people outside of their immediate social worlds, as in the aforementioned examples of K-pop fans' transnational discourse and activism around racial justice.

Practicing Global Civic Futures

This essay has aimed to contribute insights on the digital literacy practices of geographically disparate youth as they connect around global hallenges. Social media is changing the landscape of digital literacy practices for social and political organizing, including an expansion of ways that youth are communicating and learning with transnational peers. This expansion also includes ways that digital communication around and emanating from a shared affinity for a particular popular culture has become a lingua franca and global social practice among youth (Kim, 2016a, 2016b). Participating in transnational online communities can also be an avenue for youth to explore *global civic futures* and practice *global civic learning*—interrupting investments in only one's immediate community, developing a relational view of civic learning and activism, bridging affective distances between culturally different places and people, critically examining historical and structural reasons for global inequities and crises, countering deficit views and the objectification of global "Others," recognizing non-US youth as humanitarian actors, and ultimately, supporting young people to envision and build a better, more just world.

Within social media use is a growing convergence of popular culture with transnational sociopolitical movements; the civic literacy some students are practicing within popular culture fandoms to which they belong underscore diverse ways learning can emerge in digital out-of-school environments. Students use new media for their own learning purposes (Kim, 2016a, 2016b), and we need counterpoints to deficit or disparaging views of their digital activities, particularly their use of social media, as well as their positioning as "not-yet-citizens" (Garcia et al., 2021). As popular culture has always been a source of learning for youth, and transnational media have become more accessible and popular around the world, transnational fandoms can also be sites of global civic learning. To be sure, social media is not a panacea for global problems. Indeed, its role in relation to them requires more analysis. Just as social media's low barrier entry to transnational communication has opened new ways to participate in sociopolitical discussion, it has also opened more opportunities for circulating misinformation. Surveillance and algorithms further constrain opportunities for participation in critical civic dialogue. Social media has nevertheless become an undeniably significant public forum about social change that has upended a traditional paradigm of information sharing and civic learning. It also notably reveals how young people's digital lives gesture toward expansive conceptualizations of civic engagement and identity.

The transcultural digital literacy practices of today's youth can help educators reimagine learning opportunities that build relations across cultural differences and working with the world's diverse peoples toward transformative change. US teacher education tends to hew to local and national concerns, too often precluding international perspectives for critical global education (O'Connor & Zeichner, 2011). However, English language arts teacher educators can support new teachers in recognizing transnational media texts as informal multicultural curricula (Kim, 2019) through which today's youth read the world. By nurturing a view of both the importance of transnational learning and the digital media texts as replete with opportunities for critical multicultural learning, teacher educators can move toward pedagogies that support more global civic learning. More specifically, as teacher certification and educational standards increasingly emphasize digital literacy, teacher educators can encourage literacy teachers to articulate their goals for technology use in the classroom and support their inquiry into how that use critically examines issues of equity and social change (Kim & Higgs, 2023). Curricular approaches could include inviting teachers to inquire into digital literacy practices students may already be engaged with that express their knowledge of and vision for global civic futures.

English language arts curriculum can also build on the opportunities and challenges of digital literacy practices for transnational civic discourse and learning. Literacy teaching and learning that include popular culture media texts being read and created within these online communities could examine the interplay between these texts and ways that students learn about and engage with transnational social and political concerns. Online transnational communities may be how some youth make sense of and connect with others about social change while living in different political and social contexts. As youth of varied backgrounds and locations connect online, they learn, imagine, and practice ways of being in the world—sometimes engaging in transcultural digital literacies to imagine and develop their identities across conventional geographic and social boundaries (Kim, 2016a, 2016b; Kim & Omerbašić, 2017). Within English language arts classrooms, students might analyze how the texts that they read and produce within transnational online communities embrace relationality and mutual exchange, yet these texts can also circulate misinformation and cultural stereotypes about globally distant peoples (Kim, 2019). Several questions for educators to consider in the design of activities while working with youth in and out of the classroom include the following: *How do the youth with whom you work define and engage in social media activism? As the compositions of online communities are increasingly determined by algorithms, what opportunities might be built into literacy curriculum that invite students to reflect critically on the online communities to which they belong? What are the online transnational communities in which your students participate? Why and how are these communities important to them? What civic issues and civic futures are they practicing within those communities? Whose voices and perspectives are dominant within those communities? Whose voices and perspectives are marginalized or missing within those communities? How do the youth with whom you work define global citizenship?*

Works Cited

Banks, J. A. (2017). Failed citizenship and transformative civic education. *Educational Researcher, 46*(7), 366–377.

Bean, T. W., & Dunkerly-Bean, J. (2020). Cosmopolitan critical literacy and youth civic engagement for human rights. *Pedagogies: An International Journal, 15*(4), 262–278.

Cazden, C., Cope, B., Fairclough, N., Gee, J., Kalantzis, M., Kress, G., Luke, A., Luke, C., Michaels, S., & Nakata, M. (1996). A pedagogy of multiliteracies: Designing social futures. *Harvard Educational Review, 66*(1), 60–92.

Cingel, D. P., Lauricella, A. R., Lam, W. S. E., Wartella, E., & Morales, P. Z. (2019). Online communication patterns of Chinese and Mexican adolescents living in the United States. *International Journal of Communication, 13*, 116–135.

Cohen, C. J., Kahne, J., Bowyer, B., Middaugh, E., & Rogowski, J. (2012). *Participatory politics: New media and youth political action.* Youth and Participatory Politics Research Network.

Coscarelli, J. (2020, June 23). Why obsessive K-pop fans are turning toward political activism. *The New York Times.* www.nytimes.com/2020/06/22/arts/music/k-pop-fans-trump-politics.html

Estellés, M., & Fischman, G. E. (2021). Who needs global citizenship education? A review of the literature on teacher education. *Journal of Teacher Education, 72*(2), 223–236.

Evans, S. (2022). Fandomonium: How spaces marked for fandom transformed into areas for political discourse. *The Phoenix Papers, 5*(1), 17–24.

Garcia, A., Levinson, A. M., & Gargroetzi, E. C. (2020). "Dear future president of the United States": Analyzing youth civic writing within the 2016 letters to the next president project. *American Educational Research Journal, 57*(3), 1159–1202.

Garcia, A. G., McGrew, S., Mirra, N., Tynes, B., & Kahne, J. (2021). Rethinking digital citizenship: Learning about media, literacy, and race in turbulent times. In C. D. Lee, G. White, & D. Dong (Eds.), *Educating for civic reasoning and discourse* (pp. 319–352). National Academy of Education.

Gladwell, M. (2010, September 27). Small change: Why the revolution will not be tweeted. *The New Yorker.*

Hollingsworth, J. (2020, June 22). *K-pop fans are being credited with helping disrupt Trump's rally. Here's why that shouldn't be a surprise.* CNN. www.cnn.com/2020/06/22/asia/k-pop-fandom-activism-intl-hnk/index.html

Ito, M., Soep, E., Kligler-Vilenchik, N., Shresthova, S., Gamber-Thompson, L., & Zimmerman, A. (2015). Learning connected civics: Narratives, practices, infrastructures. *Curriculum Inquiry, 45*(1), 10–29.

Jenkins, H., Purushotma, R., Weigel, M., Clinton, K., & Robison, A. J. (2009). *Confronting the challenges of participatory culture: Media education for the 21st century.* MacArthur Foundation.

Jenkins, H. R., Shresthova, S., Gamber-Thompson, L., Kligler-Vilenchik, N., & Zimmerman, A. (2016). *By any media necessary: The new youth activism.* New York University Press.

JeonAe. (2020, October 27). *3 times political issues received global awareness through K-pop fans.* Kpopmap. www.kpopmap.com/3-times-political-issues-received-global-awareness-through-kpop-fans/

Jin, D. Y. (2016). *New Korean wave: Transnational cultural power in the age of social media.* University of Illinois Press.

Jin, D. Y., & Yoon, T. (2017). The Korean wave: Retrospect and prospect. *International Journal of Communication, 11*, 2241–2249.

Kim, G. M. (2016a). Transcultural digital literacies: Cross-border connections and self-representations in an online forum. *Reading Research Quarterly, 51*(2), 199–219.

Kim, G. M. (2016b). Practicing multilingual identities: Online interactions in a Korean dramas forum. *International Multilingual Research Journal, 10*(4), 254–272.

Kim, G. M. (2019). "Do they really do that in Korea?": Multicultural learning through Hallyu media. *Learning, Media and Technology, 44*(4), 473–488.

Kim, G. M., & Higgs, J. (2023). Exploring equity issues with technology in secondary literacy education. *Technology, Pedagogy and Education, 32*(1), 1–16.

Kim, G. M., & Omerbašić, D. (2017). Multimodal literacies: Imagining lives through Korean dramas. *Journal of Adolescent & Adult Literacy, 60*(5), 557–566.

Lee, A. (2018). Invisible networked publics and hidden contention: Youth activism and social media tactics under repression. *New Media & Society, 20*(11), 4095–4115.

Lee, C. D., White, G., & Dong, D. (Eds.). (2021). *Educating for civic reasoning and discourse.* National Academy of Education.

Lee, W., & Kao, G. (2021). "Make it right": Why #BlackLivesMatter(s) to K-pop, BTS, and BTS ARMYs. *Journal of the International Association for the Study of Popular Music, 11*(1), 70–87.

Mihailidis, P. (2020). The civic potential of memes and hashtags in the lives of young people. *Discourse: Studies in the Cultural Politics of Education, 41*(5), 762–781.

Mirra, N., & Garcia, A. (2020). "I hesitate but I do have hope": Youth speculative civic literacies for troubled times. *Harvard Educational Review, 90*(2), 295–321.

Navar-Gill, A., & Stanfill, M. (2018). "We shouldn't have to trend to make you listen": Queer fan hashtag campaigns as production interventions. *Journal of Film and Video, 70*(3–4), 85–100. https://doi.org/10.5406/jfilmvideo.70.3-4.0085

O'Connor, K., & Zeichner, K. (2011). Preparing U.S. teachers for critical global education. *Globalisation, Societies and Education, 9*(3–4), 521–536.

Oh, I., & Lee, C. M. (2014). A league of their own: Female supporters of *Hallyu* and Korea-Japan relations. *Pacific Focus, 29*(2), 284–302.

One In An Army. https://oneinanarmy.org

Otmazgin, N., & Lyan, I. (2013). Hallyu across the desert: K-pop fandom in Israel and Palestine. *Cross-Currents: East Asian History and Culture Review, 9*(1), 68–89.

Robb, M. B. (2017). *News and America's kids: How young people perceive and are impacted by the news.* Common Sense Media.

Shapiro, S., & Brown, C. (2018). *The state of civics education.* Center for American Progress.

Tierney, R. J. (2018). Toward a model of global meaning making. *Journal of Literacy Research, 50*(4), 397–422.

Tierney, R. J. (2020). Notes on global reading: Critical cultural traversals, transactions and transformations. In L. I. Misiaszek (Ed.), *Exploring the complexities in global citizenship education: Hard spaces, methodologies, and ethics* (pp. 38–68). Routledge.

Index

About the Editors

LaMar Timmons-Long is a high school English teacher in Brooklyn, NY, and a doctoral student at New York University. He is passionate about working with Black and Brown students in urban public schools. His teaching centers on Black feminism, ethnic studies, and the voices and experiences of Black and Brown youths. He works hard to create warm spaces for students to engage in critical conversations, write, and thrive. As a scholar, his research interests include Black feminist thought, Black educators and their pedagogical practices, Afrofuturism, and speculative thinking. His work has been published in *The ALAN Review*, *English Journal*, *Journal of Adolescent & Adult Literacy*, *Queer Adolescent Literature as a Complement to the English Language Arts Curriculum*, and on the NCTE blog.

Antero Garcia is an associate professor in the Graduate School of Education at Stanford University. His research explores the possibilities of speculative imagination and healing in educational research.

Nicole Mirra is an associate professor in the Graduate School of Education at Rutgers University. Her research utilizes participatory design methods in classroom, community, and digital spaces to collaboratively create civic learning environments with youth and educators that disrupt discourses and structures of racial injustice and creatively compose liberatory social futures.

About the Authors

Meg Booth is a program manager at Alliance for Refugee Youth Support and Education (ARYSE), a Pittsburgh-based nonprofit that develops out-of-school-time programming for youth from forcibly displaced backgrounds. During her career, she has worked both directly in schools and universities (within the US and Ecuador) and within community-based educational institutions. She aspires to be an ever-evolving learner-practitioner and is interested in the creative possibilities that exist within community-based contexts to connect with and engage youth in critical dialogues and radical imaginations that propel us to action.

Fabio C. Campos is a Brazilian researcher affiliated with the Transformative Learning Technologies Lab (TLTL) at Columbia University Teachers College. His work focuses on the design of technologies and learning experiences to strengthen political knowledge and democratic debate. He worked for more than twenty years as a practitioner in education, specializing in interventions for low-income young adults at Rio de Janeiro, Brazil. At Rio's municipal government, Campos directed the Schools of Tomorrow, a program for over 100,000 students and 155 schools spread throughout Rio's most violent favelas. He holds a PhD in education technology from New York University, a master's in learning, design, and technology from Stanford, and a BA in social communication from Rio's Federal University.

Emily Plummer Catena is an assistant professor of English education at Florida State University. Her research focuses on digital writing with educators and youth and emphasizes participatory methodologies. She is a National Writing Project teacher consultant and was previously a high school English and communication teacher.

M'mah Cisse is a high school student currently attending Abraham Lincoln High School. Since 2021 she has interned at New City Kids, a nonprofit organization that offers high schoolers a year-long, paid, part-time internship. While working with New City Kids, she was a keyboard teacher and art teacher, working with kids in grades 1–8. Her interests include crocheting, baking, and reading, as well as making and coding video games.

Jen Scott Curwood, PhD, is an associate professor of English education and media studies in the Sydney School of Education and Social Work at the University of Sydney in Australia. Her research explores the intersections of literacy, creativity, and technology to advance social change and build more sustainable futures. She began her career as a secondary English teacher in the Midwestern United States, where she strived to cultivate students' digital and critical literacies in order to foster cross-cultural learning opportunities.

Dr. Michael Dando is an associate professor of English and education at St. Cloud State University in Minnesota. An education researcher with a doctorate in curriculum and instruction from the University of Wisconsin-Madison, Dr. Dando specializes in culturally responsive pedagogy, multicultural education, and critical design practices. His scholarship integrates language arts, speculative education, and antiracist teaching, with a strong emphasis on creating inclusive and culturally sustaining learning environments for students through popular culture, specifically comics and hip-hop culture. Dr. Dando's scholarship has been published in leading academic journals and publications including *Literacy Media and Technology* and with NCTE. His research and teaching combine his passion for culturally relevant pedagogy with a commitment to advancing innovative practices that bridge the arts, education, and social change.

Beth W. Gafford is currently an assistant professor in the education department of Randolph College, where she works with preservice teachers seeking initial teaching license(s) in special education and/or elementary education in the state of Virginia. She holds an EdD in curriculum and instruction from the University of Virginia, where her research focused on the identification process of twice-exceptional students. Beth is currently furthering her research in this area, as well as exploring other research interests, including disparities identified by Black students and educators in schools today. Her passion for research lies in action research that directly impacts the field and practice of education.

Megan Heise is an assistant professor of English rhetoric and composition at Utah Tech University. She holds a PhD in composition and applied linguistics from Indiana University of Pennsylvania and an MFA in creative writing from Naropa University. Her current research focuses on multilingual and multimodal forms of expression with refugee youth and undergraduate writing students, building off of her TIRF award-winning dissertation, "Transmodal Zine-Making with Resettled Refugee Youth." She served as a coeditor for *Writing Spaces* volume 4, and her work has appeared in *TESOL*

Journal and the edited book collections *Professionalizing Multimodal Composition* and *Critical Pedagogy in the Language and Writing Classroom*. She has presented her scholarship at conferences around the world, including the Conference on Community Writing, Conference on College Composition and Communication, TESOL Convention, and the American Association for Applied Linguistics Conference.

Karis Jones, PhD, is an assistant professor of English language arts for the School for Graduate Studies (education department) at SUNY Empire State. As a teacher educator, literacy consultant, public humanities scholar, and community activist, she studies issues of equitable literacies learning across disciplinary, fandom, and gaming spaces. Her research has been published in the *Journal of Literacy Research, Equity & Excellence in Education*; *Teaching and Teacher Education*; *Journal of Language & Literacy Education, Linguistics and Education*; *English Teaching: Practice & Critique*; *Journal of Adolescent & Adult Literacy*; *Contemporary Issues in Technology and Teacher Education—English Education*; *English Education*; and *English Journal*. She has been a member of NCTE since 2017.

Grace MyHyun Kim is an associate professor of language and literacy studies in the Department of Curriculum and Instruction at the University of Texas at Austin. She also serves as both a core faculty member of the Center for Asian American Studies and a faculty affiliate of the Department of Asian Studies. Her research focuses on adolescent literacy, new media, and cultural diversity within a global context, with particular interests in the intersections of language, identity, and power. She is a proud former high school English teacher and fellow of NCTE's Cultivating New Voices among Scholars of Color (CNV) program.

Julia Lynch, EdD, is a visiting assistant professor at the University of North Carolina, Wilmington. Her interests are guided by a focus on the identity of the Black women teachers and students and their lived experiences across their educational experiences. Her scholarship explores culturally sustaining literacy practices within rural education contexts. She operates primarily from a Black*Mother*ing framework to engage in critical qualitative research that promotes equity and social justice in rural education teaching and learning. A Black poet scholar, she engages in critical qualitative research that attempts to center the lives and experiences of other Black scholars while also disrupting normative research that doesn't honor the authenticity of the researcher or culturally sustain the community of participants.

Kimonye Mays is currently enrolled at the School of Visual Arts (SVA) studying 3D computer animation and VFX for her second year. During her high school career, she interned for New City Kids as a team leader assistant, keyboard teacher, and tutor for three years. She's currently interested in 3D animation, *Chainsaw Man*, and collecting Build-a-Bears.

Dominique Skye McDaniel (she/her) is an assistant professor of English education at Kennesaw State University. She is a former middle school English language arts teacher with additional licensure certifications in elementary education, reading education, and high school English. Now, she works with preservice teachers seeking initial certification and inservice teachers pursuing master's and doctoral degrees. Her research focuses on adolescents' activism on social media, critical approaches to digital literacies, and justice-oriented teacher education. Her recent scholarship can be found in *Reading Research Quarterly*, *Journal of Adolescent & Adult Literacy*, *Journal of Language and Literacy Education*, *English Teaching: Practice & Critique*, and *English Journal*, among others. She has also published public-facing scholarly work in *The Conversation* around youth of color's social media activism.

Dr. Astrid N. Sambolín Morales is an assistant professor at Kent State University's Cultural Foundations of Education program. She received her PhD in educational equity and cultural diversity from the University of Colorado Boulder and a master's in English education at the University of Puerto Rico Mayagüez campus. Her research provides a more nuanced picture of the agency, resistance, and empowerment enacted by Latine women in the US, centering community-research partnerships and critical cycles of problem posing, dialogue, and problem solving for the sake of participants' expanding community cultural wealth and their children's schooling/education experiences. Several grants funded her work, including ones from the University of Colorado Natural Hazards Center, the BUENO Center for Multicultural Education, the URBAN Research Network, and the NAEd Spencer Foundation.

Shanna Peeples, the 2015 National Teacher of the Year, taught middle and high school English in low-income schools in Amarillo, Texas, for fourteen years. She is an assistant professor of educational leadership and the Dr. John G. O'Brien Distinguished Chair of Education at West Texas A&M University, where she also serves as the director of the Route 66 Writing Project. The project uses place-conscious writing to address issues of spatial and educational equity. Her research focuses on adaptive leadership to support belonging and inclusion in schools and organizations.

Anais Santiago is currently enrolled at the Rochester Institute of Technology (RIT) studying graphic design for her second year. While she worked with New City Kids as a Teen Life Intern, she was a reading teacher working primarily with students between the ages of five and eight years old, focusing on having the students understand fandom spaces and becoming more engaged in the media they consume. While in school, she still focuses on her hobbies such as making art for fandom spaces, reading, and playing video games.

Neisha Terry is an assistant professor of English education at Stony Brook University. She is a consummate educator with over fifteen years of experience working with youth in formal and out-of-school settings. She also has experience working with preservice and inservice teachers to develop their critical pedagogy skills. Her research explores the affordances of multiliteracies in supporting Black immigrant youth as they interrogate and respond to dominant discourses about their identities.

Ankhi G. Thakurta is an assistant professor at the Boston College Lynch School of Education and Human Development (Teaching, Curriculum, and Society Department). A bilingual Indian American immigrant and former ELA teacher, her community-centered research explores the civic literacies, learning, and dreaming of immigrant, migrant, and refugee youth. Her work has been supported by funding from NCTE, a National Academy of Education/Spencer Dissertation Fellowship, and other sources. She can be found on X (@AnkhiThakurta) and Instagram (@art_as_method).

Dr. Francisco L. Torres has worked with the Akron community for the past three years. His research has focused on the injustices children and youth have experienced or seen within their communities. He collaborated with an Akron nonprofit to create and lead sessions for the nonprofit's summer program for Akron youth. In this project, participants created comics in which they became superheroes capable of engaging the systemic issues they named as being important to them (e.g., school shootings, police brutality, bullying, poor school lunches, etc.). His research has highlighted the need for spaces that allow the youngest members of the Akron community to act as agents of change in their own lives, exemplifying the cross-generational coalitions needed to enact change in North Hill.

This book was typeset in PT Sans, PT Sans Narrow, and Alternate Gothic No3 by Cynthia Gomez.

The typefaces used on the cover include Franklin Gothic Medium and Avenir Black.

The book was printed on 50lb., white, offset paper.